SO-AIZ-637

13.0

VERONICA FORREST-THOMSON

Poetic artifice

A theory of twentieth-century poetry

ST. MARTIN'S PRESS NEW YORK

ACKNOWLEDGEMENTS

The publishers gratefully acknowledge permission to reproduce the following from copyright sources. Extracts from *The Tennis Court Oath*, copyright © 1962 by John Ashbery. Reprinted by permission of Wesleyan University Press. 'Anecdote of the Jar', copyright 1923 and renewed 1951 by Wallace Stevens. Reprinted from *The Collected Poems of Wallace Stevens*, by permission of Alfred A. Knopf Inc. Extracts from 'The Waste Land', 'A Cooking Egg', 'Sweeney Erect', 'Sweeney among the Nightingales', 'Sweeney Agonistes' and 'Whispers of Immortality' in *Collected Poems 1909–1962* by T. S. Eliot, copyright 1936 by Harcourt Brace Jovanovich Inc.; copyright © 1963, 1964 by T. S. Eliot. Reprinted by permission of the publishers. From 'Burnt Norton' and 'Little Gidding' in *Four Quartets*, copyright 1943 by T. S. Eliot; renewed 1971 by Esme Valerie Eliot. Reprinted by permission of Harcourt Brace Jovanovich Inc. Also by permission of Faber & Faber Ltd, London. Extracts from Ezra Pound, *Personae*. Copyright 1926 by Ezra Pound. Reprinted by permission of New Directions Publishing Corporation, New York. Extracts from Ezra Pound, *The Cantos*. Copyright 1948 by Ezra Pound. Reprinted by permission of New Directions Publishing Corporation, New York. Also by permission of Faber & Faber Ltd. Extracts from William Empson, *Some Versions of Pastoral*. Copyright © 1974 by William Empson. All rights reserved. Reprinted by permission of New Directions Publishing Corporation, New York. Extracts from William Empson, *Seven Types of Ambiguity*. Copyright, all rights reserved. Reprinted by permission of New Directions Publishing Corporation, New York. Also by permission of Chatto & Windus Ltd, London. Six lines from 'Last Words' ('I do not want a plain box . . . the pale star distance fades') in *Crossing the Water* by Sylvia Plath. Copyright © 1971 by Ted Hughes. Seventeen lines from 'Daddy' ('. . . I made a model of you . . . Daddy, daddy, you bastard, I'm through') in *Ariel* by Sylvia Plath. Copyright © 1963 by Ted Hughes. Twenty-four lines from 'Purdah' ('. . . Jade-stone of the side . . . the cloak of holes') from *Winter Trees* by Sylvia Plath. Copyright © 1963 by Ted Hughes. Also by courtesy of Olwyn Hughes, London. Fourteen lines from 'Mountains', seven lines from 'On this Island' and six lines from 'In Memory of W. B. Yeats' in *Collected Poems* by W. H. Auden. Copyright © 1977 by the estate of W. H. Auden. By permission of Faber & Faber Ltd and Random House Inc., New York. Extracts from *Crow* by Ted Hughes, by permission of Faber & Faber Ltd, London, and Harper & Row Publishers Inc., New York. Copyright © 1971 by Ted Hughes. Extracts from *The Whitsun Weddings*, by Philip Larkin, by courtesy of Faber & Faber Ltd. 'ik ok' by Robert Lax and extracts from *Concrete Poetry: an International Anthology*, edited by Stephen Bann, by permission of London Magazine Editions. Extracts from *Brass*, by J. H. Prynne, © J. H. Prynne 1971, by courtesy of the Ferry Press, London.

FOREWORD

This is a posthumous book, and a few words of introduction seem therefore to be appropriate. Veronica Forrest-Thomson died in 1975 at the age of twenty-seven. She was passionately concerned with poetry and poetic theory, and besides her Cambridge Ph.D. thesis (unpublished), on the role of science in modern poetry, she had published a number of articles and two volumes of poems. *Poetic Artifice* is her first fully developed critical work, and unhappily the last. She had a fierce and wayward intellectual energy, which drove her too hard but gave promise of a remarkable future. She worked with me for her doctorate, but beyond some purely formal contributions I had very little effect on what she wrote. Her ideas were in continual development but she was extremely tenacious of those that were occupying her at any given moment and was certainly not to be deflected by any outside influence. She was at first concerned with the way ideas of a non-poetic nature—scientific and philosophical—transformed themselves in poetry. Later she became powerfully impressed by the autonomy of poetry, its difference from any other kind of discourse, and its freedom from any necessary referential bearing. This is the phase in which she wrote *Poetic Artifice*. To my mind she pushes that way of thinking to its farthest permissible limits and sometimes beyond them. She had not, I think, discussed this work in detail with anyone, and the opportunity is now past; so although the book is complete and was carefully revised, it is unmodified by second thoughts. In the unambitious consensus of most current poetic criticism it is rare to find any train of thought pushed to its limits. This is exhilarating in itself, and originality is not won here at the expense of judgement. The commanding and extreme point of view results in a new and sharply discerning criticism of some of the best-known poets of today.

Graham Hough

This book is an attempt to talk about the most distinctive yet elusive features of poetry: all the rhythmic, phonetic, verbal, and logical devices which make poetry different from prose and which we may group together under the heading of poetic artifice. If prose often resembles the 'natural' language of ordinary speech, poetry is resolutely artificial, even when it tries to imitate the diction and cadences of ordinary speech. The poem is always different from the utterances it includes or imitates; if it were not different there would be no point in setting down these utterances or writing these sentences as a poem. Not only does poetry use techniques which would be strange or out of place in prose; it depends on a host of conventions which we apply only in reading and writing poems. It is on these techniques and conventions, these components of poetic artifice that I focus.

Every reader of poetry knows that poetry is different and that in this difference lies the source of its power. Linguists and literary critics have developed techniques which we can use to describe some of its special features. There are ways of talking about a poem's rhythmical or prosodic organisation, its phonetic patterns, its use of imagery, its semantic ambiguities, its thematic structures. But as soon as we enquire about the relationship among these various components in poetry we encounter difficulties. As often as not we rely, whether consciously or unconsciously, on time-worn principles, such as 'the sound must be an echo to the sense', which obviously do not account for the working of a vast majority of poems. Once we go beyond the relatively infrequent and obvious cases of sound patterns and rhythmic structures which seem to imitate what is being described we enter a shadowy realm where no one speaks with confidence. We recognize patterns and are certain that they contribute to the effect of poems but cannot say with assurance in what way they contribute.

If I seem to speak with confidence in the pages that follow it is because I am convinced that nothing is to be gained in this enterprise by modest disclaimers, expressions of doubt which would weigh down each paragraph. The tentative character of my proposals will be sufficiently obvious to any reader who reflects upon them and discovers their limitations and inadequacies. I am trying to devise ways of analysing the various verbal and logical devices and the literary conventions which make up poetic artifice, and if we recognise from the outset the difficulty of formulating a theory about the relations between the different strata of poetic artifice, then perhaps we may simply plunge ahead on the assumption that any theory is better than none because the disagreements it provokes will pave the way for a more adequate theory.

Although I am speaking of poetry in general, as the range of my examples may suggest, I call my project a theory of twentieth-century poetry because the poetry of this century has been especially marked by a formal experimentation with which we must come to terms if we are to understand the condition of poetry and its present possibilities. Moreover, in discussing the poetry of the past, which is already distanced from us by time, it is often more difficult to determine what belongs to artifice and what to a language which is no longer our own, whereas in the poetry of our own day the distancing accomplished by poetic language is easier to identify. Finally, twentieth-century poetry provides the best testing ground for a theory of poetic artifice because of the variety of devices it employs. Traditional metrical and rhyme schemes have become just one set of possibilities among others. In the work first of Pound and Eliot, then of the Dadaists and Surrealists, and finally of contemporary poets like John Ashbery and Sylvia Plath, the place and role accorded to irrational elements has grown; poetry has become more difficult—notoriously so—and these difficulties are due to the increasing complexities of poetic artifice. The poetry of our century particularly requires a theory of the devices of artifice, such as apparently non-sensical imagery, logical discontinuity, referential opacity, and unusual metrical and spatial organisation, and an account of the relationships between various strata of artifice. The question always is: how do poems work?

'Do not forget', says Wittgenstein, 'that a poem, even though it is composed in the language of information is not used in the language-game of giving information.' It is indeed important to remember this, but simply remembering it is no solution. We must try to describe the language-game in which poetic language is used, and here the initial difficulty is the relationship between the language-game of poetry and what Wittgenstein calls the language-game of giving information. The sentence, 'Pipit sat upright in her chair some distance from where I was sitting' could be used to give information about a state of affairs in the external world: namely, that at a particular time in the past someone named Pipit sat at some distance from the person who is uttering the sentence. But when Eliot begins his poem 'A Cooking Egg' with these lines:

> Pipit sate upright in her chair
> Some distance from where I was sitting;

the function of the sentence, and in particular its relationship to the external world, changes. The statement is altered by its insertion in a poetic context, by its use, shall we say, in this different language-game. It no longer refers to a particular time in the past (it is not simply irrelevant to ask whether the event took place on 3 April 1912 or at some other time: there is no need to suppose such an event at all). Nor need the 'I' be thought of as a particular person. For the purposes of the poem the 'I' is simply a voice.

Every reader of poetry knows that statements are changed by their insertion in a poem, that they no longer mean what they would mean in ordinary speech because of the form in which they appear. To state the relationship between poetry and the external world, however—to show precisely how poetic form and poetic context affect the sentences they include and the non-verbal world which the sentences imply—is difficult. It is the major problem of this book.

But it is not just a theoretical difficulty. It is also the problem of poetry itself. One of the reasons for the general dreariness of English verse in the 1950's and 1960's was the failure of poets and theorists to tackle this problem, to discover or admit what poetry does and how poetic artifice is justified. It is all too easy for poets as well as critics to give in to the kind of reading which criticism often proposes and to assume that the important features of a poem are those which can be shown to contribute to a thematic synthesis stated in terms of the external world. It is easy to treat poetry as if it were engaged in the language-game of giving information and thus to assume that what is important about a poem is what it tells us about the external world. The meaning of the poem is extended into the world; this extended meaning is assumed to be dominant, and if formal features are to become noteworthy components of a poem they must be assimilated to this extended meaning.

Such an approach falsifies our experience of poems, reduces the distinctiveness of poetry, and neglects many of the components of poetic language, but it is an intellectually less taxing approach which triumphs for that reason. Unfortunately, its consequences are not good for poetry. It makes extended meaning the locus of poetic experimentation and poets are expected to explore a new range of extreme external experiences (often with disastrous consequences) in order to earn the title of creative 'poet. Sylvia Plath and Anne Sexton are praised for opening up new depths of psychological insight; writers with techniques as disparate as Ted Hughes, Charles Olson, Allen Ginsberg, and Robert Lowell are held to combine such insight with a special vision of contemporary society. Whatever technical innovation they display is swiftly taken up and smothered by a critical reading anxious to convert all verbal organisation into extended meaning—to transform pattern into theme.

This critical process I shall call 'Naturalisation': an attempt to reduce the strangeness of poetic language and poetic organisation by making it intelligible, by translating it into a statement about the non-verbal external world, by making the Artifice appear natural. Critical reading cannot, of course, avoid Naturalisation altogether. Criticism is committed, after all, to helping us to understand both poetry as an institution and individual poems as significant utterances. But it must ensure that in its desire to produce ultimate meaning it does not purchase intelligibility at the cost of blindness: blindness to the complexity of those non-meaningful features which differentiate poetry from everday language and make it something other than an external thematic statement about an already-known world. There would be no point in writing poetry unless poetry were different from everyday language, and any attempt to analyse poetry should cherish that difference and seek to remain within its bounds for as long as possible rather than ignore the difference in an unseemly rush from words to world. Good naturalisation dwells on the non-meaningful levels of poetic language, such as phonetic and prosodic patterns and spatial organisation, and tries to state their relation to other levels of organisation rather than set them aside in an attempt to produce a statement about the world.

Contemporary poetry has suffered from critics' disposition to make poetry above all a statement about the external world, and therefore it is now especially important somewhat to redress the balance, to stress the importance of artifice. Poetry can only be a valid and valuable activity when we recognise the value of the artifice which makes it different from prose. Indeed, it is only through artifice that poetry can challenge our ordinary linguistic orderings of the world, make us question the way in which we make sense of things, and induce us to consider its alternative linguistic orders as a new way of viewing the world.

The best way to restore value to artifice is to find ways of discussing it which do not presuppose the subservience of form to extended meaning. And therefore my account of twentieth-century poetry offers a framework of concepts which allow us to dwell at length on the play of formal features and structure of relations internal to a poem. There is, therefore, a proliferation of technical terms which identify various aspects of poetic form and different ways of treating it in the process of reading.

'Naturalisation' I have already defined as the process of rationalising details, making them natural and intelligible in the process of interpretation. The unfortunate type of naturalisation which concentrates on extended meaning involves a dialectic of what I call 'external expansion' and 'external limitation'. In external expansion we naturalise details by expanding them into the external world, as a comment upon it; external limitation is the limitation imposed by external expansion on the formal features which we can take account of in our interpretation. That is to say, the attempt to relate the poem to the external world limits our attention to those formal features which can be made to contribute to this extended meaning.

Consider as an example these lines from Tennyson's 'In Memoriam':

> Dark house, by which once more I stand
>   Here in the long unlovely street,
>   Doors, where my heart was used to beat
> So quickly, waiting for a hand.

External expansion leads us to think of situation and its possibilities. The poet is standing before the house of a good friend, now dead. He remembers other times when he had stood there and the contrast between his past and present mood makes the scene appear dark and gloomy to him. This external expansion limits the number of formal features we can use in our interpretation to those which fit into our external thematic synthesis: the house is the main object of attention and hence is placed first; then, after a glance around, come the doors. The relative simplicity of the statement indicates directness, sincerity, and the alliteration of 'long unlovely' emphasises how long and unlovely the street appears to the poet in mourning.

The inadequacies of this external expansion and limitation become clear when we note that precisely the same thematic synthesis could be drawn from another poem which retains various features of the original:

> House, so dark, in front of which I'm standing again
>   Here in the long gloomy street,
>   Doors, where my heart used to pound in anticipation
> As I waited for him to emerge.

In order to account for the difference between the two stanzas we must undertake a process of internal limitation and expansion. Expansion must take place within the limits imposed by the poem's style, as we try to take account of any formal features we can identify; and we limit the external contexts that are brought in according to the needs of internal expansion. This is, of course, more difficult than external limitation and expansion, and the rest of the book attempts to develop ways of undertaking an internal naturalisation; but the task is essential if we want to be able to offer an account of the first stanza which is not also an account of the second or if we wish to be able to explain why the first stanza is more effective and intense than the second.

Whether we are engaged in external expansion and limitation or internal expansion and limitation we are bringing together levels of poetic organisation and moving towards some new kind of organisation. The reader is guided in this process by what I call the 'image-complex': a level of coherence which helps us to assimilate features of various kinds, to distinguish the relevant from the irrelevant, and to control the importation of external contexts. A simple example of the functioning of image-complexes can be taken from the activity of interpreting a metaphor: when we read 'Out, out brief candle, life's but a walking shadow,' etc., the level of coherence established by the lines tells us that only certain features of empirical candles are relevant to the passage (the shape and composition of candles, the shadow cast by a candle, and the purposes for which they are used are all irrelevant). The function of the image-complex is to tell us how to apportion our attention between synthesis on the scale of relevance, where we use external contexts and move up through the various levels of the poem towards the naturalisation of a thematic synthesis, and the scale of irrelevance, where we accumulate all the patterns and features which are irrelevant to this thematic synthesis and which combine to form what I shall call a 'suspended naturalisation'. In suspended naturalisation we know that we cannot create a thematic synthesis in terms of the external world but we can still observe the interaction and mutual reinforcement of the various types of pattern in the poem.

We can give a schematic representation of these processes which, if it does not clarify the argument at this stage, will at least serve as a point of reference for the discussions which follow:

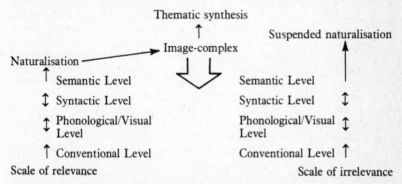

Thematic synthesis

↑

Suspended naturalisation

Image-complex

Naturalisation ⟶

Semantic Level

↑ Semantic Level

Semantic Level

↕ Syntactic Level

Syntactic Level ↕

↕ Phonological/Visual Level

Phonological/Visual ↕ Level

↑ Conventional Level

Conventional Level ↑

Scale of relevance

Scale of irrelevance

At the bottom of each scale is the conventional level: the conventions which create expectations about the particular type of poetry one is reading. Sonnets lead one to expect not only a certain rhyme-scheme but also particular themes; and thus the conventional level guides one's attention as one moves up through the other strata of artifice. Operations on the scale of irrelevance lead to a suspended naturalisation in which the conventions on content are highly stylised: in the villanelle or sestina, for example, most of the content of the semantic level will work on the scale of irrelevance rather than relevance; and this is a result of the conventions of the genre.

The image-complex is ambiguously situated in the diagram, partly because it is difficult to draw its dialectical role. On the one hand the image-complex, hypotheses about a level of coherence, helps to determine what at each of the various levels (syntactic, semantic, and phonological/visual) can work on the scale of relevance and what on the scale of irrelevance; but as a representation of the coherence of the poem the image-complex is also the road to a thematic synthesis: once the various elements have been naturalised on the scale of relevance, one can move through the image-complex to a thematic synthesis.

This schema will still be relatively unintelligible, but discussion of particular examples in later chapters should make it clearer. A set of terms does not, of course, have any intrinsic explanatory value, and the function of these is less to constitute a coherent theory than to direct our attention upon certain aspects of

poetic logic and artifice. Their scope will become more apparent in the Introduction where they are deployed in a close reading—or rather, dismantling—of a
Shakespearean sonnet.

The chapters that follow explore the various modes of Artifice over a wide
range of examples: the irrational obscurity of poems which block the process of
internal naturalisation and can be read only as examples of irrational obscurity;
the rational obscurity of poems which absorb external contexts and other types of
language, transform them, and lead to an internal thematic synthesis; and, beyond both these modes, poetry of the disconnected image-complex which
achieves integration only by making the act of writing a poem part of its theme.
This last mode is characteristic of our century, which throws into relief the role of
poet as mediator between the old languages which we inhabit and the new world
which emerges from an assimilation and transformation of these languages. The
ability of poets through their form to build bridges between various disparate
areas of concern is one of the central problems of poetic Artifice, and the last
chapter explores the ways in which recent poetry has used semantic and formal
irrelevance to produce both a suspension of old syntheses and an invention of new
orders.

Although my arrangement of chapters shows a concern with the development
of poetic artifice in this century, it should be stressed that the examples are
designed to illustrate various poetic strategies, not to provide a history or a survey
of twentieth-century poetry. Though Eliot and Pound figure largely, certain
names—W. B. Yeats, William Carlos Williams, Marianne Moore—are conspicuous by their absence. Moreover, in order to provide a focus and sense of
continuity I have taken as my central character one who would not be the major
figure in a history of twentieth-century poetry but who can serve as a continuous
stimulus and pivot to my argument: William Empson. As poet, theorist, and
critic Empson illustrates the most fruitful tensions in the poetic culture of this
century and provides many suggestive points of departure. Deeply committed to
the rationality of poetic artifice, Empson strives to demonstrate the thematic
relevance of poetic organisation with greater tenacity and ingenuity than any
other critic, and he thus invariably provides examples and arguments with which
a theory of poetic artifice must come to terms. If he is absent from my final chapter and from the fragile synthesis that constitutes the programme for a vital contemporary poetry, it is because of his inability to accept that the future of poetry
lies in the exploitation of non-meaningful levels of language.

Introduction

'About that of which one cannot speak one must be silent', says Ludwig Wittgenstein.[1] This is doubtless wise advice, but poetry is precisely the area of language where silence is impossible, and though poetry may tend toward silence, the study of poetry is the most garrulous study that exists. This book is an effort to talk about those aspects of poetry which are most difficult to articulate and which most clearly mark it as poetry. It is an attempt to talk about what is generally taken for granted because people can find no way of speaking of it except as the inexplicable. The enterprise, therefore, is fraught with peril for both author and reader, but the rewards of success may be correspondingly great.

Lest these problems of poetic form should be thought to be a specifically modern dilemma confronting twentieth-century poetry and its theorists, I have chosen to introduce my programme with an analysis of a sixteenth-century lyric, Shakespeare's Sonnet 94, and to deploy my tools of analysis upon it, so that when we come to the contemporary situation we shall feel that our problem is familiar. It is, in fact, endemic to all poetry and to the interpretation of poetry. What are the effects, what is the importance, of rhyme, metre, and all the other conventions and traditional devices which differentiate poetry from other kinds of language? If we want to provide answers to these questions, if we want to grasp the process whereby works might out-last bronze and ascend the Capitoline hill, we must first descend to the inferno of detailed analysis. To begin the journey with the greatest and most time-conscious of English poets seems, then, only just.

I   That do not do the thing they most do show

There are several reasons for choosing Shakespeare's 94th sonnet. First, it is among his best. Second, it presents us with the problem of time in its most immediate emblematic incarnation: the decay of love's faithfulness. And third, its second line—'That do not do the thing they most do show'—can stand for all those complex and elusive relations between verbal form, verbal meaning, rhythm and poetic convention which it is my business to analyse. That these cannot be analysed completely from the standpoint of linguistics is by now clear to everyone, even linguists themselves. To treat the poem as a series of sentences and to analyse their phonological and syntactic structure would not help to explain how these sentences function in poetry. Poetry is not, of course, independent of ordinary linguistic categories; if it were it would be unintelligible. What happens is that ordinary linguistic categories are subsumed and altered by rules specific to poetry. Phonological and grammatical structures have different functions in the medium of poetry. Linguists have tried to discover the rules of poetry[2] but since they have approached the problem from the standpoint of linguistics they have met with failure. Hence my contention that we must articulate the categories of poetry itself—must try to define the operations of poetic artifice—before we see how they relate to the categories of other disciplines.

The two processes are not, of course, distinct in a practice which tries to read poems as different from ordinary language. We cannot, as Eliot said we should do with Milton, read a poem once as a religious, philosophical, or linguistic statement and a second time as poetry. But it is important to distinguish in theory between the various levels of poetic discourse, for in discussing poetry we invariably tend to slip into a discussion of meaning. Precisely because we are engaged in speaking about a poem and the ways in which it challenges the categories of other discourses, we concentrate on thematic levels. And we require a strong theory that will continually remind us that we are not in fact dealing with ordinary meaningful discourse but with poetry, in which language is first of all subject to other forms of organisation.

The most obvious manoeuvre to make poetry like other languages is a Naturalisation in terms of meaning. Empson provides a splendid example of this for Sonnet 94: his interpretation is not simply a bad Naturalisation (whose value would be limited); it is a good reading which is reached by the wrong roads and supported by the wrong reasons. I propose to juxtapose it with an interpretation in terms of my own system so as to show how the appropriate reading may emerge from the distinctive features of poetic discourse. Empson instinctively guessed the reading, but a different approach can both demonstrate the meaning and lead us to see more in the poem. The first stanza goes as follows:

> They that have power to hurt and will do none,
> That do not do the thing they most do show,
> Who, moving others, are themselves as stone,
> Unmoved, cold, and to temptation slow;

Empson comments:

> It is agreed that *They that have power to hurt and will do none* is a piece of grave irony . . . 'The best people are indifferent to temptation and detached from the world; nor is this state selfish, because they do good by

unconscious influence, like the flower. You must be like them; you are quite like them already. But even the best people must be continually on their guard, because they become the worst, . . . once they fall from their perfection' . . . No doubt *as stone* goes intentionally too far from sympathy . . .

They may *show*, while hiding the alternative, for the first couplet, the power to hurt or the determination not to hurt—cruelty or mercy, for the second, the strength due to chastity or to sensual experience, for either, a reckless or cautious will, and the desire for love or for control; all whether they are stealers of hearts or of public power. They are a very widespread group; we are only sure at the end that some kind of hypocrisy has been advised and threatened.[3]

Not only does Empson anticipate 'the end' even in his reading of the first quatrain; he takes in the rest of Shakespeare's works, comparing 'They' with Angelo in *Measure for Measure*. This is because he operates at the level of meaning and thematic synthesis, naturalising the formal features straight away. Of course the poem can be read in this way, but if we value it as a poem rather than as a thematic statement we must pay closer attention to formal pattern, metrical demand, rhythmical pattern of sound and syntax. Empson gives us a good deal of thematic synthesis: ideas about the Machiavellian spiv, man's relations to Nature and to God, a poet's relation to his patron, and a lover's relation to his beloved. There is no need to deny that these are themes and meanings which the poem uses, but we must first see the tools by which it does use them. The formal structure of a poem is not a step to the end of communicating ideas from other areas of discourse; it is the other areas of discourse, as they are fed through the level of meaning, that are tools for organising the formal structure of poems. What, then, of 'as stone' and of its relation to that so ambiguous, so skilful, so ambivalent line—'That do not do the thing they most do show'?

First, it is the only image-complex in that first quatrain, and it is primarily through image-complexes that meaning and external reference are absorbed and changed; but it cannot stand out as completely different from the rest of the lines, for then there would be no coherence. We must look, then, for its place in the formal pattern, the metrical scheme, the rhymical pattern, and the syntactic pattern. And we must look through the conventional expectations of a reader of poetry.

By formal pattern, 'as stone' is linked to the prolonged *o* sound/look in 'power', 'do none', 'do not do', 'unmoved', 'cold', 'slow': a powerful combination that gives us almost all the key words in the theme. By metre 'as stone' is the last unequivocally iambic foot before the quatrain gives in—or moves up—to the metrically hesitant 'do not do', 'thing they most do show'. By rhythm. Rhythm is very much an unknown quantity in poetics, but I think it is the result of a combination between syntax,

metre, formal pattern, and conventional expectation. So that the fact that
'as stone' is metrically a sound iambic foot as well as formally strong in
the *o* pattern makes it a crux in rhythm also, since is precedes the syntactically and metrically ambivalent lines that follow. By syntax, 'as
stone' is the first comparison in straightforward statements, the first hint
that we are dealing with complex syntax. It is thus linked to the rest of the
conventional demands we make of poetry, which have alllowed us to distinguish the other levels, and is linked primarily with the level of rhyme,
where 'none' cries out for 'stone', since 'flow' must be arrested for 'slow',
which demands 'show'. And the only thing that could arrest the flow of
formal pattern is a strong image-complex.

Thus we have five very good reasons for the appearance of 'as stone'
without even touching on the thematic level. The only aspect that
touches meaning is the level of syntax; and syntax, through its creation of
meaning, is a prime agent in transforming other realms of discourse into
the realm of Artifice. Again, our conventional expectations that allowed
us to perceive these five levels and their relation to each other are part of
our apparatus for distinguishing poetry from other discourse; they could
hardly, therefore, also be used to stress its similarity. If they lead outwards to an external, non-poetic, synthesis, they also lead this external
context back into an internal synthesis where it becomes part of the pat-
terned play of the other levels. As Mr Stephen Booth remarks in his
excellent *Essay on Shakespeare's Sonnets*, our source of pleasure in reading the sonnets is a line to line experience of 'the multiplicity of organisations in which, over the course of fourteen lines, the reader's mind
participates.' In this experience there is 'a multitude of different coex-
istent and conflicting patterns—formal, logical, ideological, syntactic,
rhythmic and phonetic.'[4] So that it is inadequate to select, as Empson
does, only the syntactic, logical, and ideological strands for emphasis.

But we can see why he does so, and so can Mr Booth:

> under usual critical conditions, the critic can assume that, when he looks at
> a poem and likes it, the essential statement of the poem will be capable of
> reduction into prose . . . experience has taught him to assume that from a
> coherent poem he will be able to perceive and state a general and inclusive
> attitude evoked in the reader toward the subject matter of the poem. That
> is a hard assumption for men who are rational by profession to give up.[5]

We can see that the assumption must be given up, however, if we are to
do justice to, or even perceive, the dynamics of a poem; and that duty is
greater than our duty to professional rationality. I have said that Artifice
has its own logic, different in kind but not in degree from more respectable kinds of logic; it is equally rational in its own way, and we must now
attempt to rewrite this alluring sonnet according to the premises of
Artifice.

Since we have invoked Empsonian rationality we may as well start with the premise of Artifice which states that all norms of other kinds of discourse are changed when absorbed by a poem, and that syntax in conjunction with convention is the agent of this change. On the scale of relevance, where all poetry until this century operated, this conjunction would contribute to a thematic synthesis. I am, then, willing to concede that convention and sense of the words will be one area where Empson and I agree. Nevertheless I shall want to go one step further than Empson in bringing back into the poem the thematic synthesis which he extracts.

Empson's interpetation assumes that we should refer our reading to the external world; possible ambiguities are listed, explored, and finally related to what is taken as the final point of reference: W. H. as ambiguous beloved. It is assumed that the problem for interpretation is that of inferring what sort of person W. H. must have been. We shall learn rather more, however, if we focus on the poem itself in terms of poetic conventions. Among our frames for doing this, of course, is the fiction that this is a man talking to us about something (Why else should we care?); but we need not assume that he is talking about something outside the poem, be it his feelings or his ideas or his situation (If so, why should he bother to write a *poem*?).

The intentionally unsympathetic 'as stone', says Empson, goes too far for sympathy? Yes, but why with these first four lines should we suppose sympathy at all unless we were already smuggling in external evidence from the rest of Shakespeare's work? I do not suggest that we cannot see the rest of the poem on the page, have not read it, cannot see the poem as a poem. (If this were true we should be like those natives in Africa who cannot see a portrait of an antelope in a drawing of an antelope; we should be unable to read any poetry at all.) My suggestion is that we should go line by line as an analyst should before we see the lines as a whole. All we have in that first quatrain is a succession of relative clauses with no main verb. In order to watch the emergence—or non-emergence—of any thematic attitude, sympathy, complex irony, or anything else, we should look at the line-arrangement from which it must emerge. We may begin with the fact that by convention the first and last words in a line are stressed. If we start at this point we shall find that the formal level and the thematic emerge. Here then is the first of several anatomies:

They	None
That	show
Who	stone
Unmoved	slow

This somewhat resembles the kind of twentieth-century poem where you are given isolated words and phrases and have to make the connection between them yourself. The resemblance is not accidental; poetic Artifice does not change over the centuries in fundamentals — more will be said of this later. For the moment, however, we have the conventionally-stressed first and last words in each line; and when we look at these we shall see an interesting syntactic relation. 'They' do something to 'none' but not enough to avoid being referred to again as 'That'; 'They . . . That' show something, but not enough to complete the sentence, since they are referred to again as 'Who'. 'That', and 'Who' have some relation to 'stone' even without 'as'; and we might guess that it is one of predication and comparison since the next qualifier, 'Unmoved', implies a preceding copula and an opposition between the animate and inanimate. Finally, 'They' 'that' 'who' [are] 'unmoved' all have some relation to 'slow' (again an implied predication).

So much—for the moment—for syntax. A second convention directs our attention to formal patterns—the sound/look of both vowels and consonants—and here we find that all but two of these words contain variations on the *o* sound. Moreover, all the rhyme words contain an *o*, and it is mainly the rhyme words which tell us which vowels and consonants will be used to make up the whole formal pattern as they feed back into the rest of the line. The only exceptions to *o* are 'They' and 'That', for whose *ay*, *a* we shall shortly adduce thematic reasons; moreover, both these words contribute to the other prominent formal pattern, in hard *t* and *d*, and they are retrieved, as it were, for *o* when 'Who' appears as their one other syntactic equivalent. The important pattern in variants of *s* (also carried by rhyme words) leads us to 'as stone', a place where all patterns and levels meet. 'As stone' links 'they' etc. to 'Unmoved' and to the final 'slow'.

From the conventional and syntactic levels alone we perceive the emergence of a formal pattern and the experienced reader sees the beginning of a thematic pattern. Do not let us, however, try to gallop before we can trot. First we must take notice of another of Artifice's premises: the image-complex. An image-complex consists of a blending of two or more areas of extended meaning; like traditional metaphors, it brings various non-verbal properties together in a new verbal structure. In this first quatrain 'as stone' stands out as the only image-complex:

They	none
That	show
Who [are]	as stone
[are] Unmoved [are]	slow

From these relations our thematic synthesis begins also to emerge. They are not a class to whom the writer of the poem belongs; he is one of the 'others' whom they affect. How do they affect him? By doing something to 'none' and 'show', by being 'as stone' and 'Unmoved' and doing something to 'slow', probably by being 'slow'.

What can we make of that as regards meaning? Do an implied sympathy and ironic complexity come into the poem from this attenuated version? The fact that the pronouns are in the third person, and the image-complex a traditional one, suggests that sympathy or any close relation between the poet's 'I' and 'They', is held off as much as possible. The ambivalence is very firmly attributed to 'They' (though there is irony in that their very ambivalence makes them static, 'as stone') not to the poet. The poet is concerned to make his statements as distant and generalisable as possible. Empson himself recognises this: 'The vague and generalised language of the descriptions, which might be talking about so many sorts of people as well as feeling so many things about them, somehow makes a unity like a crossroads, . . . makes a solid flute on which you can play a multitude of tunes, whose solidity no list of all possible tunes would go far to explain.'[6]

To which Shakespeare might well have replied, in the words of Hamlet, ' 'sblood, do you think I am easier to be played on than a pipe?'

Nevertheless, however solid the pipe, the number of tunes that may be played on it is finite; the pipe's solidity depends on that very fact. And the number of tunes is as much a function of the properties of the pipe as of the listener's (reader's) ability to perceive tunes.

We are here trying to finger the stops and infer the variety of tunes they make up without examining the entire pipes as a single tune. And we have inferred that at the most basic level of organisation in the first quatrain, thematic synthesis and image-complex can be reached almost entirely through the conventional and formal levels alone. Their consequent relation strongly suggests that the generalised language and the banal image-complex, together with the syntactic pattern, is a device for distancing the poem from any particular fiction. The poem is *meant* to have a universal theme. That is, the poet has organised its levels so that he is relegated to his most entirely disinterested professional self; he is the *poeta ex machina*, and we shall see later how this recoils on his own head.

Given the stage we have now reached I think we could fill in the lines a little more in a version which retains the formal pattern, metre and general theme of the original:

> They are still and will be proved by none
> That can control the movements that they show
> Who, seeing others, make themselves as stone
> Unmovèd, keep their loving motion slow

Although this upsets neither formal pattern, metre, or theme, it does, of course, upset rhythm since it upsets syntactical arrangement. It is also horribly flat, but it does keep the theme and the image-complex as well as the first and last words. Of course, I have cheated a little by retaining 'will' 'others' 'themselves' from the original, and by introducing 'loving', but I think these tricks are valid for three reasons. First, our thematic synthesis required a contrast between motion and stasis which gives 'still', 'movements', 'motion'. From this contrast the word 'will' is practically inevitable and if we want to keep 'That' as referring to 'They'—as we do if we want to keep it referring to 'Who'—then 'none' must be part of a passive construction. Such a passive construction, in order to fit the metre, must hesitate between two and three syllables ('be proved' or 'be prov'd') and in order to fit the sound pattern it must contain either or both *o* or *d*. 'Mov'd' seemed the only alternative to 'prov'd', and there is already enough of that verb for one quatrain. Second, as already hinted, formal pattern plus thematic synthesis dictated 'proved' as opposed, thematically, to 'blamed', 'shamed', 'tamed', 'claimed', and, formally, to 'shoved', Shooed', 'loved'. 'Still', 'will', 'can' and 'control' all fit both formal and thematic requirements and help to stress the fact that a willed fixity is replacing a more appropriate emotion (the psychological counterpart of 'motion', remember); they also help to transfer the notion of movement from a merely animate to a human situation. Third, I had to preserve the contrast between 'They' and 'others' and the obvious way to do this, given a formal pattern in *o* and *d* and a thematic demand for motion versus coldness, is to introduce the notion of love. This rules out alternatives such as 'shoving motion', 'moaning motion', 'proving motion', 'losing motion'. For if all these could be connected with the experience of loving, they yet avoid the word, as, indeed, Shakespeare does here. He does it because he is afraid to admit that he is involved as an individual persona in this impersonal denunciation, but I need have no scruples in using the word in my imaginative reconstructions. With the implication of a relation between two kinds of people, 'They' and the 'others', which consists in 'They' refusing to be moved by the 'others', emotionally and physically, and carrying out this refusal by being 'as stone', the notion of a love relationship is inevitable. Especially is this so when we have a strongly marked formal pattern of *o* and *d* to which 'loved' conforms.

Now this little reconstruction seems to show two things. First, the clue to discovering the levels of priority in a poem lies in a combination of syntax, convention and formal pattern. Second, neither the thematic synthesis nor the image-complex 'as stone' alone presents 'They' in an unsympathetic light; there must be, in a poem, support from these other levels. What was lacking in my rewritten stanza was exactly the kind of support within the line from these other levels that are found in the original. My version was what Shakespeare would have like to produce—a blandly complacent, unambiguous denunciation of 'They'—and also what he would not have liked to produce: an incompetent and uninteresting poem.

What he actually produced is rather different. And we need be in no doubt now that it is different, not because the thematic synthesis or the external contexts implied by the image-complex are different, but because it has—what my version lacked—support and also dissent in the body of the lines through formal and syntactic and hence rhythmic patterns. 'Do not do the thing they most do show', for example, has a very ambivalent stress pattern even on its own; one 'do' must be stressed more than the others, but which? Is 'not' stressed? Is 'most' stressed? This uncertainty casts doubt both upon the thematic emphasis and on our way of taking the line as a rhythmical unit. When the line is placed next to its predecessor the uncertainty is multiplied until we are lost as to what meaning and attitude is intended to be dominant. And the addition of the last two lines increases doubt, since to be slow to temptation seems a good thing, but that would depend on the nature of the temptation and we are never told this. The rest of the sonnet offers a succession of polite, beautiful, and extremely sly evasions.

However I anticipate:

> They that have power to hurt and will do none,
> That do not do the thing they most do show

Again, the questions start. What power to hurt? The power of a policeman, a politician, a patron, a lover? Hurt whom? Themselves? Others? What thing? Power to hurt? Power to abstain from hurting? We can find no answer to these questions in the first quatrain (though we should not forget that, whoever is powerful outside a poem, only the poet is powerful within it). The last two lines merely increase our perplexity:

> Who, moving others, are themselves as stone,
> Unmoved, cold, and to temptation slow.

Definitely not nice people, we feel, but why? Because we cannot but be aware of the ambivalence built up around the verse which speaks of them; at least they as a subject for the poet are actively powerful enough to have produced this masterly equivocation of syntax and rhythm which gives with one hand while it takes away with the next; which cuts the reader's feet from under him even while he thought he had found a secure foothold in the formal pattern.

This supports the notion that different orders of language imply different orders of the world by supplying different imaginative contexts.

Rather than dwell on this, however, let us pass on to a further re-writing of the first stanza; this time on the level of formal pattern alone:

> Ay Oh mallal an ouch turumto foone
> Ah Ah honhol layllay mallala Oh
> Oooch muvsing uhvsing ah ten shelves ossone
> Untooved vold ond ta terumdum go

This, of course keeps the conventional level in the rhyme scheme and—as far as possible without syntax—in the rhythm. In any case, like my earlier anatomy, this is not entirely successful in eliminating all the combinations of the original. The reason for this falling short is that since metre and rhyme and sound pattern has to be kept, I had to conform to the metrical scheme and to the rules for word-formation in English (so one can tell what the sounds are). This is another indication that no two levels may combine in a poem without involving at least the vestiges of a third: here, choice of word formation.

There is, moreover, worse to come. Suppose one combines the thematic plus the image-complex alone, without attending to metre, convention, or rhythm:

> People who can hurt but refrain from doing so are behaving in an ambivalent fashion, almost hypocritically; they may be compared to stones because they are immovable, self-contained and, though they affect others, either in love or politics, they let nothing interfere with their self-control.

Like the others, this re-writing has had to include some of the connotations of the words of the original—'hurt', 'ambivalent', 'immovable', 'others', 'They'. Most important, the retention of the image-complex, 'as stone', has made it necessary to keep to the same implied external context of attitude and situation.

Nevertheless it is obvious that all three of my re-writings of this initial quatrain have failed to preserve the richness and complexity of the original. And they have failed because they tried to by-pass the internal connections of Artifice which make it such a powerful instrument for absorbing and restraining the non-poetic world. This said let us pass on to the next stanza and see if it gives us more help.

II   *They rightly do inherit Heaven's graces*

Now perhaps we are getting somewhere. The attitude towards 'they' appears to be explicitly approving, but that slyly placed 'rightly' may make us dubious about their claims, just as the strategically placed 'do not do the thing' with its uncertain stress made us dubious in the stanza preceding. But let us, by all means, have the whole stanza:

> They rightly do inherit Heaven's graces,
> And husband nature's riches from expense;
> They are the lords and owners of their faces,
> Others but stewards of their excellence.

The same opposition between 'They' and the 'others' that we found in the first stanza is reproduced here but with a subtle difference. 'Others' now occupies the important place at the beginning of the line which had hitherto been reserved for 'They' or their qualifiers. Further, the description of 'their' activities is couched in seemingly unambivalent terms of approval, but the underlying disapproval is more evident. Who can miss the sneer in 'rightly', 'lords and owners of their faces', or 'but stewards'? This irony operates on the level of the extended meaning which the words would have in prose as well as on the metrical, syntactical, and image-complicated level to which, with the exception of 'a stone', it was confined in the previous quatrain.

For this reason, perhaps, Empson sees it:

> They rightly do inherit Heaven's graces,
> And husband nature's riches from expense,

Either 'inherit, they alone, by right' or 'inherit what all men inherit and use it rightly'; these correspond to the opposed views of W. H. as aristocrat and vulgar careerist. There is a similar range of idea, *half hidden by the pretence of easy filling of the form*, in the pun on *graces* and shift to *riches*. *Heaven's graces* may be prevenient grace (strength from God to do well), personal graces which seem to imply heavenly virtues (the charm by which you deceive people), or merely God's gracious gift of *nature's riches*; which again may be the personal graces, or the strength and taste which make him capable either of 'upholding his house' or of taking his pleasure, or merely the actual wealth of which he is an *owner*. Clearly this gives plenty of room for irony in the statement that the cold people, with their fine claims, do well all round; it also conveys 'I am seeing you as a whole; I am seeing these things as necessary rather than as your fault'.[7]

Several points are to be made here. First, as the phrase I have italicised suggests—'half hidden by the pretence of easy filling of the form'—an interpretation that relies on extension into the non-verbal world cannot even see that it is by the pattern that the irony is channelled and the meanings subtly altered to suit it. Second, because Empson extrapolates to the rest of the Sonnets and to non-verbal experience including 'I' and 'you', he fails to see that *there has been so far in this poem no mention of either 'W. H.' or the poet.*

Indeed they are there by implication but the implication is a carry-over from the first stanza. And it is one thing to look for internal relations between two quatrains, one of which the reader must necessarily have encountered before the other, and quite another to jump immediately out of the poem to an external 'I' and 'you'. The second extrapolation involves the critic in dubious manoeuvres about an empirical person from which the first, simply because it treats him as an author, a poet in whom the man is absorbed, is exempt. I admit that it is hard to analyse these lines without help from outside; is, for example, to 'inherit Heaven's graces' and to 'husband nature's riches from expense' a praiseworthy activity? Or is it like moving others while being oneself as stone — admirable perhaps but not endearing? Are the three activities the same in any case? How can we decide any of these questions; what counts as evidence?

We could look at the other levels of organisation. To take choice of words first—and remember this choice is dictated by formal, rhythmical, and metrical requirement as much as by a thematic intention which cannot emerge, unless it is backed by these, because it is through them that the level of meaning filters: 'They', 'do', 'and' have all been prominent in the first quatrain, and they appear again in the second. 'Inherit Heaven's graces' and 'husband nature's riches from expense' parallel 'to temptation slow', for all three are ambiguous phrases which may well refer to the same process: the temptation might be to inherit Heaven's graces and to husband nature's riches from expense. But 'to temptation slow' is linked on all levels with 'Unmoved, cold . . . slow' and to the image-complex, 'as stone', which makes it an unattractive and despised activity. And thus on internal evidence those phrases in the second quatrain which parallel it partake also of its failings. Further, 'rightly' performs the same distancing function as 'do not do the thing' in the first stanza: it makes us wonder if we are to take these apparently admirable activities as good things, endorsed by the poet. 'But stewards' supports this effect.

Nevertheless, 'husband nature's riches from expense' and 'inherit Heaven's graces', though they may be distanced by irony, do introduce a new and rich sequence of vowels and consonants. And it is this pattern that will dominate the rest of the sonnet. The pattern also picks up the neglected *r s* which were quite overborne by the *o d* in the first quatrain; and it transforms these neglected sounds into positive dominants. It is no accident that this occurs with 'Others', for the first time in position of subject—'Others [are] but stewards'—and occupying a key position at the beginning of the last line of the octave. Whatever else the poet is ambivalent about he is faithful to his formal patterns and to the way in which, conjoined with image-complexes, they convey the attitude he wishes the reader to adopt to his theme.

'They are the lords and owners of their faces' now seems a neglected ourpost which has long been abandoned; whatever 'They' are lords and owners of, it is certainly not this poem. Empson is mistaken to extrapolate to non-verbal ownership; careerism is not confined to the upper classes; many poets had to be 'vulgar' careerists in the Elizabethan, as indeed in all other, ages. There is also a suggestion of grim humour in 'you may inherit the Heavenly graces but, by God, you miss the earthly and endearing ones'. But Empson's stress on ownership as the bone of contention between 'They' and the 'others' is correct in the sense in which it is a tug of war for ownership of the sonnet between the poet and 'They'.

The giveaway occurs in the line 'Others but stewards of their excellence': its mock-modesty does not long conceal that the 'others' have been in control from the first and that their real theme is themselves, not 'They'. And who else, pray, could be in control of a poem but its poet who organises its various levels? We have always been aware that this poet slips in equivocations and qualifications, even ironies, when he appears most to be doing straight description. He is able to do this in the way explained by using non-semantic levels of the poem's organisation: by syntactical and metrical equivocation throughout but especially in the first quatrain, by sound pattern which subtly switches the *a d* to *r s*, and by convention which equates 'graces' with 'faces', 'expense' with 'excellence', in a very neat piece of semantic ambiguity. Is 'husbanding nature's riches from expense' the same as 'excellence'? And, if so, is 'excellence' to be predicated of the other synonymous phrases, 'inherit Heaven's graces', 'to temptation slow', 'do not do the thing they most do show'? This is a strange kind of excellence. But if this is so for 'They', then what of their stewards? What does it mean to be steward to a hypocritical, rich, charming, beautiful, powerful, frigid, miser? Shakespeare, after all, knew that 'Tis mad idolatry to make the service greater than the God'.

We now move on to the final six lines which, since they are Shakespeare's attempt to consolidate his position as we have discovered it above, need not detain us so long. Thereafter the centre of gravity shifts completely from 'They' to 'Others', although until the final couplet all Shakespeare's energies—which are considerable—are bent on preventing the reader from discovering this shift.

In the third quatrain the poet abandons his claim to discursive objectivity and resorts to a comparison with natural processes. In doing so he deploys his usual equivocality of stress, as in the first two lines, while seeming to make an unexceptional statement. He then converts this into a moral commonplace (Like Dr Chasuble's, his metaphor is drawn from flowers):

> The summer's flower is to the summer sweet
> Though to itself it only live and die;
> But if that flower with base infection meet,
> The basest weed outbraves his dignity.

We can now have no doubt as to our thematic referents for 'summer's flower' and Summer': 'summer's flower' refers to 'They' and 'summer' to the 'others' (the poet). 'They' may live only to themselves—they are, as we know from the first eight lines, selfish—but really they live so that Shakespeare may write poems about their qualities and his feelings. I must stress again that these feelings are conveyed by the non-semantic levels of metre, rhythm, convention, sound pattern, not by reference outside the poem. The non-semantic levels need only be related to each other and to the level of meaning as they filter it to produce a thematic synthesis.

Similarly with the next two lines; no one need be deceived by the mock-modesty in 'basest weed' as epithet for the poet. The poet is experimenting, not botanically but with the changes to be rung on the levels of Artifice, with the movement between summer's flower and summer and the mirrored movement between 'flower', 'base infection', and 'basest weed'. The pen is mightier than the sword, mightier even than nature (Does not Shakespeare claim as much? Should we be discussing the sonnet if it were not true?). While ostensibly going to nature, having found other areas of discourse—law, feudal ownership, society—inadequate, Shakespeare is in fact going to his own realm of Artifice where new relations reinvigorate the old by absorbing them. We have been aware all along that the activities predicated of 'They' were viewed in an ambivalent way; when we get to the first two lines of this third quatrain something happens on the level of sound pattern that gives us the long concealed I/you axis and a key word in the thematic synthesis in an unequivocal manner. The pattern of x o and s is interrupted in the phrase 'live and die', and it is interrupted with an x i. We have to think about 'live and die' since it sums up 'their' activities and seems pretty comprehensive, so that whatever it is 'they' don't do must be an unusual thing. If we transfer this inference from the level of meaning to the level of sound pattern we can alter 'live' to make it conform to the o pattern, which will give us the word that has been hovering over the poem since the first line: 'love'. What we have in the line 'Though to itself it only live and die' is the almost overt statement 'I love', for the fact that the pattern is interrupted with an i together with the reader's search for the 'I' in the poem make it an easy step to transfer the i from lower to upper case.

But is loving such an unusual activity? The answer must be that for the 'I' of this poem it is. And indeed, when we remember unattractiveness of 'they' it does seem that for Shakespeare here to say 'I love' is to give the verb an unusual significance. The fact that it is concealed does something towards this also, for we can find it only by attention to the sound pattern and this predicates writing poems as well as loving of the 'I'.

This inference is possible because the reader is able to equate 'summer' with 'others' and therefore with the poet. And we must note that 'summer's flower' has given us an *l* which is repeated in the key word 'live', for this *l* reoccurs in the last two lines juxtaposed with *i* in 'Lilies'. The juxtaposition is important because it reminds the reader of the juxtaposition in 'live'. The reader asks himself, why 'lilies'? 'Flowers that fester' would have kept up the pattern of *o* and *l* and given an alliteration in *f* but 'flowers', or course, contains no *i*. So that the answer to 'Why lilies?' can only be that the poet wanted to stress that key juxtaposition of *l* and *i*. Thus the thematic statement 'I love' is kept hovering over the final couplet.

In that couplet this synthesis in and through Artifice is triumphantly asserted:

> For sweetest things turn sourest by their deeds:
> Lilies that fester smell far worse than weeds.

The image-complex is allowed to expand over two lines, flaunting its importance as a thematic analogy. The mention of the lily, which might have been banal, is boldly paradoxical: an image of perfection. This recourse to the natural world implies that 'nature bears me out', but that external reference is absorbed by the poem, which comes to assert that 'nature bears me out because I am able to reorganise it in this elaborate pattern of Artifice.' The intensification of formal patterning—'*sweetest*' '*sourest*', '*sweetest things turn*', '*sweet*' '*weeds*', '*worse*' '*weeds*'— announces the firmness of poetic control. It does not matter whether real lilies fester and give forth foul odours; nor does the image seem to relate to an empirical individual: no one, however 'debauched', as Empson calls the unfortunate W.H., would be gratified to be called a festering lily. The image brings the outside world into the poem and shows the subservience of external values to the re-organising Artifice of sound pattern and image-complex. 'Lilies that fester' are a necessary fiction which allow the poem to marshal its last two lines as support for and exemplification of the triumph of 'others', who, acting as stewards, are the masters of Artifice.

III   *Sonnet 94 and what it has taught us*

If the reader has followed the argument so far he will not need much recapitulation, but it is perhaps worth stressing what Sonnet 94 has *not* taught us. It has told us how closely Shakespeare identified his activities as poet and as lover and a good deal about how he felt about loving 'they'. It tells us nothing about how we ourselves should behave except as readers. What is has taught us further is a great deal about how to read this poem and, by extension, any poem. It has shown that neither the thematic, nor the formal/conventional, nor the semantic level working on its own is sufficient to embody the range of ideas and of reactions to ideas that most competent poems and any great poem would require language to embody.

The image-complex is the node where we can discover which of the multitude of thematic, semantic, rhythmical, and formal, patterns is important and how it is to be related to the others. For the image-complex alone operates on all the levels of sound, rhythm, theme, and meaning and from it alone, therefore, can be derived a sense of the structure of any particular poem. The conventional level that marks the rhyme-words and beginnings of lines is also crucial since from it alone, as we saw in my first anatomy, can the clue to the thematic synthesis emerge. Once put conventional and image-complicated levels together and all the rest will follow. The choice of convention and image-complex is crucial both to the poet as he writes and to the reader as he tries to interpet; for the words used in these conventionally stressed places will both work downwards to determine which formal patterns dominate, and move upwards to produce a thematic synthesis from the way in which they mesh with the level of meaning.

All this occurs on the scale of relevance and thus in accordance with critical Naturalisation. But just as traditional poetry has always, on its non-semantic levels, made provision for irrelevance, so critical Naturalisation must make provision for its own suspension. Critical reading must never try to impose meaning in the form of an extension of meaning into the non-verbal world until the reader has determined by examining the non-meaningful levels just what amount of meaning is required by the poem's structure from each phrase, word, and letter. Only when this is done can the critic hope to reach a thematic synthesis which will make contact with the poem itself on its many levels and not with some abstract, or indeed, concrete, entity created out of his own imagination.

The reader must, of course, use his imagination; that is what poetry is for. But he must use it to free himself from the fixed forms of thought which ordinary language imposes on our minds, not to deny the strangeness of poetry by inserting it in some non-poetic area: his own mind, the poet's mind, or any non-fictional situation. By examining the non-semantic levels of Artifice and by seeing how their relations lead the poem into non-verbal contexts we have arrived at a thematic synthesis very similar to the usual reading of this sonnet, but with the difference that our reading is supported by internal relations; we could get it even if we knew nothing of the author's other work. We have seen that, through the ambivalence of the stresses and the syntax in the first quatrain, the good qualities mentioned in the second are cast in doubt; that while seeming to praise 'They' the poet in fact condemns them through his image-complexes; that the sound pattern shifts of *o d* to *r s* as the poet's anxiety to make 'They' seem praiseworthy increases in the second quatrain. Further, this *r s* smothers the *o* in 'others' and makes it plain that the 'others' are in control though they be 'but stewards'. Finally in the last couplet the poet abandons his attempt to present 'They' in a favourable light, increases the ambivalence felt throughout but most strongly in the second quatrain's image-complexes ('The summer's flower is to the summer sweet/Though to itself it only live and die'), introduces a new image-complex in the festering lily, and brings together form, theme, and external reference, by making the poem cohere as a denunciation of 'They'. Thus the external context brought about by extension of meaning is filtered into the internal context of the poem's various relations. Meaning gives us 'odi et amo', and the deployment of sound in the image-complexes takes up the thematic synthesis of 'I love and am jealous of your good qualities though I think they are really bad' and gives it an internal application: 'my good qualities as poet are better than yours as beloved, as witness this skilful sonnet'. The external Naturalisation of 'you appear so good but are really so bad' is thus turned into an internal Naturalisation which we can follow through the image-complexes.

It is in the devices of Artifice as I have so far employed them that the reader will find the tools to help him build and make articulate his palace of imagination, and to this end, in the following chapter, we shall turn to the question of just how hard it is to tread the line between the imagination and the unimagined 'real', how difficult it is—since language is common to both 'reality' and 'imagination'—to attain the artifice of eternity through language.

CHAPTER ONE

Continuity
in language

> Even animals are not shut off from this wisdom, but show they are clearly
> initiated into it. For they do not stand stock still before things of sense as if
> they were things *per se* with being in themselves: they despair of this reality
> altogether, and, in complete assurance of the nothingness of things, they
> fall-to without more ado and eat them up.
>
> Hegel: *Phenomenology of Mind*

Language is common both to the realm of poetry and to the domain of
ordinary experience, and this is one of the main factors with which a
study of poetic language must deal. For our ordinary non-poetic language gives us the world which we generally regard as non-verbal: a
world of emotions, objects, and states of affairs. This is the language we
use every day (from now on I shall call it, for simplicity's sake, 'ordinary
language') and it is this language upon which Artifice must work to create
its alternative imaginary orders. Of course, poetry deals also with the
more specialised languages of, say, science, philosophy, religion, and
cookery, but these do not present the same basic problem. For in them
the non-verbal is already highly mediated, and Artifice has only to work
on their alien structures of words, which must be absorbed and transformed into poetry.

When dealing with ordinary language, however, poetry has to con-
front the assumption that there is a non-verbal situation existing outside
language which it is poetry's task to present. Ezra Pound claims that 'in
the art of Daniel and Cavalcanti, I have seen that precision which I miss
in the Victorians, that explicit rendering, be it of external nature, or of
emotion. Their testimony is of the eyewitness, their symptoms are first
hand'.[1] This may stand as the type of such assumptions (though, to do
Pound justice, he never believed that technique could be by-passed in
such external rendering).

We have already come across these assumptions in our reading of Sonnet 94 and, while it is easy to refute the notion that Shakespeare is talking
directly about his love life or any specific person or persons, it is not so
easy to do away with the idea that there is emotion in that poem, that
there are attitudes which emerge from that arrangement of words, and
that these attitudes and emotions are not entirely explicable as the result
of the words' meaning as part of technique. In point of fact it is not

entirely clear why we should want to do away with the notion that there is feeling in poetry, for we should find ourselves very quickly arguing that poetry is of no interest at all. What is clear is that we cannot locate the emotion in either our minds or the poet's mind as situations outside the poem. If this were the case then T. E. Hulme would be right to claim that poetry was shorthand for a language of feeling that would hand over sensations bodily, and we should all be dying to get rid of the poetry to enter empathetic, kinaesthetic and inarticulate rapture.

But is this the case? No. Unless we are disciples of Norman O. Brown (and in that case we should not be interested in the problems of poetic theory). Where, then, can we safely situate these troublesome emotions? Where else but in the language of the poem itself, in those non-semantic features for which I have claimed the power to select and define the thematic synthesis that the reader should insert in the poem. For these features I now claim the further power to generate the required emotional reactions and, by their relationship to the level of meaning, to delimit the non-verbal context which the poem uses as a fiction in its structure.

In a poem which begins

> From fairest creatures we desire increase

the language is working to achieve both continuity and discontinuity with a world of ordinary experience. The sentence implies the existence of 'fairest creatures'—animate beings ranked high on an evaluative scale—and suggests an attitude held by a significant portion of mankind ('we'). 'Increase' takes for granted, as elements which are fed into the poem, a whole background of natural processes. But the continuity which relates the poetic line to other situations in which its various words might be used is dominated by a discontinuity which distances and reorganises. The play of sound in 'creatures . . . increase', intensified by the vowel of 'we', creates a structural solidarity unusual in ordinary language; the conventions of verse insist that we notice this, as a distinctive value with an important role. This assertion of the form of the linguistic material itself exerts pressure on external references, limiting them to what the poetic structure requires. The phonetic solidarity of 'creatures . . . increase' acts as a kind of proof of semantic appropriateness: we need not look outside the poem for any particular creatures (from a biographical situation) or any attested desire. The desire has been made an appropriate one by the artifice of the line, and 'creatures' are simply whatever should multiply. In short, the fact that we are reading a poem rather than a letter, speech, etc., calls us to relate the formal pattern to the meaning. This is achieved by lifting the meaning away from direct reference to an external state of affairs and preparing it for its part in a thematic synthesis, where the external contexts are evoked only to be made fictional.

Our reading must work through the level of meaning into the external world and then, via the non-semantic levels of Artifice, back into the poem, enriched by the external contexts of reference in which it found itself momentarily merged. This is what continuity in poetic language means. Without it the reader would have no way of making connections between poetic language and any other kind of language or between poetic language and the experience given him by the world of ordinary language which he inhabits most of the time. He would then retreat into either tendentious inarticulateness outside poetry—as did the Dadaists—or into tendentious Naturalisation which allows no play to the non-meaningful devices of Artifice—as so many critics and even poets have done in the last fifty years. Either manoeuvre deprives poetry of its essential strength of give and take with its environment, and both deprive it of its essential power over that environment. This power depends, as our analysis of Sonnet 94 has tried to suggest, on the non-meaningful levels of language. If poetry cannot control the meanings and feelings generated by the words it uses, its worth is reduced. If it cannot control experience by verbal relationships that channel it in a structural attitude, then its worth is less than that of the latest *News of the World* 'confession'.

Poetry's dealings with emotions, objects, and situations all fall under the general problem of continuity and discontinuity: the way in which poetry retains its contact with the world articulated by ordinary language while distancing itself from these customary modes of articulation. The power of poetry depends on its ability to maintain continuity while achieving discontinuity, but it is difficult to show precisely how this is done in particular cases. The best way to approach the problem is to study the various strategies and technical devices by which poetry distances itself from ordinary language and through which it limits the kind of external material which is assimilated and subjected to new organisation and articulation.

Several of Wittgenstein's remarks can give us a perspective on the problem and help to set the stage for discussion. First, 'the limits of my language mean the limits of my world.'[2] The basis of continuity between poetry and the rest of one's experience is the essentially verbal nature of that experience: the fact that it takes shape through language. What we can know of experience always lies within language. And, correspondingly, 'to imagine a language means to imagine a form of life.'[3] The world is not something static, irredeemably given by a natural language. When language is re-imagined the world expands with it. The continuity which makes it possible to read the world into words provides that the world may be enlarged or enriched by the enlargement of one's awareness of language and/or awareness of others' enlargement of their awareness of language. However, 'awareness' and knowledge' are perhaps the wrong words if they suggest that this expansion involves simply an accretion of information. As Wittgenstein says, 'the grammar of the word "knows" is evidently closely related to that of "can", "is able to". But also closely related to that of "understands" ("Mastery" of a technique).'[4] The knowledge of both the poet and the reader of poetry is a kind of mastery, an ability to see how a use of language filters external contexts into the poem and subjects them to new distancing and articulation. The knowledge of readers and writers of poetry is an ability to exclude and to include and to grasp imaginative relations which are implicit in the words of the poem when they are read in terms of the conventions of poetry. It is mastery of these conventions that underlies the experience of 'seeing as' which the poem produces. To quote from Wittgenstein once more, ' "Now he's seeing it like *this*", "now like *that*" would only be said of someone *capable* of making certain applications of the figure quite freely. The substratum of this experience is the mastery of a technique.'[5]

A study of the way in which the conventions and formal devices of poetry direct the assimilation of external contexts and produce the discontinuity which gives poetry its power over those contexts will also be an account of the kind of mastery which is required of the reader of poetry. Learning to read poetry is a matter of acquiring the ability to hold together, simultaneously, continuity and discontinuity in the requisite proportions.

To see what is involved in the achievement of continuity and discontinuity, to see how poetry modifies and distances itself from the external contexts it assimilates, we might start with the most elementary case of poetic convention. If one takes a passage of prose and rearranges it on the page as verse, the language itself remains the same and hence any changes in its effects can be attributed to the new type of awareness with which we approach the verse passage. Any differences, in short, can be identified as effects which result from the conventional level: it is by convention that we read and organise the verse passage in ways that make it different from prose.

In a book on *Metre, Rhyme, and Free Verse*, Mr George Fraser tries this experiment of rearranging a passage of prose as free verse and claims that the rhythms which remain are those of prose. Poetry is absent, except insofar as the prose original contained pure stress rhythms and poetic figures.[6] In one sense this is perfectly true. If we rearrange prose as poetry in order to bring out rhythmic patterns we can only bring out elements or patterns which were dormant in the prose. Indeed, this is why the convention of free verse was developed in the first place: to make us aware of the poetry in our prose, of the imaginative alternatives that exist even in ordinary language. But the fact that resulting poetic rhythms were already there in the prose only makes more evident the fact that the differences between the prose and verse passage are the result of a change in conventional expectations, modes of attention, and interpretive strategies, rather than the result of any alteration of the linguistic material itself.

By way of example, I propose to rearrange as free verse what no-one, except perhaps certain members of the journalistic profession, would claim to be latent literature: a paragraph from a *Times* leader. The first paragraph of the first leader for Friday, December 15th, 1972, in its original form runs as follows:

AT THE HEAD OF THE BBC

The Government have taken their time in appointing the new chairman of the BBC, which is a measure both of the importance now attached to the office and of the difficulty in persuading somebody of the necessary quality to take it on a part-time basis at £6,000 a year. But in choosing Sir Michael Swann they have made a good selection, and a very much better one than might have been expected after such a delay. Both his record at Edinburgh, where he has been Principal and Vice-Chancellor of the university since 1965, and his comments on his appointment suggest that he will bring the right approach to his new responsibilities.

I have not kept the original line-endings but this is immaterial since the alignment is governed by the requirements of the printer which have no relation to the matter in hand. That is, no violation of material rules is involved since there is no continuum in newspapers between the meaning of the paragraph and the way it is arranged. Quite otherwise with the rules of rearranging the paragraph as verse, as a poem entitled 'At the head of the BBC':

> The Government have taken their time
> in appointing a new chairman of the
> BBC
> which is a measure both
> of the importance now attached to the office
> and of the difficulty in persuading somebody
> of the necessary quality
> to take it
> on a part-time basis
> at £6,000 a year

There is no need to look, as Mr Fraser did in his re-writing of a passage from a novel, for poetic figures or traditional stress rhythm as used, for example, in Eliot's verse plays. For twentieth-century poetry has evolved a whole new set of conventions for showing which words are dominant on any scale. Poems may or may not use traditional metre, rhythm, and rhyme, but they do generally stick to the convention that beginnings and ends of lines are marked as important in the thematic synthesis.

In the example above this is seen in lines 1, 3, 6, and in the body of the other lines where there is an ironic tone. 'Taken their time' stresses the Government's dilatoriness; 'BBC' casts a sardonic eye on that institution; 'somebody' suggests a frenetic haste to find 'anybody'. As for the other lines, 'necessary quality' suggests, given the previous ironic tinge, that the Government is being self-important; 'to take it' suggests that they have been begging anybody to accept it (which is at variance with the pomp); 'on a part-time basis' still contrasts the supposed importance with the casualness it has in fact. And 'at £6,000 a year' increases the irony (especially for those who are underpaid and overworked) by implying that £6,000 a year is a paltry sum for anyone to accept for a part-time job.

This ironic tone could be made blatant by increasing the use of poetic conventions:

At the 'head' of the BBC

The Government
　　　　　　have taken their 'time'
in appointing the
　　　　　　'new chairman' of the BBC
which is a measure both
　　　　　　of the 'importance'
now 'attached'
　　　　　　to the 'office' and of the difficulty
of persuading
　　　　　　somebody of the 'necessary quality'
to take it on a 'part-time basis' at
　　　　　　£6,000 a year
　　　　BUT
In choosing Sir Michael Swann
　　　　　　they have made a
'good selection' and
　　　　　　a very much better one
than might have been expected
　　　　　　after such a delay.
BOTH his record at Edinburgh
　　　　　　where he has been
'Principal and Vice-Chancellor' of the university
　　　　　　since 1965
AND his 'comments on his appointment'
　　　　　　suggest
that he will bring 'the right approach' to his new 'responsibilities'.

The line-spacing across the page, which is the first thing to catch the eye, is a formal convention much used in all poetry but especially in poetry of this century, where neither stress or syllable metre is accepted as the norm and where other means must therefore be found to signal the importance of phrases and, if possible, to distinguish a dominant rhythm. The title already introduces another important convention, by no means confined to this century, but which has come to have a much greater importance that it had before: the use of quotation marks. Here they indicate the distance, the ironic distance, of the poet from the world of officialdom which he (for convenience's sake let us stick to one gender) regards with amused and slightly embittered annoyance.

How do we know that this is his attitude? From the way in which he uses the poetic convention of quotation marks to enclose official jargon. This is another mark of continuity between poetry and other languages: the conventions of poems see to it that the other languages are subordinated. And it is another instance of the way in which we can deduce from internal relations an attitude that might be supposed to exist outside the poem. The line-endings themselves would not do this, for they do not tell what kind of stress should be given to the words that end and begin, and I have chosen not to feed through these words into the formal pattern, for this is difficult without metre and would be obfuscatory for the present purpose.

The irony is increased by the use of capitalised 'BUT', 'BOTH', 'AND', which use necessary breaks in syntax to give the rudiments of a formal structure to the layout and thus link the levels of theme, meaning, and form to preserve continuity. The same is true of the italics; the focus attention and determine which contexts are appropriate. My suggestion that 'somebody', for instance, could imply a frantic search for 'anybody' is now converted into a definite thematic implication by the conjunction of three kinds of contentional features: line-breaks, which give importance, quotation marks, which by that stage in the poem have established ironic distance, and italics. The point is that these conventions do not conjoin in a void; they operate with meanings of the words to modify and filter the external contexts which the meanings involve; only thus is a thematic synthesis possible. Naturally it is not much of a synthesis since we have left out image-complexes and formal patterns, but bringing these in would have swamped and obscured the austere demonstration that even so slight a re-arrangement can open up imaginative possibilities in a dull piece of prose. And it would have obscured the more important point that it is through linking conventional expectations and the external contexts implied by syntax and lexis that these contexts may become indicators of the emotion or attitude the words are to carry.

By taking another poem which uses rhythm and its semantic feed-back to increase formal pattern and relate it to the conventional level and image complexes, we can see that the thematic synthesis becomes more complicated when the poet does not merely stand back to satirise but includes himself as a persona in the poem. This step also increases the number of external contexts which contribute the creation of a general fictional context, for the poet is not committed to the single stance of the satirist but may include alternatives to satire. The poem is Pound's 'Homage to Sextus Propertius', from which I shall quote lines that include a sneer at officialdom but go no further than 'At the "head" of the BBC':

Out-weariers of Apollo will, as we know, continue their Martian generalities,
    We have kept our erasers in order.
A new-fangled chariot follows the flower-hung horses;
A young Muse with young loves clustered about her
    ascends with me into the æther, . . .
And there is no high-road to the Muses.

Annalists will continue to record Roman reputations,
Celebrities from the Trans-Caucasus will belaud Roman celebrities
And expound the distentions of Empire,
But for something to read in normal circumstances?
For a few pages brought down from the forked hill unsullied?
I ask a wreath which will not crush my head.
                And there is no hurry about it;
I shall have, doubtless, a boom after my funeral,
Seeing that long standing increases all things
            regardless of quality.[7]

Naturally this is better than my little exercise; its operations involve speech-rhythm in the taut syllable metre of the verse and in the two mythologies of Greece and of Propertius' Rome. These appropriate the conventional and the thematic level without needing to use cruder devices such as capitalisation for emphasis, italics, and quotation marks. The personages and decor of the lines are already distanced from the reader by the fact that they come from a world remote from him in time and situation. In time, because the reference is to mythology and history and this brings in an area of alien discourse which is not as readily assimilated to the present world of ordinary language; in situation, since the stance is that of the poet, Pound/Propertius. The reader must work through these initial thematic fictions before trying to naturalise.

This distancing, this halt, imposes a suspension which makes us examine the formal features before we are certain of their relation to any thematic synthesis, whereas in 'BBC' the formal features were taken from the extension of meaning into an already given theme. I say 'theme' rather than 'thematic synthesis' because a conjunction that does not use image-complex or formal (sound/look) pattern deprives itself of the most important tools for reminding the reader that he is maintaining a balance between continuity and discontinuity with the world of ordinary language. Syntax was seen to be the most malleable aspect of poems, for it can lead either out from or into the other levels, but if syntax is used—and punctuation marks are included in syntax—to provide the organisation for all the other levels, the poem becomes locked in a stance that makes movement inside it impossible. In 'BBC' the conventional level is dictated by a single purpose: to use the plain fact of being written as poetry to induce the reader to adopt a particular attitude towards the language of officialdom; to adopt the ironic stance which the poem enforces. In the Pound example, however, we find much more freedom due simply to the fact that the conventional level varies; it does not always support a single attitude.

First we have the ironic stance in the two opening lines, but this is modified within these lines by 'as we know' which, besides establishing a contrast between 'we' and 'they', converts the line-pause at 'their' into a thematic implication. That is, the levels give and take among themselves so that the conventional level may either rise to support a thematic implication or remain content with the one inevitable function of indicating that this is a poem. 'Martian generalities' is isolated by the conventional level—set off as an independent line—but connected through syntax and diction with the lines immediately preceding and following. Since this example works on the scale of relevance the reader is justified in assuming an external context which will be fictionalised by the relation between the various levels and traceable on the level of meaning. He assumes, that is to say, not simply the existence of meaning but the relevance of areas of the external world to which the meaning refers. And while 'Martian generalities' implies a continuity with classical myth as found in the first line's reference to Apollo, its overtones of pomposity contrast its external context with that of 'we'.

'We' and 'they' are brought into the lines both as references and as correlates of thematic oppositions among which the poem can move and which it can develop. Whereas in 'BBC' the conventions of meaning lead us to infer a poetic mind existing outside the poem, here the conventions which lead one to imagine referents for 'I', 'we' and 'they' are absorbed into the poem as a set of shifting relations through and around which it moves. Sometimes the convention of poetic stance is used to make diction imply an attitude, as in the polysyllabic 'expound the distentions of Empire'; sometimes diction is used to change the convention, to enforce a shift in stance, as, for instance, in the quickened rhythm and near colloquialism of 'And there is no hurry about it'.

All this is part of a process which I shall define as *internal limitation and expansion*: what happens when the world of ordinary language is drawn into the poem's technique so that those parts of that world implied by the meaning of words and phrases are limited by their function inside the poem but also expanded by the power released when levels other than meaning become important. Opposed to such a process is the *external limitation and expansion* which, relying upon pre-conceived ideas about the necessity of relating a poem to the world that exists outside it, limits the movement of internal organisation to those patterns which can be made relevant in a move into an external, non-poetic world. In 'BBC', for example, such areas were our knowledge about the contemporary world, about the way people use punctuation marks to indicate their attitude to what they say, and about the ways a poet might use his techniques to support his external stance. The Pound lines do almost exactly the reverse, since they include the external world as part of the poem and thus make it fictitious. I say 'almost' since there is not an exact correspondence between the twin processes of external limitation/expansion and internal limitation/expansion; if there were, then we could neither read the world into the arrangement of a poem nor distinguish the various levels at which the poem's technique reorganises the external contexts it has assimilated. In short, continuity in language—the relation between poetic discourse and other kinds of discourse which directly imply a world—requires discontinuity, a dislocation that occurs when one passes from the latter to the former. This is the central paradox of poetry. Mr Booth puts it thus:

> Art must distort; if it is to justify its existence, it must be other than the reality whose difficulty necessitates artistic mediation. It must seem as little a distortion as possible, because its audience wants comprehension of incomprehensible reality itself. We do not want so much to live in *a* world organised on human principles as to live in *the* world so organised. Art must seem to reveal a humanly ordered reality rather than replace a random one.[8]

Such a general statement of the paradox helps us to see why our particular problem of poetry's situation between fact and fiction needs the special solution towards which I am working, for it highlights the questions of mediation. We have all been taught, by Marx, Freud, *The Golden Bough*, and contemporary developments in Anthropology and Linguistics, that the human consciousness cannot get at reality itself without mediation. This applies whether the agents of mediation be, as for a pattern inherent in the human mind which imposes binary form on the inchoate, or, as for Marx, the self-justifying ideological structures which produce a social class's 'objective reality', or again, as for Freud, the operations of condensation and displacement which order the world as figures of desire. Most relevant for us, perhaps, is the insistence of Benjamin Lee Whorf and of the linguists who attend to semantics that as a language changes from one society to another so does the world in which the members of the society live.[9]

'All this the world knows well yet none knows well to shun the heaven that leads men to this hell', for literary theory has not kept up, has not kept that fact of mediation firmly in view. Critics have been slow to realize that literature, being based on language, cannot—to use a Poundian phrase—get at the things behind language in some special way and that there may, in fact, be nothing (at least for the human mind) more real than forms of language. We find, for example, J. P. Sullivan praising the lines from 'Homage' which I have quoted as a triumph over 'artificial diction': 'because Pound's style is an individual creation and emerges from a living language which is felt in all its nuances, because it has for background the colloquial speech of everyday', Pound's 'Homage' is able to get at the 'reality' of emotional experience and situation behind Propertius' poeticising.[10] Need one emphasize that it is scarcely praise to tell a poet that his greatest genius lies in not being a poet, in transcending those features of his art that make it an art, in lapsing into dependence on the level of meaning as 'BBC' does, and thus immersing and obscuring his art so that it becomes a 'comment on life'. This view makes his art subservient to life as we know it rather than a subversion and reinvention of that life through artifice; it makes us ignore mediation and take the 'reality' given us by ordinary language as the final court of appeal.

Luckily not all poetic theorists have succumbed to this view, and I shall hope to show that not all poets have put their theories into this realistic straight-jacket. In some literary styles, notably, but not entirely, those developed in this century, the connection between verbal form and the extension of verbal meaning into the non-verbal world may be openly questioned. The implication that 'reality' is a product of linguistic rules may emerge. As Paul de Man claims, 'literature, unlike everyday language, begins on the far side of this knowledge; it is the only form of language free from the fallacy of unmediated expression'.[11] De Man goes on to connect this fact with the priority of form over meaning and sees this latter as an analogue, essential to our understanding of literature, of the priority of fiction over reality.

This is the theme of my book, and my task it to develop a method of demonstrating it in practice. To such an end I have set forth my system of Artifice as deployed in the analysis of Sonnet 94 in the Introduction. Nevertheless, a further schematisation now seems needed, and in order that there may be no dichotomy between this and the system of Artifice I shall rechristen internal limitation/expansion as *artificial limitation/expansion* and external limitation/expansion as *realistic limitation/expansion*. We must remember that the difference between my 'BBC' and the lines from 'Homage' lay in the former's use of conventions, that already exist in non-poetic language, to signal that it was a poem and then to lead out through these extended-meaning conventions. This made artificial thematic synthesis impossible (so that I spoke of 'theme' rather than 'thematic synthesis') and we shall not be surprised that premature and external Naturalisation corresponds with the process of realistic limitation/expansion, while suspended and internal Naturalisation corresponds with artificial limitation/expansion.

We might now try to identify these operations more explicitly by schematising the good and bad Naturalisations of the lines from Pound. First, the process of realistic limitation/expansion or bad Naturalisation.

I

First presupposition: poetry uses the language of a man speaking to men and therefore I can understand these lines by relating them to ordinary language and to the non-verbal world.

First stage: what is the poem about? *Method:* Look at the title; it will sum up the theme. *Result:* 'Homage to Sextus Propertius'. These lines were written by a poet who felt he had something in common with Propertius.

Second stage: What did Pound in these lines give us to understand that he had in common with Propertius? *Method:* (this follows from the first presupposition). This common factor must be situated in the external world. Look at external contexts, bring external knowledge to bear on the poem. *Result:* Pound is comparing his situation as a poet writing in London in 1917 with the situation in Propertius' Rome. What is Pound's situation? Answer: he thinks he is in an uncongenial environment; he is embittered by the fact that 'the pianola "replaces" Sappho's barbitos' (lyre), that 'we see *to kalon* displayed in the market place', and that inferior writers are elevated and true merit ignored. What has this in common with Propertius' situation? Answer: Propertius was less appreciated by his contemporaries than Virgil and Horace, whom he considered inferior poets; one of the reasons for this attitude was the fact that they engaged in the Latin equivalent of Mr Nixon's advice to 'Hugh Selwyn Mauberley'; the 'buttered reviewers'. That is, they toadied Maecenas, the greatest patron of his day, and through him, the Emperor himself, and they did this by writing poems on the Emperor's military triumphs. Propertius' bitterness was not made less by the fact that, in order to succeed at all in a poetic career, he had to accept Horace's influence to approach Maecenas. In this also he resembled Pound who had to conform to *some* of the poetic orthodoxies of his day. (And note, in passing, that this is all external evidence from what we know of first cen-

tury Rome and the first two decades of this century.) *Result:* Pound and
Propertius share a dislike of officialdom.

Now, how can we read this attitude into the actual lines? Answer:
'Annalists' who 'will continue to record Roman reputations', 'Celebrities
from the Trans-Caucasus' who 'will belaud Roman celebrities/And
expound the distentions of empire' are set against 'something to read in
normal circumstances', 'a few pages brought down from the forked hill
unsullied', 'a wreath which will not crush my head'. The casual colloquialism of Pound/Propertius' diction is set against the pomposity of
the official jargon. But they inhabit the same world, as is made plain by
the mention of the laurel wreath that crowns poets and the 'forked hill'
(where Helicon springs) in the colloquial part of the lines. And therefore
both the ironic poet and his victims inhabit the same world as the poet
behind the persona and the reader outside the poem. The scene is
fictional, certainly, but it is the fiction that reproduces the illusion of reality by modelling its technique on the techniques of those other languages
which structure the world, and especially on the techniques of a critical
reading which is anxious to stress the continuity between poetry and the
'real' world—so anxious that it ignores or smothers the differences.

We know, of course, that this fragment is part of a poem, but that is
entirely because it uses line spacing—the conventional level. Apart from
that, it seems as though the piece might just as well have been written in
prose as was, originally, 'BBC'. The process of realistic expansion/
limitation has produced nothing to show us that special skills are
involved or that these lines are different from my rearranged 'BBC',
because no attention has been paid to devices that do not lead the level of
meaning upwards into themes in the non-verbal world. Pound and Propertius expressed their disgust and bitterness at their contemporary literary 'scene' by writing verse satire. That is all we know on earth and all we
need to know. As far as realistic limitation/expansion is concerned,
indeed, it would be impossible for us to know more, since the formal keys
to the other levels of Artifice are deliberately obfuscated by the blanket of
our already-known reality.

Let us see what artificial limitation/expansion can do with the lines.

II

First presupposition: poetry is different from any other language though it
may use all others for its own ends; it stresses the artificial nature of the
world we make through language. *First stage:* What is this poem doing?
Method: look at the conventional level and see what initially separates and
distances this piece of language from others. *Result:* First, the title indicates a literary genre: an 'homage' is as much a formal 'kind' as an elegy,

ode, or sonnet.[12] Second, the spacing of lines on the page indicates that this is a poem and therefore, to go a step further than in realistic naturalisation, that it is a sample of the kind of artifice which links the modern poet with the ancient and leads him to write in homage. For a poet to write a *poem* rather than a prose tract in praise of a poetic predecessor is, at the very least, a significant act which enjoins us to ask in what respect the process of writing poetry, the techniques of composition, act out the homage and display the relation to the predecessor.

Third, why Propertius rather than other poets of the day? What is the connection in artifice? Sullivan says that Propertius 'is a poet who should appeal very strongly . . . to the romantic and post-romantic sensibility, and it is indicative of Pound's flair for what is relevant to a poetic tradition that he should have become interested in Propertius.'[13] The qualities that distinguish Propertius from his poetic competitors and make him more relevant than they to modern versification are, as Sullivan says, his 'Alexandrianism', a refusal to be carried away, or to pretend to be carried away, by a simple desire to utter, an insistence on the importance of his stylistic craftsmanship and his arcane scholarship. This can be seen in Pound's invocation of the Alexandrians elsewhere in the 'Homage', as well as in a kind of imitation: Pound's own obscurity on the thematic level corresponds to Propertius' frequent obscurity and to the crabbiness of his style on the formal level. The 'Homage', in short, asserts at the conventional level and occasionally at other levels a poetic ancestry with a technical forebear.

Second stage (in internal Naturalisation): how is the conventional level related to the formal level? By giving a value to the disposition of the poem on the page, the conventional level stresses the break at the end of a line and isolates each line as a semi-autonomous unit with a beginning and an end (in a way that lines of prose are not isolated). Through the conventional level lines come to function as units which are set in relation to one another as rhythmical blocks. For example, after the line, 'Aňd expóund thĕ diśténtiŏns ŏf Empíre', comes the next rhythmical block, 'Bút fór sómethiňg tŏ réad iň nórmăl círcŭmstàncĕs'. After the three strong anapaests of the first line, the second begins with two anapaests, suggesting that it is cut from the same pattern and enforcing the possibility of similarity between the two lines. But the resounding firmness that characterised the first line is quickly lost, as the second shades off into two iambs and the general metrical collapse of 'circumstances'. Taken by itself, 'círcŭmstàncĕs' is an extended dactyl with a secondary stress on the third syllable, but in context, where the stressed initial syllable belongs to the previous foot, the secondary stress is not strong enough to compose a rhymic unit from the last three syllables. This contributes to a sense of lightness, as opposed to the heavy regularity of the first line; and the effect created by a purely formal, metrical variation induces, in conjunction with the pattern of diction, a contrast between the pompous and the colloquial. That in turn, feeding up into the level of poetic stance and its connections with theme, produces suggestions of irony, which might be defined as the simultaneous presence of two orders which, by their mutual reflection, criticise one another.

In terms of realistic naturalisation these rhythmical and metrical patterns are irrelevant, but in internal or artificial naturalisation they assimilate the meanings of words and, while ordering these towards a thematic synthesis, restrict the aspects of meaning which might be relevant. For example, given the functions imposed by other levels, it makes no different what are the 'distentions of Empire' that might be expounded, nor what should count as 'normal' circumstances.

Metrical and rhythmical patterns are in one sense irrelevant to meaning, yet they also use the meaning of words to lead up towards thematic synthesis. The tension between these two facts is what I have called the necessary combination of continuity and discontinuity between poetry and other kinds of language. In this case, continuity is provided by the way in which formal and conventional devices take up and assimilate various kinds of discourse, weaving them together into a poem whose movement is the movement from one moment or kind of discourse to another. Discontinuity derives from our awareness that by being cited, as it were, the various kinds of language are no longer what they would be in isolation and are subjected to a different form of organisation.

One might say, in fact, that Pound is using his language itself as the level of image-complex. That is, rather than offer a single image or set of images which, by their way of joining together two domains, indicate which aspects of each are relevant to a potential thematic synthesis, and rather than use images of this sort to indicate the dominant order of meaning, he employs switches in diction and rhythm which serve as the central point of reference in the poem and control the extensions of meaning. His switches in diction not only blend with the formal level; they also blend with and control the selection, arrangement, and order of words' meanings and thus make this mode of organisation an image-complex which leads the formal levels through meaning towards a thematic synthesis.

Moreover, even the officially pompous lines tend to have the discourse of the ironic poet inserted in them. In the first line, for example, 'as we know', brings him into the line in complicity with the reader; similarly 'a few pages brought down from the forked hill unsullied' casts an ironic glance on the party-line of official mythological inspiration, while the last four lines quoted not only do this but also sneer at official societal patronage and Virgilian/Maecenian views of poetry. And the point (shall I say it again, I shall say it again) is that the image-complexes are created internally: the conjunction between the levels of meaning and of formal pattern creates an image-complex which has no need of metaphor, simile, allegory, and all the other agents of the image-complex, for the diction is itself its own image. The thematic point emerges from this image-complex of the diction itself as it varies.

To some extent this answers our query about how the conventional level is related to the other levels and through these to an internal thematic synthesis. And it stresses the difference between bad and good Naturalisation by showing how a skilled poet can innovate internally while an unskilled one—myself as author of 'BBC'—has to rely on the devices of extension of meaning into the non-poetic world and so runs the risk both of failing to fictionalise the external contexts thus invoked and of leaving the reader stranded in the world and the language he already knows. We are now in a position to compare the thematic syntheses attained by realistic expansion/limitation and artificial or internal expansion and limitation III is the overall result of bad Naturalisation resulting from realistic limitation/expansion.

III

This is a poem written by Ezra Pound and entitled 'Homage to Sextus Propertius'; we know that Ezra Pound was an expatriate American poet and that the poem is dated 1917, at which time he was living in London; we know that Sextus Propertius was a Latin poet living in Rome and writing in the first century A.D. These facts make an external context. We are not such bad naturalisers as to think that the context can have nothing to do with the words on the page, and so what do the words on the page tell us? Official and respected poets are mocked along with their patrons, i.e. ultimately, society; the reason for this is plain when one recalls the fact that both Pound and Propertius were relatively unknown and unpatronised. Both were better poets than those who were so belauded, and they felt this was the fault of society for wanting 'a worn-out poetical fashion' and of the official 'Annalists' for providing the want. What of the style of the lines? They are obviously rather loose free verse, and that is explained by the fact that Pound/Propertius's grievance was caused partly by their attempt to write in new and experimental ways. That is all we need to know about the style, and we can move straight on our external thematic interpretation. Pound expresses his bitterness towards his society by an 'imitation' of an earlier author who also wrote obscurely and expressed bitterness at his society. Pound was quite right, because pre-war England was very like Rome in the last days of the Republic and the beginnings of the Empire: I refer you to Professor X's book, *First-*

Century Rome and Twentieth-Century England: Some Parallels (Sheep, Rotterdam, 1964). Note that this is still the orthodox opinion on the 'Homage', still purveyed to undergraduates reading English in universities.

Artificial limitation/expansion, on the other hand, grants precedence to the reflections of II and allows the internal organisation to filter the external contexts evoked in III, selecting as relevant those which can be taken up and fictionalised by the poem's structure. The conventional and rhythmic levels call our attention to the ironic contrast between the pompous and the colloquial, not as attitudes of the historical individuals Pound and Propertius but as a major component of poetic technique. It is not important, for example, whether anything in pre-war Britain corresponds to the 'distentions of Empire' in Roman times. Artificial naturalisation excludes that external reference in order to permit an internal expansion focusing on the contrast—metrical as well as semantic—between 'distentions of Empire' and 'normal circumstances'. And ultimately, as I have said, the language itself—the language which Pound/Propertius the poet uses—becomes the image-complex around which levels of the poem are co-ordinated.

We can see this if we consider how the pronouns 'we', 'they' and 'I', whose normal function is referential, work in this case. The idea of continuity and the notion of limitation/expansion help us to formulate the problem. Limitation suggests that limits are imposed on an interpretive reading while expansion shows that these very limits can be used to expand the reading. If we undertake external naturalisation, then the external contexts to which the poem is taken as referring limit the internal features which can be included in a thematic synthesis, and the expansion takes place in the world outside the poem (we tell ourselves empirical stories to fill in an interpretation). This is realistic limitation/expansion. If, however, we call upon artificial limitation/expansion then it is the internal and distinctively poetic artifice which limits what our reading may import from the outside world, and this limitation allows our reading to expand in terms of internal features.

Artificial limitation/expansion helps us to see how the pronouns work in Pound's lines. Personal pronouns rank with demonstrative adverbs and adjectives—'here', 'there', 'that', 'now', 'yesterday'—in the category of what those concerned with linguistics call 'shifters' or 'deictics'. Shifters are orientational features of language which refer to the situation of utterance: 'I' means the person speaking, 'now' the moment of utterance, etc.[14] In ordinary, non-poetic, utterances these references are easily supplied, and deictics indicate the importance of supplying an external context. In poetry, however, there is no empirical situation of utterances. The 'now' of a poem does not refer to the moment when it was penned or set in type, or to the date of the first edition. The time of the 'now' is a purely relational linguistic fiction with no referent in the external world. In poetry, as Jonathan Culler says, 'the deictics do not refer us to an external context but force us to construct a fictional situation.'[15] They become formal devices for organising a work. A contrast between 'now' and 'yesterday' or 'five years ago' in a poem does not lead us out into an empirical situation but tells us that a temporal contrast will be an important device for thematic organisation; and the same holds true for references to 'I', 'we', and 'you': these oppositions, lifted away from external contexts, limit the invasion of the external world and provide scope for internal thematic expansion.

In our Pound lines we have a clash between a reference to the non-poetic world—'Out-weariers of Apollo . . . continue their Martian generalities'— and the shifter 'as we know', which is sandwiched between the two portions of this reference. Though the primary function of this shifter is to provide a tone, we could no doubt recover it as a reference to the poet and his readers—though even that class is a fictional one (not so much a reference to a given class of people as an attempt to create internal complicity between the reader and a poetic 'I' which he is led to postulate). But the second 'we' of 'We have kept our erasers in order' shows that the poem is not referring to an external class of persons, however nebulously defined. Functionally and internally it asserts a contrast between 'we' and 'you', addresser and addressee, and hence produces a class of 'poetic voices'.

The 'we', one might say, is a shifting reference which comes to refer to all those who have 'kept their erasers in order'; within the poem that reference is organised around the language itself as image-complex; the negation of ironic juxtaposition which 'erases' one linguistic sequence by ringing changes on its formal organisation in the next line, the implication of austerity and craftsmanship as against pomposity and prolixity, crystallize here.

The fictionalized 'we', which refers not to an external class of persons but to a shifting function within the poem, helps to distance the language from particular external contexts and to associate first-person pronouns with the self-reflexive process of reading and writing poetry.[16] And it thus becomes difficult to avoid associating the first-person singular pronouns with the same process: 'A young Muse . . . ascends with me into the æther', 'I ask a wreath which will not crush my head', and 'I shall have, doubtless, a boom after my funeral'. The 'I' which ascends with the young muse is any poetic voice which ranges itself against the other forms of verse displayed and parodied here. It is, of course, the author whose artifice takes place in the same de-temporalized present as the ascent, but it is also, since this is an Homage, a figure of continuity in artifice:

Propertius/Pound, a mythical figure which the poem itself aims to create and which can only exist within the realm of artifice. As soon as it re-enters time or becomes an empirical figure it is subject to irony: 'I shall have, doubtless, a boom after my funeral,/Seeing that long standing increases all things/regardless of quality.'

As in every good poem, the process of artificial naturalisation is sus-pended inside the poem, so that the reader takes account of the way in which levels of organisation assimilate possible external contexts and filter them into a thematic synthesis. The reader is made aware of the process of naturalisation so that he may sense both the requisite con-tinuity between poetry and other languages and the requisite dis-continuity. If he gives the poem its due and allows artifice to work on and through him, he will never engage in that bad naturalisation which con-sists in stranding the poem like a whale when the tide retreats on the deserted beach of the ordinary world ('How high the seas of language flow here', as Wittgenstein says).

Empson himself is well aware that 'the process of becoming accus-tomed to a new author is very much that of learning what to exclude in this way' and that 'the selection of meanings is more important to the poet than their multitude, and harder to understand.'[17] If he himself tends to prize the multitude rather than the selection, to multiply ambi-guities instead of seeking to determine which enrich the poem in the relevant ways, it is because it is hard to select properly, hard to exclude, if one operates entirely on the level of meaning. The process of exclusion—and the internal expansion which it permits—can operate only if other levels of organisation are brought into play, which is why I have stressed so much the importance of non-semantic features. In the next chapter we shall encounter more directly problems of meaning: modes of obscurity in twentieth-century poetry and their relation to the problems of continuity and discontinuity. I shall end here simply by restating the basic premise of artificial limitation/expansion.

Artifice tells us that selecting and ordering external contexts is one of the basic manoeuvres in writing and reading poetry. When we naturalise well it is because we are aware that primary among these contexts is the existence of poetic art itself: the fact that we are reading a poem. When we get behind the surface of a poem we encounter not another kind of meaning nor a different non-poetic world, but another organisation of the levels of language that produce meaning. Through the relation be-tween these levels, language and the world may be changed, changed utterly. A terrible beauty is born. Often, of course, the birth is slow and obscured; it may seem a blur rather than a change. As Empson says, using a visual metaphor, you have an impression of a thing's distance away, which can hardly ever be detached from the pure visual sensation, and when it is so detached leaves your eye disconcerted (if what you took for a wall turns out to be the sea, you at first see nothing, perhaps are for a short time puzzled as with a blur, and then see differently)[18]

The distancing of artifice produces dislocation and, of course, discomfort. 'The reading of a new poet, or of any poetry at all, fills many readers with a sense of mere embarrassment and discomfort, like that of not knowing, and wanting to know, whether it is a wall or the sea.'[19] Like Empson, I want to know whether it is a wall or the sea.

Two types of obscurity and two types of imagery

> Classical dance requires an ordered balanced form in which a calm spaciousness of movement animates the dancers. In its purest form it is without emotional content or character. Any expression it may show arises solely through the inspired personality of an artist who has mastered his technique.
>
> Ninette de Valois

In the previous chapter it was suggested that emotion in a poem must come, as Dame Ninette says it does in ballet, entirely from the interactions between the various levels of language that make up a technique. We tried further to establish a spaciousness of movement inside these levels which, if it was not calm, at least enabled us in some sort to realise how poetic language absorbs and transforms the world of everyday experience. I shall now turn to the problem of obscurity in poetry, which has obvious affinities with the notion of continuity in language. For if a poem is obscure then it is because it is discontinuous with our other areas of language. It is necessary to distinguish at least two ways in which it may be discontinuous; for the sake of convenience I shall call these the irrational and the rational. And within each there are two distinctive types of imagery which I shall call discursive or empirical. Let us consider first a case of irrational obscurity using empirical imagery; my example is David Gascoyne's 'The Rites of Hysteria'.

I   Irrational obscurity and Naturalisation

Whereas many poets write in complicity with the process of realistic limitation/expansion and thus invite bad Naturalisation, Gascoyne is determined not to be naturalised, determined to stress his discontinuity:

> A cluster of insane massacres turns green upon the highroad
> Green as the nadir of a mystery in the closet of a dream
> And wild growth of lascivious pamphlets became a beehive
> The afternoon scrambles like an asylum out of its hovel
> The afternoon swallows a bucketful of chemical sorrows
> And the owners of rubber pitchforks bake all their illusions
> In an oven of dirty globes and weedgrown stupors.[1]

In his introduction to Gascoyne's poems, Robin Skelton says that this passage 'uses a rhetorical tone and, by means of bizarre and near-nonsensical imagery, produces a powerful effect of social and moral dislocation. It is as much a poem about the state of society as many of the more explicitly didactic poems of Auden.'[2] We see here an interpretation of irrational obscurity which immediately naturalises it and translates it into the language of ordinary statement, albeit at a very abstract level. The fact that on the formal plane the poem appears disconnected—a series of isolated lines— and on the semantic plane appears to make no overt statements is immediately transferred to an external context. The technique means disorder, mirrors social and moral dislocation. No doubt Gascoyne himself was relying on such an interpretation to give meaning to his incoherence, but it is very much an instance of what Yvor Winters calls 'the fallacy of imitative form'. Form does not directly mirror a world; the connection can only be made through the other levels of poetic discourse.

Wishing to avoid such a lapse, we must look to other levels, and at first sight we might hope to find significance in the way the level of meaning relates to both the level of image-complex and the level of formal pattern. Afternoons, vegetation, lunacy, and destruction are all dominant, and they provide several external contexts which might be fictionalised. But the agents of fictionalising are not working. The level of convention suggests nothing except that these lines ought to interact in some way, so we are left with the levels of formal pattern and of image-complex. Nevertheless, fighting one-handed, let us see what may be done with these. All the vowels in the alphabet and many of the consonants are present but we have no way of telling which are important and which are not, since the conventional level—rhyme, rhythm, line-endings are all inert—does not help. If 'hovel', 'sorrows', 'stupors', or any other word that ends a line were to feed back its sound/look into the rest of the lines—which would be indicated by metre and rhythm—we might find glimmerings of a formal pattern, but they do not do so. There is as much a case for claiming that *l* is prominent as there is for *s*, for *e* as for *o* or *i*. And as little, for in the absence of metre and rhythm the reader cannot tell which sounds come to the surface in the poem's movement.

The same dead-end is reached when the reader tries to get a clue from the image-complexes. Once more there is a cluster (forgive the metaphor) of ideas about mysteries, destruction, insanity, dreams which smother the level of meaning, but these clusters are not worked out through a gradual build-up of selection and restriction of connotations as happens in Sonnet 94 and the extract from 'Homage'. And it is difficult to see how the process could take place when the other non-semantic levels are frozen. Such being the case, it is impossible for a thematic synthesis to take place in the area of continuity and artificial limitation/expansion.

Of course, Gascoyne may ignore these requirements and write as he pleases to stress his discontinuity, but the price, as I have suggested, is complete unintelligibility and loss of any incentive for the reader to continue. This is not a deprivation lightly accepted by any writer lacking the arrogance of James Joyce, who said that it would take anyone a whole devoted lifetime to understand *Finnegans Wake*. To which the only answer is that, however highly we rate *Finnegans Wake*, we have other things to do with our lifetimes. In any case, the critical reader will not adopt Joyce's extreme position, and it is notable that Mr Skelton does not do so: he attempts a weak and abstract naturalisation.

What happens, in fact, is that the irrational obscurity of 'the Rites of Hysteria' can only be naturalised as an example of irrationality. Since rhythm and sound patterns exert no control, we cannot tell how to organise the images, and the only recourse is to treat them as empirical images—as references to the world—which, because they are so incomprehensible, reflect a state of chaos in the world. This is an extremely abstract naturalisation in that it does nothing with the details of the poem and could apply equally well to any set of 'bizarre and near-nonsensical' images.

Mr Skelton does not even try to naturalise the lines internally. He is content to say that they express the 'social and moral dislocation' of society and apparently does not realize that by this vagueness he is situating his critical reading quite outside the scope of the poem itself. Social and moral dislocation belongs to the language of sociology, politics, and psychoanalysis; it may reach into the realm of poetry only if the poetic technique can accommodate it and change it into its own world.

We can see this from a much more certain example than 'the didactic poems of Auden':

> Unreal City,
> Under the brown fog of a winter dawn,
> A crowd flowed over London Bridge, so many,
> I had not thought death had undone so many.
> Sighs, short and infrequent, were exhaled,
> And each man fixed his eyes before his feet.
> Flowed up the hill and down King William Street,
> To where Saint Mary Woolnoth kept the hours
> With a dead sound on the final stroke of nine.
> There I saw one I knew, and stopped him, crying: 'Stetson!
> 'You who were with me in the ships at Mylae!
> 'That corpse you planted last year in your garden,
> 'Has it begun to sprout? Will it bloom this year?
> 'Or has the sudden frost disturbed its bed?
> 'O keep the Dog far hence, that's friend to men,
> 'Or with his nails he'll dig it up again!
> 'You! hypocrite lecteur!—mon semblable,—mon frère!'[3]

It may be objected that the comparison is unfair, that to set one stanza of a minor poet against one of the greatest passages in English poetry is not simply bribing the jury but bringing Pompey's legions into the law-courts to intimidate them in session. But persons who speak of 'a powerful effect of social and moral dislocation' should pause to consider the seriousness of these claims and have some idea of what they are talking about.

The above passage from 'The Waste Land' also uses 'bizarre and near-nonsensical imagery' but it takes good care that this be related to the other levels of Artifice and that the image-complexes move through these in a newly alive and potent verse line which progresses inexorably through citadel after citadel of social and literary heritage, leaving each in crumbling ruin, only to shore them ('These fragments I have shored against my ruins') by its technical re-shaping.

One example must suffice. The echo of Dante in the fourth line quoted—'I had not thought death had undone so many'—immediately follows an echo of Baudelaire.[4] Both these literary allusions on their own might have taken us to the originals, were it not for the fact that they are caught up in a fictionalised contemporary London context: 'A crowd flowed over London Bridge, so many'. And all three contexts are made fictional by the blend of levels of Artifice. The conventional level is used to link sound/look to meaning, as in the management of *o* in 'flowed', 'crowd', 'London', 'so'. The repetition of 'so many' in the two lines, set off by metric and syntactic pauses, produces a single fictionalized context. This makes the diction itself, as in the lines from 'Homage', part of the image-complex, and with the same result: 'I' can be used without reference to any individual external to the lines; 'I' is Dante, Baudelaire, Eliot as poet, Tiresias as Eliot's persona, the man who knew Stetson at Mylae, and all of these simultaneously. 'I' is also 'you', 'hypocrite lecteur', who perceives and organises these lines as a poem and who knows how to supply the physical context of London Bridge as a contemporary lead into the lines.

We have here, in fact, a technique which I shall describe in Chapter Three as the disconnected image-complex but which I may mention briefly at this point since it shows how poetry may actually achieve, through the work of its various levels, the effects rather naively claimed for Gascoyne's irrational obscurity. In Gascoyne the formal levels exercise no control, so that one cannot tell how the external world is filtered through the language of the poem. Without a sense of what is dominant and what is ancillary one cannot distinguish empirical from discursive imagery and so one must, as I suggested, abandon the attempt to make use of details of imagery and assume that all the imagery is abstractly empirical: an evocation of chaos in the real world.

In Eliot's lines we encounter potential examples of both discursive and empirical imagery. Literary allusions can be naturalised as discursive imagery: we make sense of them by thinking of the mind moving among literary monuments. But London Bridge, crowds, King William Street, and St Mary Woolnoth ask to be read as empirical references. And it seems impossible to produce a synthesis in either an empirical or a discursive mode. If we say that this is a description of an urban scene enlivened by allusions and metaphors we miss much of the strangeness of the passage; if we say that it is the poetic mind musing over the fragments of its experience we neglect the specific details. We are left with a hesitation between empirical and discursive modes, but that hesitation is not unproductive, as it was in the case of Gascoyne, nor should it be arrested by a blind leap into one abstract possibility. The verse form, as in the repetition of 'so many', and semantic parallels, as in the 'death' of the allusion to Dante, the 'dead sound' of the empirical (?) bell, and the 'corpse' of pseudo-empirical discourse, assert a connection which is not to be worked out in rational naturalisation. Similarly, the first 'I' of the passage is Dante cum poetic persona, the second is poetic persona cum empirical character, and the third (of 'mon semblable, mon frère') is Baudelaire, the poetic persona, and also the empirical character who 'speaks' these lines to 'Stetson'. The logical development of the sentences asserts that these are a single 'I', but we cannot work out an identity for it in terms of our models of rationality. It is a disconnected image in that it holds together at the level of fiction which the poem asserts; it is a fictive and depersonalised 'I'.

We might sum up this effect by saying that the lines are obscure, but they have not the irrational obscurity of Gascoyne's lines which offer the reader no hold; nor have they the rational obscurity of the poems to be discussed later in this chapter where arcane information resolves dificulties and makes possible rational integration. Their obscurity comes from the use of disconnected image-complexes which leads us to feed a context of contemporary London and a range of literary fictions into the poem and to leave them suspended there, unified only as fictions within a linguistic structure.

To such examples we shall return in Chapter Three. Having offered a glimpse of the paradise to come, an example of what irrational obscurity is not, we must try further to specify what it is.

Irrational obscurity does not mean simply bad poetry which makes no sense, though Gascoyne's lines might seem to suggest this. Skilful verse which makes use of formal patterns may still be irrationally obscure, as is, for example, Edith Sitwell's 'Fox Trot':

                    Old
                         Sir
                              Faulk,
          Tall as a stork,
          Before the honeyed fruits of the dawn were ripe would walk
          And stalk with a gun
          The reynard-coloured sun[5]

These lines, unlike Gascoyne's, use formal patterns which, by convention, stress the difference between poetry and ordinary language. The control imposed by 'Faulk', 'Stork', 'walk', 'stalk', or the rhyme which makes the sun what is stalked with a gun, insists on the fictionality of the hunting gentleman and his landscape: a scene determined by sound pattern and the general language of hunting. The level of formal pattern, that is to say, is least developed to the point where the reader can perceive some meanings as more important than others. The idyllic landscape, for instance, is more important than the hunter himself because it fits better with the technical pattern of stress on sound.

However, there seems little way to move beyond this perception to a thematic synthesis which would take account of details. Miss Sitwell's editor, who would dearly like to produce a respectable thematic interpretation, encounters little success and is led to engage in the kind of bad naturalisation which seemed the only possible response to Gascoyne. 'The conjunction of images', he writes, 'becomes as violent as the clash of symbols (sic), as violent as often the effect of the rhythm, and the clanging bells of the internal rhymes and assonances.' As might be expected of one who talks with such awkwardness of formal patterns and image-complexes, he makes these lines signify social and moral dislocation. They are 'satiric', trying to escape the 'rhythmical flaccidity, the verbal deadness of contemporary tradition'. He feels 'a deeper consequence between the surface inconsequence (as in the 'nonsense' poems of Edward Lear), and sometimes a note of strange sadness and mystery comes hauntingly through'.[6]

Such reaching after a way to feed the poem back into the already-known world—of objects of satire, of emotions of haunting sadness—is the result of an uneasiness provoked by the style's refusal to offer an alternative way of reading. In Eliot's lines the formal control helps to indicate what (from the external world of urban scenes and other literature) is to be fed into the poem where it takes up a fictional existence; but here when one attempts to interpret one is compelled—even when one has first attended to formal features—to make a leap into a vague external world. One cannot blame Miss Sitwell's editor, for he does at least make the attempt to work from within the poem, but finally he must, like the interpreters of Gascoyne, retreat to an external thematic synthesis because the poem itself presupposes this kind of interpretation.

Empson provides another kind of naturalisation for irrational obscurity of this type: elements of the poem are justified and unified in terms of the poet's mind. The mixture of disparate sensations throws the reader back

> upon the undifferentiated affective states which are all that such sensations have in common . . . one is thrown back on a series of possible associations, as to the social setting in which these sensations would be expected, or the mood in which they would be sought out. Miss Sitwell seemed often to use the device rather as a flag of defiance, to insist that the main meaning is not what she valued, and the reader must put himself into a poetic or receptive frame of mind. ('These two things are alike in that, for quite different reasons, they harmonise with my mood'.)[7]

It is ironic, and quite characteristic, that Empson tries to make irrational obscurity into a kind of rational obscurity: if he had enough supplementary information about the poet's mind and mood, then the poem would be rationally coherent and thoroughly explicable. How this might work in practice for a poem like 'Fox Trot' is, fortunately, not clear— fortunately, for the description of a mood which gave each element of the poem associations that could be developed as a rational argument would be excessively circumstantial and fantastical. The notion that aspects of the language itself might be dominant, rather than the associations of objects to which the poem ostensibly refers, seems not to have occurred to Empson. And this is perhaps some indication, albeit a tenuous one, that the formal patterns do not in fact succeed in organising a process of internal limitation/expansion.

Before turning to the kind of rational obscurity which Empson prefers, we should see what happens when irrational obscurity is carried to its logical extreme: in 'Concrete Poetry'. Here too, interpreters have little to do on an internal scale and must, if they are to offer an interpretation at all, resort to the kind of abstract external expansion encountered in Skelton's reading of Gascoyne: the meaninglessness of verbal arrangements on the page imitates or reflects a meaninglessness of objects in the world.

Concrete poetry has carried discontinuity with ordinary language to its limits by seeking a point where language ceases to be language and becomes simply material, visual or aural, for making patterns. The beginnings of the movement are based, like so much else in twentieth-century poetry, on the break-up of the poetic line initiated by Ezra Pound. But the practitioners of concrete poetry go further than Pound wished or imagined because they deny that poetic technique is all-important. Having, as it were, established discontinuity with the world of language by simply ignoring the urgency of continuity and meaning, these 'poets' have found it necessary to establish a more radical and spurious continuity with the physical world normally mediated through language. They treat words as physical objects; they try to avoid mediation altogether. And this resort to the concrete implies, I think, that Concrete poetry is a regression rather than a liberation. Rather than let Artifice loose on the world of ordinary language to create a new world through non-semantic levels, their production of words and letters at literal three-dimensional objects subjects Artifice slavishly to the world of physical limitation/expansion normally mediated through language and to an utterly simplistic ordering of language itself. Needless to say both theme and image-complex are totally absent, so that neither the conventional level or the formal level can rise above the level of mere noise. And it is totally impossible for a thematic synthesis to take place.

I shall quote some of Robert Lax's 'poem', *'ik ok'*, which comes as close as possible (while remaining in black and white on the page and therefore not, like three-dimensional moving poems, quite unquotable) to this pseudo-simplicity that tries to deny meaning:

ik	ik	ik	ik		
ik	ik	ik	ik	ok	ik
ik	ik	ik	ik	ok	ik
ik		ik			ok
ik	ok	ik	ok	ik	
ik	ok	ik	ok	ik	
ik	ok	ik	ok		ik
				ok	ik
				ok	
ok	ik	ok	ik		ok
ok	ik	ok	ik	ik	
ok	ik	ok	ik	ik	
ok	ik	ok	ok		
ok		ok			
ok	ok	ok	ok		
ok	ok	ok	ok		
	ok		ok[8]		

Of this Mr Stephen Bann remarks that unlike orthodox Concrete poets, who aim to create objects out of letters and thus use language without linguistic mediation—an aim whose absurdity is apparent as soon as stated:

Robert Lax comes closer than any other poet [sic] whose work is included
in this collection to achieving an almost 'abstract' style. By 'abstract', I
mean something significantly different from 'concrete': something which
is in fact almost the antithesis of concrete, since, as Arp has pointed out,
the 'abstracting' tendencies of Cubism are opposed to the procedures of
Concrete Art, 'qui a son point de départ dans l'inconscient de l'artiste'.
One might say that the concrete procedure is inductive, while that of the
abstract is reductive. And it is this element of reduction which is the
remarkable feature of Robert Lax's work. His poem, 'ik/ok', with its
strong reminiscence of the Latin 'hic/hoc', is reduced to a minimum
content—both visually and phonetically—so that it appears as a kind of
ultimate in equivocation.[9]

The movement of Mr Bann's Naturalisation is very like the clouds of
Skelton and Gascoyne: minimum content, both visual and phonetic, is
interpreted as an 'ultimate in equivocation'. One can feel the phase
'social and moral dislocation' hovering over Mr Bann's typewriter. His
attempt to remove Mr Lax's 'poem' from Concrete poetry by the distinction between abstract and concrete is a dead loss, for neither process
can be seen as objective and both, if they are not so seen, must, on an
external limitation/expansion, have their point of departure in the sub-
conscious of the artist. We have seen Empson himself doing this with
Edith Sitwell; and Mr Bann's equivocations about hic/hoc are archetypal
instances of external Naturalisation.

Totally irrational obscurity cannot be fought with critical interpretation, nor can it fight critical interpretation since it is deprived of the
levels of meaning, image-complex and thematic synthesis; it is perhaps
even more abject than the work of, say, Philip Larkin in its submission to
the everyday world and to the interpretations of the critic with his
ready-made notions of 'the poetic'. Mr Bann's reductionism applies to all
Concrete poetry insofar as it fulfils its aims of total discontinuity with
other languages. The opposite of extended meaning is not nonsense but a
different kind of sense (organisation of linguistic levels) and the opposite
of Mr Bann's induction is not normally reduction but deduction, which
brings us back to our distinction between empirical and discursive imagery. But before taking up that problem I should like to complete this discussion of Concrete poetry by briefly mentioning the views of a scholar
who can treat the topic with the necessary detachment. Leonard Forster
accepts the orthodox version of Concrete poetry as, 'an extreme example
of the use of language as material'.[10] Nevertheless he also sees that poetic
technique must absorb and transform the external contexts in which they
are used: 'words become dirty because of their associations and the contexts in which they are used. If they can be placed in other, not necessarily directly meaningful, contexts they may be made clean again.'[11]
Alas, Professor Forster himself provides—may I say this without

offence?—the type case of critical discourse making words dirty by placing Concrete poetry in the historical tradition of multilingual, medieval,
renaissance, baroque poetry which is read as 'revolutionary' (the ghosts
of 'social and moral dislocation' and 'deeper consequence beneath surface inconsequence' still hover). The cleansing process must come from
Artifice, from within; indeed, filtering is a more apt analogy, for the
external world is filtered through the levels of technique and especially
by selection on the level of meaning and image-complex.

Concrete poetry is one extreme of irrational obscurity where we go
beyond meaning and rationality altogether, so that it seems almost point-
less to talk of obscurity. Once all pretence to meaning is abandoned, the
artifacts themselves are not obscure—though why someone should have
bothered to produce them may be obscure. They lie beyond meaning, as
Stephen Bann cheerfully admits, and their empirical reference is even
more abstract than the kind adduced for Gascoyne's lines: they do not
even mirror social and political dislocation but only 'physicality' in general.

The other extreme, the other limit of irrational obscurity is one which,
unlike Gascoyne and Concrete poetry, works industriously with meaning
and other levels of artifice so that, while remaining extremely obscure, it
gives the impression of attaining a deeper rationality. It is not rational
obscurity of the kind which we shall come to next, for there appropriate
information resolves difficulties and creates a logical structure. It is,
rather, the successful pole of irrational obscurity.

Consider, as an example, these lines from 'Of Sanguine Fire' by J. H.
Prynne:

> Swift as a face rolled away like
>   pastry, turned up the stairwell oh
> cough now room for two &
>   faced with bodily attachments:
> evidence hovers like biotic soup, all
>   transposable, all like. The pastry
> face takes the name Pie (crust folded
>   like wings over the angelic sub-
> strate, all so like pasties they
>   hover again), is younger by a
> specific aim. From upstairs the
>   face crossed by banisters
> counterclaims in re Outwash, it
>   foils downward, round the newel,
> to a fierce vacancy guarded
>   on legal & moral grounds which
> run to the limits of perfect zeal.[12]

Immediately one comes up against the fact that these lines are obscure in a special way. They have not Gascoyne's obscurity of chaos, nor the obscurity of fantasy we encountered in Sitwell. And they use meaning in a way that sets them poles apart from Concrete poetry. They are ten-dentiously obscure. They resist the reader by making him work; they positively repel him by implying that no amount of arcane knowledge will help him produce an interpretation, that however hard he tries he will not get away with (or through) these lines into a non-poetic realm. He will have to recognise that he is stuck with the lines on the page, that these words have a meaning but not an extended reference to the world outside, and that his limitation/expansion will have to take place within the levels of the poem, internally and artificially. In other words, Prynne uses his obscurity in order to promote a good naturalisation which works, as I shall attempt to show, in terms of suspended levels of poetic organ-isation. Levels do not mesh to produce a thematic interpretation which leads out into statements about scenes or events, and if one were to attempt a critical reading in these terms one could only conclude, as did a reviewer in the *Cambridge Review*, that the poem is obscure and that only one eighth of it is interpretable.[13]

We must, then, have recourse to levels of Artifice. And first of all, since the poem is tendentiously obscure and discontinuous with ordinary language, we must situate ourselves on the scale of irrelevance, which means that there will be no thematic synthesis internal or external and any naturalisation will be tentative and suspended.

The opening line is a parody of the beginning of Shelley's 'The Triumph of Life':

> Swift as a spirit hastening to his task
> Of glory and of good, the Sun sprang forth

The allusion prepares the reader for the use of literary allusion found, for instance, in 'The Waste Land'. This is to be Prynne's 'Triumph of Life'; and, knowing what we do of Shelley's poem, we shall not expect it to be optimistic. No; we are prepared for the savage irony of 'The Waste Land'—simultaneous acceptance of the literary tradition and des-truction of it by the brutal contemporary world.

But what do we get? 'pastry, turned up the stairwell oh'. Is Prynne making fun of the reader? Evidently not, for the poem runs to four full pages and contains much that is sincerely climatic in its author's work as whole: meditation on the nature of evidence from the physical world, for example, and on the problems of equating knowledge with love. Is he simply sniggering at our expectations on one level while fulfilling them on another? Again, no, for the lines are very skilful on all levels and elude any attempt to give them a theme. Does the poet want to juxtapose the world of literature with the 'real' contemporary world and thus cast doubt on the value of both, as does 'The Waste Land'? No, again, for no one thinks of the world of the kitchen as a microcosm of the great globe itself; pastry would not be adequate for this function. We can rule out the notion of a simple juxtaposition of poetry and physical life. They do indeed intermingle ('evidence hovers like biotic soup') but the clash would have come much more fiercely had this been the objective. Nor does the poet want simply to upset our expectations; he wants to create new ones as the skill of the verse shows. The distinctiveness of these lines lies in their style. It is that which makes them transcend these other limiting possibilities and it is that which we must now try to analyse.

The first line gives a speed in the *i s f t* of 'Swift' and a stability in the motion described, 'rolled away', with its open vowels and trilled *r*. These are combined in the last two words, 'away like', which then lead into the second line where the syntactic level is beautifully combined with the rhythm and meaning of the words. The pause after 'pastry' isolates that word, which is also isolated as the first indication that we are getting something very strange indeed. 'Turned up the stairwell' gives us our first glimpse of a particular scene in the 'outside' world while we know that we shall never be allowed more than a glimpse (surely we know that!); while the final 'oh', not heralded by a comma, only by the pause in rhythm after our glimpse of the stairwell, seems to introduce a persona speaking. This spurious persona persists into the next line—'cough now room for two &'—where it seems to be addressing someone else. But who else? We are not even sure of the person's credentials, still less of his interlocutor's. But why 'cough'? Is it the reader who ought to cough, in order to signal his presence on the stairwell, perhaps? And why now? Has there not previously been room for two, on the stairwell? Elsewhere? Are the two the poet and Shelley? or the poet and the reader? or the persona and some other persona?

And how absurd all these questions are when the function of the words is to provide a particular combination of sounds for the formal level to work on. The next three lines with their 'all/transposable, all like' offer a statement which questions the validity of any comparison, makes plain the absurdity of trying to differentiate scenes and characters. And when 'The pastry face' between words and the world takes the name Pie, it is obvious that no attempt is to be made to reproduce an analogue of 'reality'.

But if these image-complexes and the syntactic arrangment are only an excuse for formal pattern, is this not to reduce 'Of Sanguine Fire' to a Concrete poem or to Edith Sitwell's 'Fox Trot'? Does it not matter at all what the words mean and what external contexts they 'imply but to exclude', to quote one of Empson's poems? In which case why the wilful obscurantism? Why doesn't he just say what he wants to say instead of prevaricating like this?

The clue lies in the fact that the obscurity is wilful: a 'fierce vacancy', as line 15 has it. Since language has appropriated the non-verbal world and distorted it to suit the requirements of society, Prynne is engaged in restoring language to the condition of reality in its pre-mediated state. Whence the refusal to have any complicity with the demands of critical Naturalisation for meaning and sense. But he is too clever to believe that any poem, however chaotic, can simply, like Gascoyne's piece, resist recuperation by working on the formal level alone; he is too serious to restrict himself to fiddling about with pretty patterns that, as I keep saying, insist that poetry is the one form of language free from the fallacy of unmediated expression. This, of course, must be said and is always repeated by poetic form, but Prynne has other things to say as well, and he proposes to say them under cover of his wilfull obscurity.

He says that our knowledge of the physical world is uncertain but that we are constrained by that world more than we know.

'From upstairs the / face counterclaims in re Outwash', and one of the meanings of 'in re' is 'with reference to things'; the legal and moral senses of the phrase are brought out in the contrast between the implied human and the 'angelic sub-/strate' and both are contrasted with the alienation from the body imposed by legal and moral superstructures and incarnated in the pomposity of 'bodily attachments'. In fact Prynne's obscurity, while apparently irrational and discontinuous, has a good deal of rational obscurity in it also. Clearly, the names 'Pie' and 'Outwash' are chosen on the principle of annoying the reader, but other words are not. We have mentioned 'in re' and 'all like'; and these have the effect of making any future occurrence of 'like' in the poem—and there are many—reflect the theme of distrust in either the physical world or the world of other languages. As the poem moves to its climax the theme is summed up in a series of short lines which describe the unknown protagonists as like the angels in:

> evading with the
> quickness of
> the morning the
> bounded condition
> of name.

It is no accident that these short lines contrast with the majority of longer lines and so produce an effect of speed. The conventional level is used to support a thematic point drawn from the level of meaning. Such conjoined effort to be both obscure and totally direct supports my contention that Prynne's obscurity is an attempt to make language real again for the poet and reader, not simply by cutting him off from the discourse of the critic or frightening him, but by making poetry again an area where even the despised 'great thoughts' may fittingly dwell. Here irrational obscurity is a cover for a deeper and more profound rationality which, while discontinuous with the world of ordinary language, is continuous with a world which is an imagined alternative. So far, our reading of Prynne seems very unsatisfactory; when we return to him in the last chapter, with a fuller sense of the conventions and possibilities of modern verse, we will achieve greater success.

II   Rational artifice

Rational obscurity is perhaps the least disturbing form of obscurity because it continues to presuppose a framework of intelligibility. Problems are attributed to an absence of knowledge, and once the necessary arcane knowledge is supplied, the poem becomes rationally coherent. This is the traditional way in which poetry is difficult: once we know what the poet is talking about, and have sufficient external information about that something, then the poem becomes relatively transparent. But like irrational obscurity, rational obscurity takes different forms, of which the first is a type which leaves the world alone, which makes a gesture towards obscurity and discontinuity but ensures that this gesture will be easily evaded and read, simply, as a sign of profundity.

The best case is Wallace Stevens, and since there is no need to avoid the obvious here, I shall have recourse to Tennessee pottery:

Anecdote of the Jar

I placed a jar in Tennessee,
And round it was, upon a hill.
It made the slovenly wilderness
Surround that hill.

The wilderness rose up to it,
And sprawled around, no longer wild.
The jar was round upon the ground,
And tall and of a port in air.

It took dominion everywhere.
The jar was gray and bare.
It did not give of bird or bush,
Like nothing else in Tennessee.[14]

I do not propose to enter into the critical battles that rage around this poem;—whether it is a critique of the human ordering produced by the jar or a celebration of art's mastery of wilderness. Both positions assume that this is a poem meditating on the relation between art and nature, between human and natural reality. The process of interpretation involves accepting the world of ordinary experience as given, finding in it various already-known attitudes to the problem of which the poem speaks, and clarifying the poem by relating it to these attitudes. In a sense the interpreters are right: the poem is written in complicity with these assumptions; it demands this type of reading.

The poet is deliberately setting out to meditate on the nature of the contrast between the artificially made object, the jar, and the slovenly wilderness, as an allegory of meditation on those other artificially made objects, poems, and their dubious relation to 'reality'. This is apparent but what is not so readily recognised is the fact that these meditations, however sincere philosophically or biographically, cannot be sincere poetically in the way that Eliot's lines are sincere, for they do not through their technique question the existence of language, reality, or the fact that poetry mediates between them. They rely on and refer to experience rather than question and explore it.

This is not to say that Stevens is a bad poet; he is not. But he is not an original poet in the sense of questioning what his readers require of him, or the reality they require him to reproduce. Even phrases like 'give of bird or bush' which display a certain formal organisation and escape from the cliché, assume that we shall translate them, relate them to our experience of the world. The poem, that is to say, takes for granted our meditations on art and nature and asks to be read as a statement of a kind with which we are already familiar. Indeed, the fact that the poem does not assimilate and re-order external contexts is indicated by critical disagreements about it. To interpret it we refer to general discussions of art and nature, and insofar as we disagree about the problem of art and reality we shall disagree about the meaning of the poem. We make it a rationally cohesive statement by relating it to positions already taken, and may find it ambiguous insofar as there exist, in the world or our experience, different positions among which the poem does not choose. The poem is not, of course, very obscure; only obscure enough to hint at profundity. But it illustrates a factitious rational obscurity which assumes a move from poem to already-known rationality.

A poem like 'Bantams in Pine-Woods' might be thought a counter-example, an attempt to work on a formal level so as to question language and its ordering of the world. But in fact it too suggests that Stevens' obscurity is a kind of coyness, an anticipation of certain interpretive manoeuvres:

> Chieftain Iffucan of Azcan in caftan
> Of tan with henna hackles, halt! . . .
>
> Fat! Fat! Fat! Fat! I am the personal.
> Your world is you. I am my world.[15]

The phonetic play is easily overcome, translated. The hint of an alternative ordering is no sooner offered than withdrawn, as one moves from 'Iffucan' to 'If you can' and 'Azcan' to 'as can'. Formal experimentation works as mere concealment, relying on discovery and effacing itself once that discovery is made. And should we be tempted to linger among bantams, the poem offers an explicit statement of subject: 'Your world is you. I am my world.' Once again we are asked simply to insert the poem in a known world of discourse, to take it as a reflection on problems whose parameters are familiar, and to grant it, because of the interpretive work it has imposed, the status of a 'profound' reflection of some kind. Stevens asks to be naturalised as a slightly obscure and figured version of a philosophical statement. He exploits, that is to say, the reprehensible and (one had hoped) discredited notion that the 'poetic' is simply an elaborate way of saying plain things; his obscurity is a kind of coyness, an attempt to stay one step ahead of the reader and so gain a reputation for daring while ensuring that the reader knows exactly where the poet is and how he can take that one step to reach him.

Reliance on the already-known is not, of course, bad in itself. It is the general mechanism of rational artifice. What one objects to is rather the tendency to make the already-known or already-thought the point of arrival, to make poetry an obscure and figured statement which one understands by translating it into the already-known. If poetry is to justify itself it must do more than this; it must assimilate the already-known and subject it to a reworking which suspends and questions its categories, provides alternative orderings. In the best rational obscurity external contexts are brought into the poem as a way of creating a new ordering which is nonetheless rational.

We might start with an example from Empson where the obscurity is only latent but where we can observe the basic mechanisms at work. Here is 'Manchouli':

> I find it normal, passing these great frontiers,
> That you scan the crowds in rags eagerly each side
> With awe; that the nations seem real; that their ambitions
> Having achieved such variety within one type, seem sane;
> I find it normal;
> So too to extract false comfort from that word.[16]

Here the implied relationship of poet to language is totally different from what is found in Gascoyne, Sitwell, Concrete poetry, or even Stevens. The relation established between author and reader in the first two lines is one of ordinary conversational statement, and this in turn implies a whole world of experience, and of the way in which that experience is dealt with in language, which can be taken for granted. The place-name of the title, the deictic in '*these* great frontiers', suggest that we are being offered reflections on a place and an experience, and that additional knowledge—about Chinese frontiers, about the Chinese-Japanese War and the ambitions of nations—will be relevant in that it is what the poem refers to. 'I find it normal' strikes one as a casual observation on Empson's experience of crossing frontiers: we are invited to expand 'it' from the rest of the poem and from knowledge of the world, and 'I' is taken on trust. Why Empson should have chosen verse to tell us about his lucubrations is not clear; they would seem to go equally well in prose, but no doubt we find it normal for a poet to address us through a poem and may even like him for adopting this unpretentious tone—unlike the hysterical Gascoyne, the self-conscious Sitwell, the smug Stevens.

So, initially at least, we concur in external naturalisation, making our critical exploration a move into ordinary experience and the world of which it forms a part, limiting our investigations to the level of extended meaning. Having thus established a continuity between the words of the poem and the world outside, Empson is in a position from which to proceed to modify, subtly to undermine, this mode of reading and the assumptions on which it relies.

The relationship between narrator and reader initially implied by the poem encourages realistic expansion/limitation and, whether or not we have ever passed these great frontiers, asks us to think about the experience and to attend in the ordinary way to the writer's reactions to it. In this context, we might find Empson's reactions unusual. 'Good Heavens, Gwendolen! What odd notions you have! Scanning the crowds in rags each side with awe! I thought that your mother had brought you up to be short-sighted; she certainly wouldn't approve of you scanning crowds in rags, let alone with awe.' All the same, poets are expected to be eccentric, and we could make sense of the oddity easily enough through the old blague about poets as 'the antennae of the race'.

It is line five, the repetition of 'I find it normal', that really pulls us up in our headlong external naturalisation. No longer, it seems, can we work in a purely conversational, non-poetic mode. It seems that Empson has been using artifice all along and very subtly. The slight surprise on the level of meaning may have prepared us for more disruption—if we remember that it is through the level of meaning that rationally obscure poems appropriate external contexts—but we should simply have ignored any discomfort were it not for the last two lines.

Line five introduces repetition as a conventional poetic device. The line is shorter than the rest, and by convention brevity and repetition indicate a kind of poetic intensity. The poem, it turns out, is not going to be simply a repetition or imitation of ordinary speech which might as well have been written as prose. And so we must try to relate this new device to the order we had previously established. 'I find it normal' also contains the 'I' we had been so sure of and which we now begin to doubt, allowing the poetic persona to displace the empirical individual. We must go back to the first 'I find it normal' and begin to explore the internal network of levels which interact with one another. Having first moved into an external world and the experiences it was thought to contain, we are now led back into the poem where we begin, as it were, to climb the ladder of relations that leads to an internal thematic synthesis.

When we go back to the beginning of the poem, considering it under the aspect of Artifice, we must re-examine the theme and the poet's attitude towards it. We discover, for instance, that after 'I find it normal' has been isolated by repetition it becomes ambiguous in its two occurrences. Are the judgements of the first three lines 'normal' because of their appropriateness to the experience and the objects of experience, or are they normal because they are explicable, though at odds with the facts objectively viewed? This question seems to turn upon external circumstances, to ask whether in fact the differences in appearance which distinguish the people of two nations can rationally justify border disputes and national rivalries. But when we move back to the second occurrence of 'I find it normal' we discover that external focus was only a way of posing another question which transcends the former: is it normal and false to derive comfort from judgements that something is normal, or is it normal to extract false comfort—comfort that one knows is false? In other words, it might be an error to extract comfort from the idea that something is normal, or it might be normal to want to extract comfort, even when that comfort is false and recognised as false.

By the time we reach this point we are relatively detached from the experience of crossing great frontiers and the scanning of crowds in rags. That external context has been fictionalised, brought back into the poem as a poetic construct which leads to a posing of larger and more internally relevant questions. The subtle use of the semi-colon, which holds the verse up, postpones the completion of the sentence, and produces a suspended rhythm, preserves a relation between the first and second instances of 'I find it normal', and connects both of them with the last line which turns back, self-reflexively, on the problem of the judgement and ordering achieved through words.

The first image-complexes of meditation on this particular scene are overthrown by artifice and give way to more important ones. The emergence of the conventional level—the repetition which implies a new mode of discourse and displaces the 'I' towards a poetic persona—controls these external contexts, makes them pretexts (the bit of meat a burglar throws to the dog is Eliot's metaphor) or grounds for accepting the poem as a rational bit of poetic language. The contexts are fictionalised as we turn to the internal movement of the poem: 'I find it normal . . . I find it normal/So too to extract false comfort from that word.'

c*

This becomes the focus of an internal expansion. The apparent referent for 'it'—the reaction to crossing great frontiers—is fictionalised and becomes a more important question about the need for normality. Similarly, the phrase 'that word,' caught up in the ambiguous questioning of the final two lines, applies not only to 'normal' but to the whole process of meditating on and coming to terms with the external world through linguistic categories, such as 'normal'. The poem becomes self-reflexive, self-referential. The 'I' and the 'you', cut loose from the ties which originally seemed to hold them in a straightforward communicative contract, can no longer be situated except in relation to a generalised, interpersonal process of ordering. The poem, that is to say, has become obscure, and the only way to preserve continuity is to grasp part of its theme as an allegory of the process of writing.

The poem says 'my reaction to finding it normal to react as I do is to wonder whether the rationale which connects judgement with object should be comforting, whether that comfort should depend on truth or whether false comfort is also a comfort because of its own rationale, its normality.' We can find, at this level of fictionality, an allegory of what the poem itself does: its attempt to maintain continuity with the world of experience while investigating the judgements carried by words and trying to deal at the same time with discontinuity. The problem of the relationship between what might seem normal within a particular discursive order and what might be true (and the question of how far such discontinuity might matter) is also the problem of poetry itself. Or rather (for to speak in this way is to appeal to a generalised discourse about poetry) it is the problem of *this poem*: the problem of the relationship between the first 'I find it normal', continuous with a world of reactions and experience, and the second, which establishes an internal discursive order.

In interpreting the poem we move from empirical imagery to imagery which is discursive in the basic sense that it presents the language we normally speak; and here this very discursiveness—the fact that it is presented as an instance of our language—prevents us from making extrapolations to situations outside the poem: either to a state of society or of the poet's mind. The rationality of the imagery makes us take the arrangement of words and phrases itself as an image-complex signifying the desire to be rational and to assert continuity.

It is thus an example of rational obscurity, in which poetic technique is used to question and distance the external world. The complexity, the opening of the poem's semantic areas which can be found here, is a result of co-operation between ordinary language and poetic convention. It might be simplistic to claim that ordinary language provides poet and reader with a controlled and interpreted experiential context, while poet-

ic convention disrupts, modifies, and perhaps questions. But some such
dialectic is certainly available in Empson's style here. It is not available in
a style like Gascoyne's, where the reader is not sufficiently possessed of a
level of ordinary language to be able to weigh particular words and
phrases in relation to a general theme. Empson's technique, which
makes provision for the naturalising discourse of the critic, leads him out
into the world and then fictionalises that external context in a movement
of internal or artificial expansion and limitation. As such, it is infinitely
more powerful than any type of irrational obscurity, for it can disarm the
reader and swear him in as one of the poetic Mafia instead of just shooting
him down or showing him the door.

'Manchouli' is not, of course, an extreme example of obscurity. It may
even seem, in its closeness to ordinary language, to have affinities with
that poetry of empirical imagery and ordinary experience which has
characterised 'The Movement'. To see that this is not the case, to show,
by comparison, how artifice distinguishes 'Manchouli' from a poem
which operates entirely through external limitation/expansion, we might
look briefly at Philip Larkin's 'Mr Bleaney':

> 'This was Mr Bleaney's room. He stayed
> The whole time he was at the Bodies, till
> They moved him.' Flowered curtains, thin and frayed
> Fall to within five inches of the sill,
>
> Whose window shows a strip of building land,
> Tussocky, littered. 'Mr Bleaney took
> My bit of garden properly in hand.'
> Bed, upright chair, sixty-watt bulb, no hook
>
> Behind the door, no room for books or bags—
> 'I'll take it' . . .
>
> I know his habits . . .
>
> But if he stood and watched the frigid wind
> Tousling the clouds, lay on the fusty bed
> Telling himself that this was home, and grinned,
> And shivered, without shaking off the dread
>
> That how we live measures our own nature,
> And at his age having no more to show
> Than one hired box should make him pretty sure
> He warranted no better, I don't know.[17]

This is almost embarrassingly lucid. 'Embarrassingly' because if Mr
Larkin really does consider these reflections his most profound
thoughts—and there is every reason to suppose that he does—and if this
is a specimen of his best poetic style, as it would seem, then the notion
that he is an important poet, which had been bedeviling English poetry

for the past twenty years, is without foundation.

Naturally, we recognise a familiar world in these lines (unless we are lucky and have never been exposed to taking a bed-sitter), and we recognise the image of the contemplative poet in front of reality. Mr Larkin writes on the assumption that we will do so. The opening stanzas refer us to a known world and invite us to explore the associations of the real in an operation of external expansion. And the last two stanzas offer, as reflections that are to be added on to our own, the question of whether such surroundings should not depress the inhabitant. In their empirical reference and deliberate focus on Mr Bleaney, they too lead outward, urge an immersion in known orders rather than a questioning distance.

Of course, our conventional and time-honoured ideas of the poet's role demand that he be more than the merest obituary versifier and reporter—however much he may pretend to be no more. We may have a sneaking desire to cast Mr Larkin as prophet or seer and may even attempt to do so, though it will be uphill work (Mr Larkin is not a clever man for nothing).[18] We can take the 'I' as a poetic persona whose empirical situation (taking a bed-sitter) has been chosen to suit the theme: Mr Larkin's meditations on the vanity of human wishes. If we agree to read the last two stanzas as an instance of poetic intensity, as opposed to the fragmentary and 'realistic' notation of the opening, then we might say that watching 'the frigid wind tousling the clouds' is a poetic perception which makes life in a bed-sitter seem the more sordid. The poetic seer is more exposed, more sensitive to the failure and disappointments of empirical life than other characters, who may or may not interpret their condition, 'I don't know.'

One might object that this is a strained reading; that all Mr Larkin's efforts as the grand old man of the 'Movement' and the 'Group' have been devoted to routing the notion of special 'poetic vision' and to making the poet apologist of the quotidian. And indeed, 'the frigid wind tousling the clouds' can only count as poetic intensity if we take it as a reference to a discursive order (such as 'poetic visions of nature') and supply other more intense examples. So again, far from being led back into the poem for an internal thematic synthesis, we must move out from it in two directions: first, to an alternative vision of the world which we must ourself supply from past poetic practice (since Mr Larkin only offers hints and vague gestures towards such alternatives), and secondly to the empirical question of whether ordinary people who live in bed-sitters do in fact feel that 'they warrant no better' or whether such feelings are left to the more sensitive.

Artifice does not lead us back into the poem so as to question the empirical orders on which it is founded. There is none of the questioning, the shifting in levels of discourse and referentiality which we found in 'manchouli'. Mr Larkin is not a bad producer of verse; his technique is exact if unexciting; it fulfils the reader's expectations, leading him out towards the world and inviting him to think of it once more. But it does no more than that. It leaves poetry stranded on the beach of the already-known world, to expand and limit itself there.

We can now turn to properly obscure rational obscurity, which may even be refreshing after the limp and limpid vision of Mr Larkin. Rational obscurity which works through discursive imagery assimilates the ways in which particular 'languages' or modes of discourse (whether highly technical and specialised or more widely accepted) order the world. It explores and relates these alternative orderings, gradually subsuming particular themes to its general theme of ordering. As we found in an attenuated form in 'Manchouli', rational obscurity based on discursive imagery substitutes the reader/poet/poem relation for other explicit themes: fictionalises the latter so as to expand compass of the former. In 'Manchouli' the mode of ordering explored was that of 'normality' and ordinary judgements of rationale. In Empson's 'High Dive' we can study a more complex and radical assimilation where the dominant images come from science and mathematics:

> A cry, a greenish hollow undulation
> Echoes slapping across the enclosed bathing-pool.
> It is irrotational; one potential function
> (Hollow, the cry of hounds) will give the rule.
>
> Holding it then, I Sanctus brood thereover,
> Inform *in posse* the tank's triple infinite
> (So handy for co-ordinates), chauffeur
> The girdered sky, and need not dive in it.[19]

No one could claim that 'High Dive' is not obscure. It begins, in these first two stanzas, with a parallel development of empirical and discursive image-complexes and thus accepts its own task of mediation between language and the non-verbal world. It makes the image-complex the nodal point for creating this mediation. At first the two strands of imagery are kept apart. 'A cry, a greenish hollow undulation/Echoes slapping across the enclosed bathing-pool' presents the reader with a descriptive setting in the external world (the waves made by a plunge into the pool). The next two lines introduce scientific discourse—'irrotational; one potential function . . . will give the rule'—with an interpolation from another social 'language', that of hunting.

A primary quality of rationally obscure poetry is that when we investigate the various modes of discourse on which it draws we are able to work out rational links which relate particular phrases to general themes. By working through the languages we will be able, in these first two stan-

zas, to relate the diver's position above the pool to other instances of consciousness faced with an ordered universe: God and creation, scientist
and the physical world, poet and society, reader and a certain kind of
poetic style. From above the pool one can see it in several ways, three of
which correspond to different kinds of assumed reality. The ordinary
description speaks for itself: the water's movement is presented as it
would appear to a man who inhabits everyday experience (undulations
and slapping noises). The movement is then described in a scientific
formulation: insofar as the pool's water is 'irrotational' (without rotation)
it can be defined by one potential function which operates on the x/y axes
of the Cartesian system of co-ordinates. That is, it contains all possible
movements but any actual movement would force recourse to a three-
dimensional system of co-ordinates (x/y/z axes) which scientifically
defines motion.

This juxtaposition introduces a contrast between the physical reality
apparent to the senses and a mathematical summary of it, and it also indicates that the bathing-pool is like the world viewed from inside a closed
system of conceptual relations. We can say that it is like the world
because the third vision is equated with God's view of the creation: 'I
Sanctus brood thereover'. Like the mathemetician's formulation, this
view implies that detachment from the physical world is a precondition
for contemplating it. 'I Sanctus' leads us back away from any external
individual to a poetic persona, identified with the diver, the scientist, and
God, and insofar as the poet identifies himself with these viewpoints, he
is released from any commitment to action: he 'need not dive in it'.

The poet in his relation to society and the reader in his relation to a
poetic style have a different status from our other pairs: diver and pool,
scientist and physical world, God and creation. The latter belong to a
thematic interpretation of the meanings of words. The former, however
belong to the specific poetic activity that is undertaken here. To take a
language and organise it in rhymed stanzas, making use of a rhetorical
tone and figurative combinations or words, is a social act which emphasises formal features normally 'irrelevant' to the business of communication and, by adding this new dimension, comes to dominate the
whole problem of producing meaning, or ordering. It is at this level that a
synthesis of the various languages and their ways of dealing with the
world must be achieved.

The synthesis begins with 'potential' in the third line, which belongs
both to the specialised language of science and to the colloquial language
of everyday, as is emphasised by the sound pattern which links it with
both 'holl*ow* undulations' and 'irr*o*tational'. Play on the meanings of
'potential' also underlies the second line of the second stanza: 'Inform *in
posse* the tank's triple infinite'. And here the religious strain of discourse

is added. 'I Sanctus', brooding thereover, can give potential form to the water, grasp all its possible movements, much as the mathematical definition can, though in a different mode. Since our ability to relate three kinds of language and the three kinds of world-view they imply depends on our knowledge that we are reading a poem—our ability to undertake the kind of operations necessary to construct meaning in poetry—the poetic context as mode of synthesis is evoked. Like God, Diver, and Scientist, the poet and reader stand above language, to whose potential function they give form; stand above a text which they inform. 'Potential' in its two occurrences serves as a bridge on which poet and reader can stand while developing empirical and discursive image-complexes and bringing them together in a thematic synthesis which cannot but evoke the poetic posture—and exploitation of language not normally permissible—that permits it to take place. Similarly, the fact that 'infinity' is central to both theological and mathematical discourse brings those two perspectives together, and since this can only occur in verbal organisation controlled by poetic conventions, the stress on the style's self-consciousness is reinforced.

'Triple' in 'the tank's triple infinite' is another instance of the same operations of rational obscurity. Mathematically the expression is triple because it describes the water's movement in terms of the three axes of the Cartesian system of co-ordinates ('So handy for co-ordinates', the tank's triple infinite), just as 'infinite' relates to a potential function that takes no account of boundaries. Theologically, 'triple' relates to the tri-ple infinite of the Godhead held together by Sanctus. Again the formal similarity makes the thought possible, while our knowledge of how to interpret poetic metaphor through a rationality extended into other languages is a precondition of our giving thematic importance to the formal similarity. The synthesis serves as example of, and hence evokes, the simultaneously detached and involved stance of the poet/reader, who must draw back in order to perceive multiple relations, yet plunge in in order to mediate.

> Unless, in act, to turbulence, discerning
> His shade, not image, on smashed glass disbanded,
> One, curve and pause, conscious of strain of turning
> Only (muscle on bone, the rein cone now handed),
>
> Unchart the second, the obstetric, chooses,
> Leaves isle equation by not frozen ford,
> And, to break scent, under foamed new phusis
> Dives to receive in memory reward.

Here the dive is invoked as a real possibility—necessity even—which destroys the irrotational character of the pool. The fact that vectors are plotted by a series of rotating curves is brought together with the plain physical fact that by turning in order to dive the man creates a vortex, first in air, then in water. The facts of science and mathematics as they are made accessible through their verbal formulation to the metaphorical language of poetry are integrated by it in virtue of their very strangeness: as the representation of an order which is strange. And even a social order can be distanced by the operation of poetic integration, as is best seen in a certain type of poetic comparison. The diver is seen as a hare pursued by hounds and hunters in green coats: '(Hollow, the cry of hounds)' is related to the 'hollow' of the dive; the hunters dressed in '(green for hares) however, tear me down'; and the diver plunges into the water 'to break scent'. The hunters, following the social code which prescribes their dress, are also related to a social order by the fact that the comparison develops according to assumptions which underlie the institution of poetry. For instance, there is development from physical fact—the chlorinated water of the bathing-pool is green ('a greenish hollow undulation')—to imaginative indentification (the green of the hunters' coats) to thematic implication (the individual is pursued). Indeed, this process of development itself presents us with a contrast between the individual and a society which, through its modes of ordering, including those of poetry, defines and places him in a network of meanings.

Different kinds of diction and the poetic style itself are made to serve a thematic purpose. What seems obscure may be clarified by a reading that assumes a kind of continuity between poetic language and other kinds of discourse. So that by tracing the senses of key words through other contexts and putting this together with our assumptions about how poetry is to be read we may arrive at an interaction of meaning which shift and modify the non-verbal contexts they might imply. 'Inform' is one such nodal point, the centre of a network of possible meaning. Hovering about 'Inform' are many other similarly formed words which our thematic synthesis draws into the poem as material for internal expansion. These are: 'un*form*ed' (un-created by form), '*for*med with respect to *infor*mation rather than action', 'containing a lot of potential *in*formation because of the word's *form*', '*in*formed' either because a lot is known or because the knowledge is not yet in *form* of action (not yet *for*med but 'inform *in posse*'). Finally there is the familiar notion of poetic form as both an object and an instrument of knowledge and of action in language; in the words of Francis Ponge, 'le seul moyen d'agir est le moyen que j'ai choisi: d'écrire'.

Empson is, as he says, 'using F. M. Cornford's theory that the order behind the "physical" world was originally thought of as the life-blood of the tribe'[20] and the fear of society which is symbolised by the feeling that one must take the dive once one has climbed up. This fear leads either to empirical paralysis or acceptance of the given 'phusis' [social order]. The only way to escape these alternatives is to write poetry as a way of keeping contact [continuity] with one's society while creating new orders of imagination within the language of society, creating 'new phusis' as the last stanza quoted above puts it.

The play on *physics/phusis* has important implications for Empson, as we shall see in chapter IV. Here it is both image-complex and theme, bringing together two major strands of the thematic synthesis. 'Physics' is first of all, and especially in the opening two stanzas of the poem, an area of discourse used to provide words and metaphors which work to create image-complexes, formal patterns and ambivalence on the level of meaning. It is a standpoint for ordering the universe, the source of an order which initially clashes with everyday experience and is integrated with it only at a higher level, through poetic technique or, to give it its proper name, poetic mediation. The word 'physics' itself makes an actual appearance when the dive occurs and the need for a new technique is accepted. It appears in its original Hellenic form and sense of 'order' while ostensibly describing the swimming-pool after the dive 'foamed new phusis'. The whole cluster of ideas about physics is brought in first through the original imagery and finally through the Hellenic sense—it meant both 'the natural order' and 'the character of an individual'. Poetic convention thus evokes a group of similar words which can contribute to the thematic synthesis. 'Physicist' who in his account of the world may also be a 'physician' who cures its ills; the 'metaphysicist' who stands above and must cure the ills of philosophy as a 'metaphysician'; 'metaphysics' as both beyond and opposed to 'physics'. All these connotations are important to the idea of the poet as tribal outcast as mediator among languages and orders.

This and other image-complexes can be brought into a thematic synthesis in that they bear, allegorically, on the theme of poetry as knowledge versus poetry as action and on this opposition as an instance of the individual's situation: he must be tribal outcast in order to re-create the conceptual schemes of a society which offers him no hope of absolute knowledge or value in human activity.*

Briefly the poem's thematic synthesis is that it is impossible for the individual to cut himself off from society. He must either accept its con-

---

* 'High Dive' was first published in 1932, but 'Value is in Activity', 'Letter l', and 'Dissatisfaction with Metaphysics', all of which contain the same image-complexes and themes, though in a less developed form, appeared in 1928. And in the *Collected Poems*, arranged 'roughly in the order of their writing', 'High Dive' appears on page 13. So that it is reasonable to suppose that the paradoxical co-existence of relativism and positivism (best seen in the work of I. A. Richards, with whom Empson had a lifelong and ambivalent relationship) began its work on Empson's poetry when he came up to Cambridge in 1926 to read first mathematics, then English.

ceptual schemes and its view of him and his role, descending from the diving board by steps that are already constructed for him, or he must accept the task of creating a new society and a new personality and lose his superior perspectives, creating a new order as he dives. If he is a poet this means that he must create a new kind of technique which will make critical reading difficult and his style obscure, but the style will be rationally obscure so that the critic can, by applying his rules, eventually interpret the poem. Rationality can be preserved in such poems only by using image-complexes that are either empirical, like most of those in 'Manchouli', or discursive, so that the reader may follow their Ariadne's thread through the levels of the poem to a thematic synthesis (irrational Artifice offers only 'Ariachne's broken woof').

I have been trying to show how Rational Artifice, by being obscure on the scale of relevance, has the power to appropriate not only the meanings and ideas but also the structure of definitions that make up other languages: in this case predominantly the language of science. Because of this power it can assert continuity with the world of other languages without giving in to them. We must now turn to the exploration of techniques of discontinuity, which have a very different kind of power.

CHAPTER THREE

The disconnected image-complex: Pound and Eliot

No account of the main strands of development for poetry in this century can ignore Imagism, which flaunted its discoveries and its modernity with fervour and served as an important catalyst. The case of Imagism is the more interesting because it is anathema to Empson's brand of rationalism and might seem, because of the theories it propounded, anathema to Artifice *tout court*. What we must discover is whether, in the poems of Ezra Pound as distinct from the tendentious theorising, Imagism falls outside the bounds of artifice, or whether it does indeed make a distinctive and crucial contribution.

I   However entrancing it is to wander unchecked through a garden of bright images . . .

I quote Harriet Vane's remark to Lord Peter Wimsey because too many people think that poetry is about wandering through a garden of bright images — and too many think that they can do it unchecked. This means that poetic imagery is thought of in terms of the physical world—the world which it presents—and the checks of Artifice do not have a chance to operate. For if the reader encounters a poem which is not 'entrancing' in this way (and many of the greatest are not) he may simply stop reading and return to Keats or to whoever he thinks provides him with minute detailed physical images.

Empson certainly thinks of Imagism as an attempt to describe the physical world and therefore criticises it: 'the trouble with Imagism and all its offshoots is that it tells us that we have to be very stupid.'[1] We have to be stupid because we have to try to forget the basic facts of how language works: by connected and logical sentences. Empson continues, 'when imagery works well and is known to work well it is by leading the reader through a series of imaginative analogies until he feels he can safely deduce something, usually a very plain fact, about life from the decisiveness of the rudiments shown in it'.[2]

Now, it doesn't seem to me that either of these assertions is incontrovertible. We do not know much about how language works but linguists, logicians, and philosophers have long ago abandoned the assumption that language works through logic in the restricted sense: that is, consists of true propositions that are well-formed grammatically and can be verified, or falsified, by either an appeal to induction (the empirical method) or an appeal to deduction (the high priori road). In fact the assumptions were questioned by Sanskrit philosopher-linguists two thousand years ago (not to mention a certain Immanuel Kant). Nobody knows—least of all linguists themselves, who are trying to find out— what is the nature of language and how it works, but I haven't been talking about 'the fallacy of unmediated expression' for nothing. It seems at least reasonably certain that, however the human consciousness is related to 'reality' (and that concept is just as much a problem as language), it must be related through language; that is, the world comes to us through words and may very well be created by them. Be that as it may, our notion of how the world comes to us through words or how we come to the world has direct bearing of how poetic imagery works, for it is the canonical function of poetic imagery to—as the word suggests—image things.

The crux is that without language we can have no notion of 'things' and once they become part of language they are no longer 'things in themselves'. The word 'imagery' has other affinities too, though, and perhaps more important ones for poetry; it suggests for instance imagining things, which is not at all the same as imagining them. Or is it, as Coleridge says, that our problem is always to imagine that which we know but without an image of 'it' cannot know how to imagine 'it'? Is the 'it' we know the same as the 'it' we imagine; is it a picture of a duck or a rabbit or is it a duck-rabbit? ' "Do you see yonder cloud . . .? Methinks it is like a weasel." "It is backed like a weasel." ' Acquit me of frivolity a while; though this be madness yet there's method in it, for Ezra Pound in the Imagist manifesto did proclaim that the image is 'thought beyond formulated language', that poetry must aim at 'direct treatment of the thing.'[3] And if Empson's idea of poetic language as a process of logical inference is narrow-minded, Pound's is plain silly and quite enough to make men more patient than Empson cross.

In fact, the much vaunted theory, as is usually the case, is a pretext for a change in technique. We could do with some more of such pretexts and excuses, though, for at least they make people argue about poetry in a reasoned way. We must stick with the theory for a bit if only for a lead into the practice. Where better to start than with Pound's account of how one of his best known poems, 'In a Station of the Metro', was composed.

In his memoir of Gaudier-Brzeska Pound says that he encountered, in the Metro, several beautiful faces in succession and that he wanted to make a poem about this but gave it up after writing and discarding thirty lines. Had he been a painter, he says, no doubt he would have been able to catch the topic on canvas, but being a mere poet he had to do with words which are, according to Imagist theory, very inadequate for 'getting at the things'.[4] The curious aspect of this account is Pound's assumption that 'the things' lie somewhere outside the medium which reproduces them—between the lines, between the strokes on the canvas—and that technique is simply a way of reproducing them in a way which will make the reader see what the artist sees in 'the things': that is, his vision plus 'the things'.

We had better look at 'In a Station of the Metro' to see whether this is true:

> The apparition of these faces in the crowd;
> Petals on a wet, black bough.[5]

In a sense it is obviously true that the reader reads an external context between the lines and that what he sees is partly the poet's vision. He can only see these things, though, because both he and the poet know the rules for reading poetry. The reader connects the title with other lines as explanatory; he connects one line with the other as a metaphorical comparison. There is nothing revolutionary about this; as Empson says in discussing one of Arthur Waley's translations from the Chinese which is very like 'Metro',

> two statements are made as if they were connected, and the reader is forced to consider their relations for himself. The reason why these facts should have been selected for a poem is left for him to invent; he will invent a variety of reasons and order them in his own mind. This, I think, is the essential fact about the poetical use of language.[6]

As is clear from his earlier dismissal of Imagism, Empson believes that the intention of connections is a logical, or at least a rational process that takes place in the reader's mind just as other processes of reasoning do but, as his last sentence implies, that poetry uses a special technique to set the ball rolling. What is innovatory about 'Metro' is that it leaves out the connecting link between the statements, which would have been so easy to supply: the apparition of these faces in the crowd is like petals on a wet, black bough. That omission does not suggest a mistrust of the power of poetic imagery or of the reader's poetic competence. Nor does it suggest, as Pound believed, that Imagism had invented a new technique for 'getting at the things' through poetic language by by-passing ordinary language. On the contrary, 'Metro' relies more than other poems on these basic technical skills. It is all very well for Pound the theorist to claim that, 'the point of Imagism is that it does not use images *as ornaments*. The image is itself the speech. The image is the word beyond formulated language.'[7] There is no word beyond formulated language, and Pound the poet knew it even at his most rabidly imagist. Of course 'Metro' uses the level of meaning to lead out into the external world—

into a station of the metro and into the poet's reaction to that world—but its technique then leads us back into the poem's thematic synthesis. Of course 'Metro' makes us imagine an external context: these faces in the crowd, petals on a wet, black bough. But so do 'The Waste Land', 'Manchouli', 'Fox Trot', 'High Dive', and even David Gascoyne's lines. Empson and Eliot's techniques, however, take these external contexts back into the poem through the level of image-complex into an internal thematic synthesis.

The fact is that Pound's 'image' is an attempt to by-pass the combination of discursive and empirical imagery and the level of image-complex in order to evade bad Naturalisation—to convert the soiled language of the everyday world to a new language that will be clean. Exactly the same manoeuvre led to the 'ideogrammic method' and the *Cantos*. The aim is laudable ('In matters of similar magnitude the bare attempt would be praiseworthy') and, indeed, close to that of Prynne and other contemporary poets who are tendentiously obscure. Moreover, Pound was too good a technician, too good a poet, to fall into the trap of Concrete Poetry.

It is rather insulting to be told (and critics have been telling poets this since Plato's *Ion*) that one is too good in action to practise what one preaches; and in fact Pound, at least as a poet, cannot be accused of that: he was constantly formulating and publishing theories to justify his poetic practice from 'I gather the limbs of Osiris' (*The New Age*, 1912) and probably before, until the interviews and remarks made in the last year of his life (1972) and he is probably still doing so in his mythological paradise. We should look, however, at what the innovations of Imagism can tell us about Artifice, having disposed of the claim that these innovations 'got at the things' without linguistic mediation. Indeed, via Professor Empson, we have already seen one of its most important contributions: the recognition that disconnected statements in an unfamiliar technique will nevertheless be naturalised by the reader who is competent in poetry, and that this Naturalisation need not be bad if the reader sees how the image-complexes are leading him back into the poem.

The problem remains: what are Imagism's image-complexes that they can do this to the reader with practically none of the development in conjunction with other levels so characteristic of discursive and empirical imagery? I think the answer will best come circuitously, by a look at what Pound was reacting against when he formulated the famous 'Few Don'ts for Imagists': his own early poems. My example is taken from 'Canzon: of Incense' which appeared in *Canzoni* of 1911 but also in the repudiated earlier volumes and was therefore written long before:

> Thy gracious ways,
> O Lady of my heart, have
> O'er all my thought their golden glamour cast,
> As amber torch-flames, where strange men-at-arms
> Tread softly 'neath the damask shield of night,
> Rise from the flowing steel in part reflected,
> Sô on my mailed thought that with thee goeth,
> Though dark the way, a golden glamour falleth.[8]

Now I don't think that that is bad poetry but I can see why Pound thought so, especially when I remember that there are eight stanzas of it. In fact the poem is a very skilful adaptation of the Italian Canzone; rhythm, metre, and sound/look are well blended with each other and with the imagery, but it doesn't exactly lead out into the external world, or 'get at the things' beyond language, or make use of the language of 'real' experience. And I'm willing to bet a gold sovereign to a brass farthing that there is no actual 'Lady of my heart' or that Pound had never seen amber torch-flames reflected on the habiliments of 'strange men-at-arms'.

Of course I have been maintaining all along that the personages and decor in poems are convenient fictions, and that so are the poet and reader, but I have been dealing with poems whose diction and form would lead one to deny this: poems, that is, written in contemporary syntax and lexis and recognisably contemporary poetic forms which take account of past literature and of their own present (through 'free verse' and colloquial speech and self-reflexivity in 'Manchouli', through the language of mathematics in 'High Dive', and through tendentious obscurity in Prynne). The only exceptions are my irrational obscurities and they too are evidently modern though covert accomplices of critical presuppositions.

'Canzon: of Incense', however, uses an artificial and out-moded poetical diction and takes no account of contemporaneity in its themes and imagery. This very unreality gives it certain advantages in the freedom with which it asserts its own separateness and brings it paradoxically close to twentieth-century movements like Dada and to English poetry in the 1970's which can be characterised as neo-Dada. One might say, in fact, that both the poetry Pound recognised, such as the *Cantos*, and the poetry he repudiated, such as early Canzoni, are relevant to our situation today. This matter must wait for another book, though, which will concern Pound, the 'Nineties, and the great fictionalisers, Tennyson, Swinburne, Rossetti, who lie behind them. ('And I also will sing war when this matter of a girl is exhausted.)

To return to the image-complexes of Imagism. The first thing to strike one about the contrast between 'Canzon' and 'Metro' is their difference in title; the former stresses its formal, generic, and artificial affinities, while the latter stresses its descriptive intention, its scene and setting, its references to the world of everyday experience. The same is true of the stanza form—if one can call the two lines of 'Metro' a stanza—which in 'Canzon' and 'Metro' asserts the same things as the respective titles, as do also the syntax and choice of words. Note, however, that we have already stumbled on a difficulty: 'if one can call the two lines of "Metro" a stanza'. Our assumptions about poetry are being questioned. Are we or not to call these two lines a stanza? They do not rhyme: they have no recognisable metrical regularity, nor are they overtly connected by syntax or metaphor. In 'Canzon', contrariwise, the rhymes, rhythm, metre are unmistakable—even, Pound must have felt, oppressive; the lines are unmistakably connected, syntactically as well as artificially. In 'Canzon' all the levels of Artifice mesh smoothly and, if there is not much of a thematic synthesis or very striking image-complexes, the reason is that it is no mean feat to produce such highly mannered verse which is also syntactically correct. The trivialisation of theme and image-complex may be not just a venial sin but a positive advantage.

In 'Metro', however, nothing meshes smoothly. Is this because the poem reflects the unmanageability of 'things in themselves'? The poet would like to think so, but I'm not so sure. For a start there is the traditional poetic pact between the poet and the reader, as shown by the relation between the title and the first line. According to Imagist aesthetic this proves that the poem is descriptive of an external scene—we are all familiar with crowds at Metro stations—but it is also the performative act of making a pact with the reader. Of course it may be both things simultaneously. I should never deny that poems may be about subjects other than writing poetry, but I do deny that they can be about other things without also being about writing poetry, in the sense of employing Artifice in their organisation. And I think that the 'other things' are apt to take, rightly, second place to the organisation of the poem.

Moreover, for a second start, there is a perceptible use of Artifice in these lines despite their insistence on the language of everyday life. This would be true even if the formal arrangement were restricted to the conventional level alone—spacing on the page, initial capitalisation—but it is not so restricted; the poem could not be good if it were, for 'no verse is free for the man who wants to do a good job' as Eliot said. Metre and rhythm are present if we look hard enough. As usual rhythm can only be defined as the interaction of metre and syntax but about these we can be more definite:

> Thĕ appărĭtiŏn ŏf thĕse fácĕs ĭn thĕ crówd;
> Pétăls ŏn ă wét, bláck boúgh.

We could say that the metre was loosely anapaestic but with small justification, for the first line consists of three extended anapaests each with one extra unstressed syllable. There are only three strong stresses in a line of twelve syllables, which is not usual; there are three strong stresses to nine weak stresses. And the effect of this is to mark most strongly the words that are stressed, 'apparition' 'faces' 'crowd'. These words are central to the theme and to the image-complex. Indeed, as in 'Papyrus', the poet could have gone as far in disconnectedness as to write:

Apparition faces crowd

The reader would arrive at the same meaning and with more chance of being stranded in an external context. I think it is significant that Pound did not go as far as that, as he did in parts of the *Cantos*. And the reason for both the holding back and the later advance is that at that time he lacked the skill to make disconnected words and phrases cohere—'Papyrus' is not a success—and was reluctant to abandon the skill he did have with traditional metres that require unstressed syllables.

It is not an accident that there is great metrical contrast between the two lines: four stressed and three unstressed syllables in the second to three and nine in the first. The metre works together with the syntax to isolate 'petals', with its strong initial stress. And 'wet, black bough' is set off as a unit both by its final position and by the metrical equivalent of the three stressed monosyllables. But what of the link between these two lines? The semi-colon is a very odd punctuation mark to have picked for a metaphoric relation. The semi-colon, as my schoolmistress taught me, is used when one wishes to break a sentence more strongly than with a comma and less strongly than by ending it with a full stop. It is used to organise rather long sentences whose subjects are either identical or closely connected when one doesn't want to break up the sequence of thought by introducing a full stop. What the semi-colon is not used for is to refer to some phrase as the object of attention or the point of comparison; for that the colon or the dash is used.

But Pound uses a semi-colon. Why? He could have compromised with a comma or gone all out with a colon or dash. The only reason must be that he was hesitating between the demands of Imagism for disconnected phrases and the demands of traditional verse for a comma at the end of the line and a capital letter at the beginning. It is very unusual to use a capital letter after a semi-colon in written prose or transcription of speech. Moreover, this hesitation connects with a deeper hesitation in the type of his image-complex, the style of his mind. The poem hesitates between discursive and empirical imagery and between rational and irrational Artifice, for it presents a sequence of thought and the objects of thought but does not work these into the structure of the poem's image-complexes. The three strong stresses at the end represent a return to the object of comparison once the comparing mind has distinguished scene and vision, but for the reader they convey a strong metrical and rhythmical pause. The rhythm moves swiftly through the first line till held up by the semi-colon and by the dactylic reversal in 'Petals'; it then recovers for a moment the anapaestic speed only to be lifted into those three final strong stresses.

The second line has seven syllables, four of which are strong; this is in noted contrast to the first line. In a way Pound's account of the time and trouble it took him to make this poem is significant: all the action, as it were, takes place between the two lines so that we have the impression of a very much more substantial and lengthy piece. This is perhaps the true innovation of Imagism: to be able to say in two lines what another writer—the early Pound—could not have said in fifty. But my use of 'say' is suspect for two reasons. First, according to the Imagist aesthetic, the important thing is not to say but to show some aspect of the external world. Second, according to Artifice, poems can only say something (reach a thematic synthesis) by working through the development of image-complexes on other levels in connected sequence, and this is not what an Imagist poem, 'Metro' with its two juxtaposed statements, is meant to do.

I think, however, that 'Metro' does in fact do this and for the reasons stated: the extreme skill in blending metre and syntax and in handling rhythm; the impression of spaciousness created by disconnected statements and alternate discursive and empirical imagery; the fact that it manages to be both rational (the statements are perfectly grammatical) and irrational (they are connected only by juxtaposition). In fact, Imagism as practised by Pound (of others I do not speak) represents a valuable contribution to the resources of Artifice by its creation of a new type of image-complex, which might be called the 'disconnected image-complex'. It is not, as we intended, a new road to 'reality', but a new road to the possibilities of language and to the techniques that make them available to us. It does clean up words by freeing them from the constraints of the connected image-complex, while it keeps them in order by trimming their garden with new metrical experiments which keep it from lapsing into the incoherent minimalism of Concrete Poetry.

The notion of 'disconnected image-complex' may help to clear up some of the confusion that results when critics try to naturalise lines from Pound. In Eva Hesse's collection, *New Approaches to Ezra Pound*, which would be better entitled *Glimpses of Chaos in the Literary World*, we find a bewildering variety of presuppositions and methods of Naturalisation. Albert Cook, for example, accepts Pound's aesthetic of the Ideogram and

argues that Pound's image-complexes are not signs which can be interpreted:

> Ideogram exists, then, 'paratactically' [i.e. in juxtaposition] on an absolute
> level with *persona*, so that one cannot be signifier and the other
> signified . . . Each ideographic unit, by carrying so many connections,
> possesses the sheer indecipherability of 'L'Art, 1910', even when ideas
> dominate it: because the ideas have their poetic function, *as distinct from
> their signification*, only by juxtaposition to other ideas.[9]

There is some truth in this, but only some. Mr Cook speaks of the 'sheer
indecipherability' of 'L'Art, 1910' because the images operate in ways
that he does not expect—because, shall I say, he lacks the concept of the
disconnected image-complex.

L'Art, 1910

> Green arsenic smeared on an egg-white cloth,
> Crushed strawberries! Come, let us feast our eyes.[10]

It is, of course, crucial to good health as well as to good poetry that only
the eyes should feast. Mr Cook has been led astray by Pound's aesthetic
of 'getting at the things'. He takes the three noun phrases as empirical
images and finds them indecipherable because he cannot imagine what is
being described. Thus he is forced to assume that he is dealing with indecipherable and juxtaposed ideas. But in fact we are confronted with a case
of the disconnected image-complex. The poem hesitates between empirical reference to a scene and assimilation of another linguistic system.
The phrases, we can say, are metaphors for a painter's colours; the scene
is one created by the poem which puts us into an imaginary picture gal-
lery or painter's studio. The title employs the traditional tool of summing
up the topic, in a way that indicates the co-existence of possible scene and
assimilated discourse. The lines lack 'Metro's' rhythmical excitement
and syntactic surprise; they use the convention of capitalisation and traditional poetic metaphors (to feast one's eyes on visual beauty), and once
we have grasped the nature of their disconnected image-complex,
nothing makes the poem hard to interpret.

Consider, by way of contrast, an example from John J. Espey's work
on Pound's sources. In 'Ezra Pound and the inheritance *to kalon*' Mr
Espey writes about late nineteenth-century influences on Pound:

> 'Beauty is difficult, Yeats' said Aubrey Beardsley
> . . .
> So very difficult, Yeats, beauty so difficult.
>
> 'I am the torch' wrote Arthur 'she saith'. (Canto LXXX)

The direct statement, with all its Nineties associations and its return to Symons' 'Modern Beauty' comes late in *The Cantos*, but the 'Difficulty' of beauty—*to kalon*/order—is their most profound theme, and a search for a solution of that difficulty underlies all of Pound's political, economic, and historical reading.[11]

Mr Cook could have nothing to do with 'direct statement', 'profound theme', and 'search for a solution', nor, one imagines, could Mr Espey accept 'sheer indecipherability'. Indeed, his avoidance of unintelligibility leads him to neglect the obvious discontinuities in the passage he cites. Both Mr Cook and Mr Espey have grasped half of the problem; they each perceive one effect of the disconnected image-complex, but neither grasps its dual function. Language in *The Cantos*, as in some of the earlier poems, is used disconnectedly with a very distinctive mingling of rational and irrational Artifice, of discursive and empirical imagery, which makes the techniques themselves their own subject and past literature one strand in the network. The ideas *are* there in order that continuity may be preserved; and they exist both as part of the form and as an assertion of discontinuity which enables the technique to be creative. That is why I have introduced the concept of the disconnected image-complex which suspends our reading between empirical and discursive imagery and forces us to make connections which neither discourse itself nor the world already contains.

The image-complex of Imagism, which is of course almost entirely the image-complex of Ezra Pound (H. D.'s poems are the only notable exception), has played an important role in the poetry of our century; and I should now like to examine a more radical use of it in Eliot's quatrain poems, which are not usually considered imagist at all.

II   Eliot and the disconnected image-complex

Views of Oxford Colleges
Lay on the table, with the knitting.

'A Cooking Egg' is one of Eliot's quatrain poems which shows very clearly the use of the disconnected image-complex in apparently traditional verse. 'Apparently' since, unlike Pound's Imagist productions, these poems preserve traditional stanza norms, rhyme, rhythm, and the use of persona, while in fact separating these features from traditional poetry. In 'Metro' we saw that beneath the innovation in technique links with past poetry were preserved; in Eliot's quatrain poems almost exactly the opposite occurs. 'Almost' because these techniques still make use of the image-complex and, indeed, by making it disconnected take it further than overtly tendentious experimental poetry like orthodox Imagism can do. One does not find Eliot making silly claims about poetry getting directly at things beyond language.

On the contrary, his concept of the 'objective correlative' is a direct transposition into poetics of the ideas expressed in his *Knowledge and Experience in the Philosophy of F. H. Bradley*, where he adopts Bradley's claim that

> the Nature studied by the observer and by the poet and painter is, in all its sensible and emotional fullness, a very real Nature. It is in most respects more real than the strict object of physical science. For Nature, as the world where real essence lies in primary qualities, has not a high degree of reality and truth.[12]

Eliot contrasts science (objective knowledge and expression of things in themselves as it was then considered to be, at least by Pound) whose aim is 'to reduce reality to one type of object, and the ultimate type of object I should suppose to be points in mathematical relation', with those activities such as metaphysics, history, and literary studies which involve a 'transformation of object type'.[13] (As we shall shortly see, he thought of poetry also as belonging to this class.) The mind altering alters all; there is no physical reality independent of consciousness—and for the poet consciousness is language—or consciousness independent of physical objects. So that both objects and language co-exist as mutually dependent and an idea or emotion cannot help but alter the object, and vice versa.

Thus we get the idea of the objective correlative, the verbal form which evokes an articulated emotion. Though it may seem and has seemed to influential critics[14] to claim that poetry by-passes language in order make a direct correlation between the poet's mind and external reality, in fact the objective correlative insists on their dependence on language as the area where this activity takes place. Indeed, Eliot's emphasis on the 'new art emotion' as a linguistic and poetic construct should make this plain.[15] Eliot could never have believed the Imagist aesthetic of thought beyond formulated language, and in fact never did so; his philosophical background was too firm. Similarly, the insistence on the mutual modification of past and present literature has its roots in this 'transformation of object type', and it is behind Eliot's constant endeavour to assimilate the past of world literature, an endeavour which reached its climax only in *Four Quartets*.

But it is present too in the quatrain poems, where traditional forms are used in a radical experiment in assimilation and dislocation.

A Cooking Egg

Pipit sate upright in her chair
  Some distance from where I was sitting;
Views of Oxford Colleges
  Lay on the table, with the knitting.[16]

I don't propose to discuss the questions any reader must ask himself: who is Pipit? who is 'I'? and later, 'Where are the eagles and the trumpets?' These questions have exercised literary critics since the poem was first published—until Donald Davie had the wit to point out that the scene is imaginary.[17] That it doesn't matter whether 'Pipit' is the poet's mistress, friend, old nurse, pet dog, or even F. H. Bradley himself, is clear, for it is a shorthand name for a level of organisation that fictionalises the scene and may—as we shall see when we analyses the poem in detail—change from one level to another like Edward Lear's Jumblies. It need not matter because we do not expect disconnected imagery to give us a normal thematic synthesis, and if ever imagery was disconnected, this is.

First, the title explains nothing; it is Eliot's first dig at the reader who cannot be expected to know—as critics have zealously found out—that 'a cooking egg' means one which is slightly bad. Even when we do know this it doesn't help much; perhaps it might be connected with the epigraph from Villon, 'En l'an trentiesme de mon a age/Que toutes mes hontes j'ay beues', and with the prevailing atmosphere of defeatism. But this is assuming that the poem is trying to be connected and coherent and that scholarly information is useful, whereas it contains indications (much clearer than the disconnectedness of 'Metro') that it is not trying to be coherent:

> Daguerrotypes and silhouettes,
>   Her grandfather and great great aunts,
> Supported on the mantelpiece
>   An *Invitation to the Dance*
>
>   .   .   .   .
>
> I shall not want Honour in Heaven
>   For I shall meet Sir Philip Sydney
> And have talk with Coriolanus
>   And other heroes of that kidney. . . .
>
> I shall not want Society in Heaven,
>   Lucretia Borgia shall be my Bride;
> Her anecdotes will be more amusing
>   Than Pipit's experience could provide.
>
> I shall not want Pipit in Heaven:
>   Madame Blavatsky will instruct me
> In the Seven Sacred Trances;
>   Piccarda de Donati will conduct me.
>
>   .   .   .   .
>
> But where is the penny world I bought
>   To eat with Pipit behind the screen?
> The red-eyed scavengers are creeping
>   From Kentish Town and Golder's Green;

> Where are the eagles and the trumpets?
>
> Buried beneath some snow-deep Alps
> Over buttered scones and crumpets
> Weeping, weeping, multitudes
> Droop in a hundred A.B.C.'s[18]

Those four dot breaks are only the most obvious instances of disconnectedness. A bewildering variety of scenes and personages is invoked; they have nothing in common except their inhabitation of the same poem; and the poet's contemporary London brought into the last stanza is a veritable 'unreal city'. Nor is this ironic writing. The poet has left himself no safe place from which he can heap scorn on anything; no place at all except in the verse form. This gives a new twist to the famous statement in 'Tradition and the Individual Talent' that 'no poet, no artist of any art, has his complete meaning alone. . . . you must set him, for contrast and comparison, among the dead.'[19] By using traditional stanza and metre in conjunction with this vicious parody—parody, as we shall see, is a form which leaves the poet his techniques but prevents him using them seriously—Eliot has veritably placed himself among the dead and is demonstrably musing: 'I had not thought death had undone so many' ways of writing. That is the real topic of these disconnected stanzas.

The four dots between the second and third stanzas and between the sixth and seventh indicate spaces between three different ways of writing, just as Pound's disconnected lines indicate reflection on methods of articulating attitudes in poetry. But there is no deviation from normal syntax or from the conventions of the stanza form. This is enough to prevent the type of discontinuity found in Gascoyne and Sitwell; critical reading is allowed to penetrate the poem as the formal continuity offers assurance of coherence. Because the image-complexes are disconnected, however, the process of reading is blocked at the image-complex level, and we realise that each section requires an alteration in our Naturalisation: the empirical images of the first section give way to discursive imagery in the second, and the third section is a mélange which can be read neither as composed scene nor parodied discourse. Eliot uses a more radical type of disconnected image-complex than Pound's 'Metro', for he has led us further into the poem before we realise that it is not an ordinary poem in quatrains and that therefore more areas of our experience and assumptions are involved in the cross-examination.

The first two stanzas are not exactly straight satire; they satirise the poet's situation, which includes knowing Villon, knowing archaic diction ('sate'), and knowing how to write quatrain poems. Thus the poem has already moved out of satire towards parody. After the four dots it moves into parody simple. The thematic level is a parody of meditation:

What will I find in heaven? with parodic answers stressed by rhymes like 'Sidney'/'Kidney'. We can see a thematic connection between Honour and Sir Philip Sydney or 'Coriolanus'; so the lines could not be called irrational or discontinuous. But the conventional level itself, the techniques of writing in verse, becomes an image-complex which is disconnected from the thematic level. There is a gap between the ostensible theme and the image of writing the lines present. Both poetry and meditation are parodied by 'Sidney'/'Kidney'. If the traditional discourse of poetry is parodied, where are we?

Possible naturalising strands may be distinguished. They range from the extremely generalised notion that the poet is contrasting present society with his notions of 'Heaven', to the extremely particular strands of knowledge about how to connect Sir Philip Sidney, Coriolanus, Lucretia Borgia, Madame Blavatsky, Piccarda de Donati, not to speak of Sir Alfred Mond, with this general notion of 'Heaven'. But we have no idea how these may be connected with Pipit and 'I' unless we accept the external Naturalisation which tells us that the poet is talking about his reflections, feelings, or states of society. And the empirical image-complexes of the first two and last two stanzas will not let us do so, for they are clearly unrealistic, using the conventional level to detach their contemporary references from non-verbal reality.

It may seem banal to insist on this unreality because, of course, Pipit is an imaginary character. But if one looks at her role one will see that she is not a 'Character' at all. She stands for a thematic strand which may be naturalised as the commonplace world and is thus opposed to the 'heavenly' characters, who also are reduced to their attributes. There is a kind of 'transformation of object type' here, in which characters fail to fulfil any of the functions of empirical individuals and become nodes in a poetic technique parodying itself. The reader must be guided by other levels on the scale of Artifice. We need one kind of Naturalisation for the relation between the title and the theme, and it appears that this will involve empirical imagery—and imagined scene—although we are never left in doubt that the conventions of reading poems underly empirical imagery. We need discursive image-complexes to see that the poem requires a disconnected Naturalisation after the first two stanzas; and this too is signalled by the conventional level. Instead of Pound's semicolon in 'Metro' we have four dots which may indicate a change of scene but in fact indicate a different use of the stanza to parody itself by using poetic diction as imagery. Such a process is more subtle than the overt breaks in 'Metro' because it parodies the reader's assurance that writing in traditional stanza involves the conventional level in an internal thematic synthesis that is consistently empirical or discursive. In fact the types of synthesis alternate, so that no sooner have we decided that the obscur-

ity is to be elucidated by the poet's satire on his own state of mind by jux-
taposing empirical with discursive imagery, than we realise that he does
not use either consistently.

In fact the quatrain poems and their disconnected imagery are a
smoke-screen to prevent us from extracting a thematic synthesis at all. In
'The Hippopotamus' it is uncertain whether the satire is directed against
the 'True Church' or against those who, by ignoring the physical world,
rely on its shady proceedings. In 'Sweeney Erect' and 'Sweeney Among
the Nightingales' the same switch from discursive to empirical imagery
prevents us from making the poem internally consistent, at the same time
as it makes us recognise the impossibility of anything other than an internal consistence. The variety of types of Naturalisation involved—in
terms of empirical scenes, modes of external discourse, or the discourse
of poetry itself—keep the reader constantly self-conscious as a reader of
poetry. Two obvious instances must suffice. The first from 'Sweeney
Erect' presents an imagined scene which might be taken as descriptive of
the non-poetic world were it not for the fact that we are already expecting
a parody of meditation from the previous stanzas:

> Sweeney addressed full length to shave
>   Broadbottomed, pink from nape to base,
> Knows the female temperament
>   And wipes the suds around his face.
>
> (The lengthened shadow of a man
>   Is history, said Emerson
> Who had not seen the silhouette
>   Of Sweeney straddled in the sun.)[20]

Another discourse, Emerson's, intrudes and provides a discursive
image-complex, only to be mocked by the awareness that for this poem
'Emerson' is as much a fiction as 'Sweeney', whose silhouette, as Eliot
says, he did not see. Eliot thus makes amazingly literal statements seem
full of importance while obscuring the fact that they are literal statements, and yet literal statements of a special kind because they occur in a
poem. In 'Sweeney Among the Nightingales' the shift from empirical to
discursive imagery occurs within a single stanza:

> The circles of the stormy moon
> Slide westward toward the River Plate,
> Death and the Raven drift above
> And Sweeney guards the hornèd gate.[21]

The equation of Sweeney with Cerberus shows that he is an allegorical
personage and thus continues the strand of allegory in the line preceding.
But the scene in which 'Apeneck Sweeney spreads his knees' is empirical
imagery. A 'mélange adultère du tout' indeed!

Disconnected imagery needs both empirical and discursive types so that it may straddle the two scales of Artifice and so preserve limpidity in obscurity by oscillating between rational and irrational obscurity. This is the easiest way to explain the alternation between limitation and expansion which is observed in these poems, and which puts us as readers on our guard. The appropriate kinds of Naturalisation involved make us quite forget the weariness, the fever, and the fret that result from trying to force an external Naturalisation on this style, and show how radical breaks with habits of reading poetry may be built into a new technique which takes account of the past but assimilates it. Rational obscurity, still less irrational obscurity, cannot do this, for they both rely on presuppositions external to poetry. And although rational obscurity at least can allow the other non-semantic levels of organisation to assimilate these presuppositions, they remain as mutual enemies.

Only a compromise between these two types makes contemporary poetry possible. 'Metro' is one such and the quatrain poems another. The first uses apparent discontinuity to insist on empirical imagery while the second uses apparent continuity to absorb both empirical and discursive imagery. In the latter not only do the conventional and formal levels involve the reader in internal limitation/expansion, but also the thematic, syntactic, and image-complicated levels, by the shifts of focus I have described, make many Naturalisations possible and none certain. Such disconnected imagery immerses the reader more surely in the poem than the images of 'Imagist' poems, which are apt to satisfy the reader's theoretical demand for formal organisation simply by using, as does 'Metro', traditional rhythm and metre beneath the disjunction.

For the poet such techniques involve a rather complex relation to past poetic techniques; their breaks and assimilations parallel the reader's jumps from one level of organisation to another. The poet cannot avoid his ghosts; he can only evolve techniques to photograph them, and various strategies to set the past against the present. Consequently the reader must watch and constantly be alert to perceive and test the evidence. The scale of Artifice is such an apparatus for testing, and we shall now see what it can do with a central case in this century's poetics: the canonisation of John Donne.

CHAPTER FOUR

The poet and his tribe: tradition and the disconnected image-complex

Ros: Well, really—I mean, people want to be *entertained*—they don't come expecting sordid and gratuitous filth.
Player: You're wrong—they do! Murder, seduction and incest—what do you want, *jokes*?
Ros: I want a good story, with a beginning, middle and end.
Player (to Guil): And you?
Guil: I'd prefer art to mirror life, if it's all the same to you.
Player: It's all the same to me, sir.

Tom Stoppard

Aye, there's the rub. For most people do prefer art to mirror life and—to speak of the present problem—poetry doesn't. Nor, to repeat, can it forever avoid our attempts to make it do so. Delaying tactics are its only resource, and we have examined some attempts and some failures in order to reach the notion of the disconnected image-complex, which stretches the reader between the conventional level and thematic synthesis and sends him back to rediscover the other levels of organisation. Poems which use such techniques cast the reader in the same role as the poet: the poet as scapegoat, as tragic hero, as tribal outcast, or, in more practical terms, as mediator between his tribe and the re-creation of the world through language.

The case of Donne is particularly crucial if one wishes to trace this idea and make it a guide to the relation between technique and poetics. Donne's poems offer what many poets in this century felt they needed if they were to cope with contemporary experience both as an idea (the modern world of discourse) and immediate situation in life (the modern empirical world). In Donne they found a blend of discursive imagery and empirical imagery, or rather discursive imagery disguised as empirical imagery, which seemed to them of quite exemplary value. The famous fusion of thought and experience to which Eliot alerted the century, the interaction of discursive and empirical imagery, seemed to provide a way of articulating immediate experience while engaging in the process of mediation. The result was the conviction that innovation in technique, which detaches the poet from his reader's idea of poetry and its relation to experience, could be made to retain its hold on the accepted world of discourse if one asserted a connection with past poetry. The reference to

Donne made poetic innovation part of an already existing culture and thus helped the poet to play the role of tribal mediator; he would be both detached from and involved in his society through its assumed techniques of writing poetry. He would grasp the empirical and subject it to a new ordering.

'Donne,' as Eliot says, 'was such another', 'expert beyond experience' and thus a poet who found ways simultaneously to innovate and to keep in touch with his readers in poems that use argument plus the presentation of empirical situations. The mainstream of English poetry in this century flowed from Donne for that reason. Eliot, of course, is the key figure, who made the need explicit in his essay on 'The Metaphysical Poets'[1] and pointed the way for Leavis's *Revaluation* and *New Bearings in English Poetry*, not to mention a host of other critical books. But most poets share with their readers the desire to naturalise innovatory techniques in terms of the external world, and this is what happened to readings of Donne: Empson could argue for example, that Donne's techniques showed that he 'needed to be allowed to recognise the variety of life in the world.'[2]

This inference fastens on an external context, which by now should not surprise us, but in fact what is important in Donne's technique, especially in the 'metaphysical conceit', is that it blends empirical and discursive imagery and at the same time keeps them apart by producing that suspension of Naturalisation which I have called 'disconnected imagery'. As we saw with Eliot's 'Pipit', this gives us many possible external contexts and assimilates them to poetic structure, but prevents there being any certain or dominant external context. The external contexts remain fictions. This is still, in its way, a method of 'recognising the variety of life in the world' (though not in an external Naturalisation), for it reproduces many worlds in many word-arrangements. This is what was needed, since poets in this century were faced with many worlds in many and contradictory languages.

Naturally most people, like Guildenstern, would prefer art to mirror in already-known ways an already-known life, and thus they emphasise technique as a means rather than an end. Empson himself claims that the conceit was a device for reproducing non-poetic states through a contradictory limitation/expansion conveyed by the grammatical complexity. Grammar itself could be taken as a kind of mirror, whose complexity (to put it crudely) reflected the complexity of modern life. 'I myself', says Empson, 'being concerned with verbal analysis, thought I could take this part of Donne's mind (which was part of the atmosphere in which I grew up as an undergraduate at Cambridge) for granted; and all the more, of course, when I was imitating it in my own poems, which I did with earnest conviction'.[3]

The minor point is the evidence, casually mentioned in parenthesis, that Donne's techniques were taken for granted as the way of coping with being a poet. The major points are how they were so taken in practice and how the disconnected image-complex is related to the metaphysical conceit. The first step is to return to Eliot with Donne in mind and to explore Grishkin's Maisonnette.

I *Grishkin's maisonnette*

Like Pipit's chair, Grishkin's abode is the supposed 'contact possible to flesh' which introduces the non-verbal world into 'Whispers of Immortality'. But the fever of our bones is not thereby allayed, since the poem is an extreme example of the use of disconnected imagery. Extensive quotation will be necessary:

> Donne, I suppose, was such another
> Who found no substitute for sense,
> To seize and clutch and penetrate;
> Expert beyond experience,
>
> He knew the anguish of the marrow
> The ague of the skeleton;
> No contact possible to flesh
> Allayed the fever of the bone.
>
> . . . . .
>
> Grishkin is nice: her Russian eye
> Is underlined for emphasis;
> Uncorseted, her friendly bust
> Gives promise of pneumatic bliss.
>
> The couched Brazilian jaguar
> Compels the scampering marmoset
> With subtle effluence of cat;
> Grishkin has a maisonnette;
>
> The sleek Brazilian jaguar
> Does not in its arboreal gloom
> Distil so rank a feline smell
> As Grishkin in a drawing-room.
>
> And even the Abstract Entities
> Circumambulate her charm;
> But our lot crawls between dry ribs
> To keep our metaphysics warm.[4]

By the end the only image-complex remaining is the fact of writing in 'rhyme and regular strophe', for the others have been undermined. Grishkin, the jaguar, the marmoset, are clearly fictions, but they do not obey the laws of consistency in fiction; they appear and disappear when required by the conventional level, and there is no attempt to make them look real, to provide them, as in a naturalistic novel, with internal relations as surrogates for external relations. We could try to start at the other end, abandoning these figures and look to thematic synthesis for a clue. This is what Empson does:

> 'Value and *a priori* knowledge are not known through sense; and yet there is no other mode of knowledge. No human contact is possible to our isolation, and yet human contacts are known to be of absolute value.' This I take to be the point of the poem, and it is conveyed by the contradictory ways of taking the grammar.[5]

'Contradictory ways of taking the grammar' is as close as a realistic naturalisation like Empson's can get to the details of the poem, and, ironically, even it does not get very close, for it relies on a misquotation. Putting a semi-colon rather than a comma after 'sense' and a comma rather than a semi-colon after 'penetrate', Empson produces the following stanza:

> Donne, I suppose, was such another,
> Who found no substitue for sense;
> To seize and clutch and penetrate,
> Expert beyond experience,

Lines three and four may either go forward, as the syntax suggests, or backwards, as the stanza form implies. But with the correct punctuation line three is firmly tied to lines one and two, and the syntactic construction which links line four with the following stanza is made much more normal and inescapable.

Similarly, in attempting to turn this poem into rational artifice, to naturalise it in terms of meaning, Empson strains to find an ambiguity in the opening stanza which can serve as a rational expression of thematic indeterminacy:

> Webster was much possessed by death
> And saw the skull beneath the skin;
> And breastless creatures under ground
> Leaned backward with a lipless grin.

'Leaned', he argues, may either be an active main verb or a past participle in a noun phrase that serves as another direct object of 'saw' (Webster saw creatures who had been leaned backwards), and thus the breastless creatures may be either active or passive. This shows what happens when we try to impose a bad Naturalisation on a poem. 'Leaning' is not, in any case, very active, and the problem arises only if we try to imagine real creatures and give them an external history, neither of which the poem does. We are dealing with emblems of death, with figures lacking the relations normally necessary to establish a fiction. In fact, the lack of relations and of empirical imagery helps to indicate that we are confronted with a 'transformation of object type' in which serious things are ordered in ways which question their seriousness. We cannot take refuge, as Empson does, in the poem's 'I suppose' or in its apparent meditation on Donne or on Grishkin or, finally, on 'our lot' and 'our metaphysics'.

This is not to say that we don't think of these things; disconnected imagery is not irrational obscurity nor is it discontinuous with other languages. It is simply that we can't, without engaging in bad Naturalisation, fit them together with glue; as Galileo said, *E pur si muove*. This is the distinctive feature of a poem written in disconnected imagery; it moves the reader constantly from one to another view like a kaleidoscope. All poems, of course, do this to some extent; they move up and down the scales of Artifice, but at least they allow us to distinguish each several level, to separate before relating, and then to find an image-complex that will guide us to a thematic synthesis that takes account of all levels. Disconnected imagery, however, will not let us reach a thematic synthesis: not, like irrational obscurity, because it is too chaotic to let us compare levels at all, but because its image-complex is a wall with nothing behind it. Far from offering the comforts of rational obscurity and discursive imagery, it evokes only to discard and unites only to sever (it also murders to dissect, but so must the poet-physician in the dissecting-room of his society). Nothing, it should not be necessary to say, could be further from the canonical notion of the metaphysical conceit which uses every level in the armoury to unite, make cohere, reaffirm order by the transcendence of disorder.

In any case no thematic synthesis can be reached without taking account of the relations between every level as these are displayed in the image-complex. And when the image-complex is disconnected these relations cannot be distinguished. Paradoxically, the disconnected image-complex, by radical subversion, destroys the power of the image-complex as we have so far been tracing it and substitutes a pattern that is new in every moment. When the conventional level (the techniques of verse) operates as a disconnected image-complex, it excludes the normal interaction between it and other levels. We are left with the continuity provided by the simple continuation of the stanzaic form. All the levels are present but all are bracketed and all are kept apart from each other. So that, as we saw, disconnected imagery looks very like Imagism's juxtaposition of disconnected phrases but goes further in that it effects this within the conventions of rhymed stanza.

In 'Whispers of Immortality', for instance, Grishkin's maisonnette is coupled with scampering marmoset by rhyme and metre; we think that the comment which is offered in the next stanza is implied by this juxtaposition, but who knows? Similarly, in the last stanza the conjunction

'But', which should state a contrast, serves simply to increase the confusion; why or who or which or what is 'our lot'? Is it Eliot/ Donne/Webster versus Grishkin, or the same trio versus 'the Abstract Entities'? How could 'our lot', if opposed to 'the Abstract Entities', 'keep our metaphysics warm', for surely 'the Abstract Entities' are part of metaphysics? Doubtless, 'metaphysics' here is not the intellectual discipline, but what is it then, aside from something which might, in some sense, be kept warm? A reference to our metaphysical poets? The eschatological obsessions of Webster & Co., as described in the previous stanzas, making a thematic comeback? Neither, I think, for those four dots between the Donne part and the Grishkin part are not there for nothing; they mark a shift in the relation of the poet to his discourse. In the first part he has a persona—'I'—of a literary man meditating on his own literary progenitors; in the second part he retreats to a seemingly detached symbolic contemporary description though he is, of course, still there in that he continues writing in the same stanza form; in the last two lines he wants to make a come-back in his first persona as one of 'our lot' and in the last stanza as a whole he uses the disconnected image more strikingly than ever before with that 'But'.

These speculations, however, depend on our interpreting 'lot' to mean 'group' when it could just as well mean 'doom' and on our assuming that coherence, relation even, is required. The only coherence, finally, is on the level of technique. I think that 'our metaphysics' is this new technique of disconnected imagery which is the doom of fate of the twentieth-century poet, who must simultaneously be detached and involved with language. This means that he has all the tricks of rhetoric and the skills of language but he must not make the mistake of thinking that they solve anything. He has the level of meaning—all the words in 'whispers' make sense—without its extension. Before he can appropriate the external world he must deny it to himself, and this requires him to 'learn', as one of Empson's poems has it, 'a style from a despair'. He must develop new techniques in order in the end to be able to use the old; as Bradley said of the speculative philosopher, to converse with shadows he must himself become a shade.

I say 'he' because he is a mythical figure, a familiar compound ghost, metaphysicist-metaphysician, tribal outcast; and as such we shall encounter him again at the end of this chapter. But I also mean Thomas Stearns Eliot, for it is he who developed both the theory and the practice of the disconnected image-complex and who is responsible for linking it to the work of John Donne and the idea of the metaphysical conceit. Every poet in this century has had to come to terms with the problem of mediation—we have seen one such attempt in Imagism and another in the theories of Empson—but only Eliot, until the early 'sixties, was able to rob the past in order to patent in practice the innovation of disconnected imagery, and his use of it in relation to the metaphysical conceit makes us now turn to Donne.

We have seen a little of how completely disconnected imagery is the opposite of what is usually considered—and not least by Eliot himself—as the metaphysical conceit. I want now to look at two attempts to relate Donne's technique to the needs of the twentieth-century poet. The first attempt will take us into fairly detailed reading of pieces by Donne and Empson, of Donne by Empson. The second will examine the *Scrutiny* essay by Mr James Smith on metaphysical poetry which remains the most intelligent study of the conceit available; this will then lead back to Eliot and Donne.

II   The separate planet

Empson thus designates a special image-complex of Donne's which, he claims, shows the power of poetry to validate imaginative freedom; 'The separate planet' refers either to the pair of lovers as a universe in themselves, or to the individual as Christ, and most profoundly to the poet as tribal outcast, for which these other states are symbols.[6] It is through these themes that Empson tries to make Donne relevant; he strives to make any discontinuity into rational obscurity which can be drawn out into a thematic statement.

In Donne's poem 'The Crosse' Empson focuses on a favorite antinomy: between the uniqueness of Christ as an historical and theological reality and the pervasiveness of Christ as Logos, as reflected in the rhetorical claims that a single individual (e.g. Elizabeth Drury in the 'Anniversaries') or a pair of lovers are suffused throughout the universe as its lifeblood. The poet as author of these claims becomes mediator, Christ figure, and there is a clash between the Christian sacrifice, which makes Christ scapegoat and hero, and the similar sacrifice which casts the poet in these roles. If Christ through his sacrifice has become the Logos and his blood supports the order of the Universe, then there is a rational connection between physics, as the intelligible ordering of the Copernican universe, and physic which orders and heals, which lets and restores blood. And the poet, in making this connection, becomes the node of a rational Logos. As Empson says, quoting the couplet

> Who can deny mee power, and liberty
> To stretch mine arms, and mine owne Cross to be?

'the cross here seems quite independent of Christianity; it is essential to man's mode of apprehending the world.'[7] He gives great weight to the pun on *physic/physics*, which enables him to relate 'The Crosse' to the themes we encountered in 'High Dive'.

> Donne makes the pun on *physic* and treats the cross (it is an old fancy) as underlying the natural order.
>
>> All the Globes frame, and spheares, is nothing else
>> But the Meridians crossing Parallels.
>> Material crosses, then, good physic be,
>> But yet spiritual have chief dignity.
>
> Space, itself, the type of explanation, is shown to hold dissolved through-out it, as the differential equation of its structure, the impenetrable tangle of ideas about the sacrifice of the scapegoat and hero.[8]

Now this 'differential equation' and its ground in the discourse of physics is Empson's metaphor; Donne's metaphor is drawn from geometry and his pun on physics from medicine. The fact that Empson stresses the physic/physics pun shows that he himself needed to absorb the mathematical formulations of physics which surrounded, and threatened, poetry in his century. Differential equations were not known in Donne's time, and Empson uses them in 'The World's End' to absorb the scientific world by making it part of a strand where Christian mythol-ogy and Classical mythology come together. The last stanza of 'The World's End' goes:

> Apple of knowledge and forgetful mere
> From Tantalus too differential bend.
> The shadow clings. The world's end is here.
> This place's curvature precludes its end.[9]

And the author glosses thus: '*Differential*: they follow his movements exactly, as if calculated like the differential coefficients used in forming this [Relativity's] view of the world. *Precludes*: "stops from happening" and "already shuts". *End* in space but blurred onto end in time con-ceived as eventual justice—"what there is of it occurs here" '.[10]

Such an interpretation shows discursive imagery as we have already found it and illustrates that a naturalising interpretation which leads the poem into other languages (instead of from other languages to the poem) can be referred empirically only to the poet's mind: 'Empson is dis-tressed by the fact that everything is relative and that the mind is enclosed in its own conceptual frameworks'. This strategy belongs to rational Artifice when Artifice is restricted to the level of meaning. It is one way of coping with the predicament: by using the traditional techni-ques of symbolism, persona, and a form expressing solidarity with the past, one brings the conventional level into play and can use ordinary image-complexes to reach a variety of external contexts. These strategies, as we have seen, can produce good Naturalisation if the external contexts are led back into the poem to form an internal thematic synthesis. They are not, however, the best techniques, which are found in the disconnected image-complex; these we have glimpsed in Eliot, and they will preoccupy the rest of this book. The disconnected image-complex is a particular twentieth-century phenomenon and uses the conventional level to block without destroying our assumed techniques of Naturalisation. In fact, it allows a constant revaluation and re-creation of poetic Artifice which takes the reader into the technique, thus forcing him to recognise that the world is constantly re-created through language and that our only hope of continuity lies in the fact that this process of re-creation maintains, through its non-semantic levels, its contact with the past.

To return, however, to Empson's dealings with Donne's 'The Crosse'. When read as a whole that poem firmly subordinates the pun on physics/physic to the conceit about the cross which leads through a combination of discursive and empirical imagery to a thematic synthesis identical with Empson's equation of pantheism and deism. However, in Donne's case the process depends on an apparently random punning which shows trust in poetic devices to catch thematic acrobatics and thus reminds one of the traditional image-complex:

> Since Christ embrac'd the Crosse it self, dare I
> His image, th'image of his Crosse deny?
> Would I have profit by the sacrifice,
> And dare the chosen Altar to despise?[11]

So far the poem is relying on empirical imagery and its 'I' is a meditating Christian (though note the other 'I' which uses metre, rhyme, and rhetoric to state his problem). The following lines take us to the extreme of empirical imagery—a reference to Donne's physical body—while using discursive imagery to introduce another meaning for 'cross':

> From mee, no Pulpit, nor misgrounded law,
> Nor scandall taken, shall this Crosse withdraw,
> It shall not, for it cannot; for, the losse
> Of this Crosse, were to mee another Crosse;
> Better were worse, for, no affliction,
> No Crosse is so extreme, as to have none.
> Who can blot out the Crosse, which th'instrument
> Of God, dew'd on mee in the Sacrament?
> Who can deny mee power, and liberty
> To stretch mine arms, and mine owne Crosse to be?

After this the poet searches the rest of the material universe for crosses that occur in nature and thus provides Empson with material for a synthesis of pantheism and deism (what I believe is known as 'Natural Theology'). And here the physic/physics pun occurs.

But this is really the traditional operation of poetic logic in which the external world (empirical imagery) is made a symbol for an argument (discursive imagery), so that the activity of writing poetry is proved with reference to both the non-verbal and the highly verbal, its great competitors in organising the world.

This has nothing to do with disconnected imagery as a specifically twentieth-century manoeuvre. And it is rather ironic to find Empson, one of Donne's most ardent disciples both in theory and practice, not only providing a bad Naturalisation of his guru but also totally ignoring the differences between his situation and Donne's. Consequently he tries to reproduce Donne's type of traditional Artifice rather than, as did Eliot with his disconnected image-complex, building a new Artifice out of the relation. Before we look more closely at these new constructions, however, we must demonstrate my claim by a comparison between Empson and Donne. And I should in the process take Donne's advice: 'When thy brain workes, ere thou utter it/Crosse and correct concupisence of witt'.

I shall take some stanzas from 'A Valediction: Forbidding Mourning' and Empson's 'Letter V' so that we shall see to what extent Empson does copy Donne and then how Empson's interpretation fails to account either for Donne's manoeuvres or his own.

> If they [our souls] be two, they are two so
>   As stiffe twin compasses are two,
> Thy soule the fixt foot, makes no show
>   To move, but doth, if th'other doe.
>
> And yet though it in the center sit,
>   Yet when the other far doth rome,
> It leanes, and hearkens after it,
>   And growes erect, as that comes home.
>
> Such wilt thou be to mee who must
>   Like th'other foot, obliquely runne;
> Thy firmnes makes my circle just,
>   And makes me end, where I begunne.[12]

Empson naturalises this compass comparison as both empirical and discursive imagery, limited and expanded in each case by an external context. Empirically, 'the reality, the solidity, the usefulness and the intellectual uses of the compasses, their reliability in a situation where native intuition cannot guess the answer unaided, are all relevant to the comparison.'[13] This empirical aspect is cancelled out in the argument, however, for the physical aspects of the compasses must be thrown aside in the last line 'And make me end where I begunne.'

The final point in drawing the circle is where the pencil began, but not also the centre, whereas Donne means that he will return to his wife. What he chiefly wanted to imply by the comparison is that his argument about true love is not a fanciful convention, such as he has laughed at in earlier poems, but something practical which he has proved in experience.[14]

Of course, Empson would say something like this, but one is entitled to question it, and the best way to question it is to look at the stanzas in question. 'Donne means that he will return to his wife': this claim about an empirical situation is offered as the central point in a thematic synthesis. The discursive imagery is therefore supposed to offer proof of the empirical point.

I have already said, of 'The Crosse', that a combination of empirical and discursive imagery is poetic logic's substitute for referential or inductive proof in more respectable kinds of logic. Thus we have to look at the levels in these stanzas to answer Empson's Naturalisation with a better. What (it is a pun he endorses) does Donne do? The first thing to note is that Empson's external context is indeed present; the lines do give us the situation of a lover taking leave of his beloved, but already this is fictionalised by the use of the persona. 'Thou' and 'mee' are no more Donne and his wife than they are the legs of a pair of compasses. For this the use of discursive imagery in conjunction with the conventional level is responsible. From the first line we are in the presence of what appears to be a reasoned argument: 'If' conceals a syllogistic form and 'then' hovers over 'so'. The stanzas abound in rational words ('Yet', 'though', 'Such', 'if'), and they are so placed in the line-to-line progression as to be prominent.

But it doesn't require much perspicacity to see that the argument is specious: it may have taken in 'Donne's wife' but no one else is likely to be deceived, for, as Empson so rightly remarks, a pair of compasses is not a very good analogy for the link between the beloved who remains and the lover who will return. If carried to its logical conclusion it would mean that he wouldn't return. And so the obvious step is to say 'Yes, but as the last line shows he does want to say he will return and he gives up his development of the image-complex to make sure that that is said.' But does he throw out the compasses in the end? 'Thy firmness makes my circle just', the penultimate line, shows that he is concerned to develop his image-complex and knows how, in poetry, to use a pair of compasses. Moreover even the last line is descriptive of the return of the pencil to the point from which it began in drawing the circle. It looks as though Donne was more concerned with writing his poem than with 'soothing his wife'.

The supposed external situation of the 'I' and the 'you' is absorbed by the poem as a way of organising itself. The level of meaning is extended just sufficiently for the reader to reach into the poem by way of an implied

external context, but once there the other levels absorb both him and the
extension. The image does not prove anything about possible empirical
behaviour. Rather, empirical images are used to develop the argument
about 'justness', and completion, and this is the crucial point about
Donne's artifice as well as the thematic assertion of the poem. The conjunction of empirical and discursive imagery allows Empson's interpretive reading but prevents us from stopping there with the conclusion that
'Donne means that he will return to his wife'.

Let us see what happens in 'Letter V':

> Not locus if you will but envelope,
> Paths of light not atoms of good form;
> Such tangent praise, less crashing, not less warm,
> May gain more intimacy for less hope.
>
> Not the enclosed letter, then, the spirited air,
> The detached marble, not the discovered face;
> I can love so for truth, as still for grace,
> Your humility that will not hear or care.
>
> You are a metaphor and they are lies
> Or there true least where their knot chance unfurls;
> You are the grit only of those glanced pearls.
> That not for me shall melt back to small eyes.
>
> Wide-grasping glass in which to gaze alone
> Your curve bars even fancy at its gates;
> You are the map only of the divine states
> You, made, nor known, nor knowing in, make known.
>
> Yet if I love you but as Cause unknown
> Cause has at least the Form that has been shown,
> Or love what you imply but to exclude
> That vacuum has your edge, your attitude.
>
> Duality too has its Principal.
> These lines you grant me may invert to points;
> Or paired, poor grazing misses, at your joints,
> Cross you on painless arrows to the wall.[15]

The first thing to note about this is that it is much more difficult than
Donne; where Donne explains and expands Empson contracts, and
we shall see this process as we trace the development of circle-
circumference-envelope-tangent, which is the Einsteinian version of the
compass analogy. The second point is the equation of knowledge with
love, which is as old as humanity. The third is the fact that the levels of
formal patterns, rhythm, syntax, rhyme, are not used with anything
approaching Donne's skill. The reason for this is no doubt that Empson
is so involved with his puns and image-complexes and so unaware of the

need for semantic play to be related to these other levels that he has no attention to give them. The matter is not susceptible of demonstration, but note the lack of verbs that might contribute to the image-complex; the copula is the most frequent verb, and this prodices a feeling of stasis where Donne's lines are all movement. Note, also, that every line except the third—which, even so, as an elided 'is'—is end-stopped, whereas Donne's stanzas have four run-on lines out of the twelve and more lines which could belong in either camp.

I don't think that these differences are accidental or merely attributable to the fact that John Donne is a better poet than William Empson (if that were the reason it would not be germane to the general thesis I am advancing). I think that the lack of movement on the non-semantic level and the lack of technical innovation is directly due to Empson's taking, as he admits, the rhymed stanza form for granted and to his anxiety to put all the complexities into the level of meaning. That also is the reason the poem is obscure, for, however indebted to Donne, it was written in the early nineteen-thirties and there was a good deal more to combat in the way of other languages claiming to tell the truth about the world than there had been three hundred years earlier.

Further, as I have said and shall again, the only way to cope with the complexities of these other languages was and is to use the non-semantic levels of form to absorb and alter; which means innovation in technique. And this Empson does not do; it is against his principles. Instead of making the complex external contexts filter through the levels of Artifice and in the end produce a new form, Empson congests them on the level of meaning and thus paralyses his image-complex. First we must anatomise the mathematical image-complex, and then see why innovation in content unaccompanied by innovation in form is insufficient to produce powerful poems.

The mathematical image-complex hinges on the differences and similarities between definition by locus and definition by tangent. It is, therefore, discursive. But, because of its mingling with the empirical love imagery and its debts to rhyme and metre, it is not entirely subservient to other kinds of discourse. Empson notes that 'a locus defines a surface by points and an envelope defines it by tangents';[16] this must be elaborated if we are to understand how Empson has made Donne's compass metaphor come 'true' so that the centre is also the point of return on the circumference. A single circle may be defined by all the tangents one can draw to it; it may also, as in Donne's conceit, be drawn by extending a line from its centre which is the locus for the circle's radii. Futher, an extension within the circle of any of the points where tangents touch it produces a radius leading to the centre. Thus the apparent paradox of Donne's circle whose circumference ended at its centre is elucidated by an imaginative development of the possibilities of another discourse: mathematics.

This is not a reference to an external situation but the development of discursive imagery. As in 'Forbidding Mourning', the implied lover/ beloved situation is absorbed into the development of the image-complex: the lover 'may gain more intimacy for less hope' because a tangent can reach the centre (the beloved) with a glancing touch extended into a radius, although the tangent line itself seems to lead away from the circle. Such is proof in the area of poetic logic, and to such an extent Empson does the same as Donne, although the fact that he concentrates his operations on the level of meaning makes his stanzas less flexible and his image-complex more obscure.

This obscurity can be followed further. In mathematics an 'envelope' can itself be the line of locus joining the points where a series of consecutive circles intersect. An envelope can therefore be seen both as a tangent to each individual circle and a locus for a consecutive series of circles. A definition by tangents is wider than a definition by loci, and the third line—'Such tangent praise, less crashing, not less warm'—is justified both in these terms and in terms of a second image complex from physics, introduced by the mention of heat and bombardment. That this concerns the nature of light is already hinted in the second line—Paths of light not atoms of good form'. Light is both wave and particle, and photons change the structure of the atoms they bombard, so that at the subatomic level one can never actually see a particle: in the time that the light takes to travel the particle is already changed, and so one's only hope is a tangent and relative perception. Hence the exploitation of the paradoxical envelope, which is a locus but looks like a tangent, holds the stanza together, and these two image-complexes produce the thematic synthesis that indirect perception may be more true to its 'object' than direct analysis. From the dual nature of light, we have a hint that the ultimate thematic synthesis will be that intellectual distinctions, such as that between locus and envelope, are really a matter of looking at the same thing in different ways and that the ways, being different, make the thing different also.

The second stanza, however, chooses to dwell on the empirical facet: the beloved is best loved impersonally. Discursive imagery is still present, though, in the pun on 'enclosed letter': both envelope and the epistle as a poetic genre. And this self-consciousness of technique is exploited in the third stanza: obviously in 'You are the grit only of those glanced pearls/That not for me shall melt back to small eyes', which echoes 'those are pearls that were his eyes', and less obviously in 'You are a metaphor and they are lies'. This line is very difficult to analyse. 'They' can only mean the lines of the poem, as these make up its image-complexes; and they can be lies for the canonical reason that all poems tell lies, or because in the modern world any attempt to tell the truth, through science, philosophy, religion, ethics, has to accept that truth is never absolute, or finally because the poet uses image-complexes as fictions for talking about his love. Indeed the following line—'Or there true least where their knot chance unfurls'—stresses this aspect. Empson's note says, '*Knot chance*—where the connection of thought they make possible spreads itself into an actual meaning; pun with "not" '.[17] That is, their best truth is knotted-up in image-complexes. If one attempts to give an external meaning (bad Naturalisation, external limitation/expansion) outside the structure of the poem, outside the standards of truth created by poetic lying, the strands of ideas lose any validity; in the poem, like Sir Lancelot, faith unfaithful keeps them falsely true.

In fact all these interpretations of 'they are lies' co-exist, and can help us to understand 'You are a metaphor'. For 'you' is metaphor, a fiction, an image-complex when absorbed into a poem; at the same time metaphors, in a world of lying, can be used as cognitive instruments. And this provides an explanation both for 'You are a map only of the divine states/You made, nor known, nor knowing in, make known' and for the claim in the last two stanzas that poetry can reach the external world through technique. By making 'you' a metaphor, 'I' give myself the only chance of touching the external you.

We can see this by one further excursus into the language of mathematics. The 'Principle of Duality' states that any proposition made about points may be converted into a proposition about lines, and this gives a new twist to the image-complexes of tangent/locus and of the dual nature of light. For the duality of the lovers—the fact that they are two—symbolised by the complexes comes to suggest the themes of love as knowledge and of poetry as the only possible mediation between the known and the unknown: as the note says, the lines are in part the lines of the poem. The mention of vacuum, of Cause unknown, and of 'Cause has at least the form that has been shown', brings in another mathematic law: the 'Law of Projection' which states that any proposition made about lines may also be made about plane surfaces. Taken in the context of this poem, this means that a tangent line can be converted into a tangent plane so that the circle defined by the sum of plane tangents becomes in consequence a sphere, the sphere of curved space-time. Similarly the points of radius and the point at the centre of the circle can become the situation of modern man trapped in the curved universe. As 'The World's End' has it:

> Each tangent plain touches one top of earth,
> Each point in one direction ends the world.[18]

But note how 'Letter V' claims to transcend this dilemma by bringing in the 'Principle of Duality' so that the lines of the poem become instruments of knowledge by reflecting on poetry's endemic fictionality. Nevertheless it does not succeed in the way that Empson wants to think; poetry, as Auden says, makes nothing happen; 'you' remain a metaphor. The semantic congestion prevents the poem from offering a powerful enough alternative to the world of Relativity, for we get caught up in meaning to such an extent that both the discursive and the empirical image-complexes restrict us to movement between mathematics and the fact that the poem is about writing a poem. This is the only way to escape an external Naturalisation about Empson's love-life.

Now the point (if I may use the term as a dead metaphor) is that Empson's imitations of Donne are limited by his desire to impose an external Naturalisation, and we shall shortly see that the non-semantic aspects of Donne's poems give him greater freedom. But the reason for that is that Donne lived at a time when the devices of rhetoric and Artifice were accepted as part of poetry, assumed by the poet and linking him with his tribe of readers; Empson did not. In his and our time the only way to restore this awareness of the importance of poetic devices and to make a creative poetry possible is by a radical innovation which starts from those features of the conventional level which can still be assumed as shared (line endings, rhyme, stanza form, etc.). With the conventional level secured as a basis of continuity, one can develop disconnected image-complexes as Eliot did, dislocating and parodying levels of meaning and thematic synthesis, and eventually even parodying the conventional level (the activity of poetry itself). Passed through the alembic of the disconnected image-complex, poetry is restored as Artifice, as a repertoire of techniques both inherited and created, whose value and continuity lie in their ability to undermine facile syntheses. This, of course, involves more than the level of meaning alone, so that the orthodox version of the 'metaphysical conceit', which sees it as a uniting of thought and experience, is no solution.

It is useful here to look at the accepted account of the metaphysical conceit, as given in James Smith's article in *Scrutiny* (1933): 'it is an essential property of Donne and his like to maintain as even as possible a balance between two rival claimants to reality . . . within the metaphysical conceit, even when it is being dwelt on by the mind, tension between the elements continues.' What of these 'elements'? Mr Smith continues, 'a satisfactory explanation can rest only upon the nature of the elements of the conceit. These must be such that they can enter into a solid union and, at the same time, maintain their separate and warring identity. Are such things to be found? Only if reality is of a peculiar kind. But metaphysics suggests it is of this kind.'[19] More promising. The mention of 'things' is ominous, but the notion that the conceit is made up of elements both distinct and unified resembles the notion of themes in a poem which cohere at each level but progress to a thematic synthesis in which they maintain their separateness. And 'metaphysical conceit' is certainly a type of image-complex.

Even better, we learn that 'the metaphysical conceit, stating impartially and at the same time solving the problem of its context, controls and unifies that context.'[20] This sounds very like the process of fictionalising and absorbing external contexts which is basic to poetry.

All the same Mr Smith does believe in an eventual external Naturalisation; he characterises the conceit as part of a process in the poet's mind that makes itself felt especially on the level of meaning:

> verse properly called metaphysical is that to which the impulse is given by an overwhelming concern with metaphysical problems; with problems either deriving from or closely resembling, in the nature of their difficulty, the problem of the Many and the One. . . . It is conceivable, however, that there should be a few [poets rather than philosophers] who, aware of the difficulty of metaphysical problems, see them lurking behind any action, however trivial, they propose. Such people will be in a state of great disturbance or at least excitement. Such excitement may well be an impulse to poetry, and the poetry it generates be metaphysical. Such a course of events, I repeat, is at least possible. From the example of Donne I am convinced not only that it is possible, but that it has occurred.[21]

Mr Smith considers the type of this metaphysical problem and emotional excitement is to be found in the conceit of Donne's love poems: that the lovers are both separate and inseparable. Further, he claims that the roots of this conceit lie in Donne's emotional life as a man who thinks and loves.

There are two main points to be taken up here. First, Mr Smith's conception of the 'metaphysical conceit' involves the extension of the level of meaning into the external world and the playing down of non-semantic features; we shall see this taken further when we arrive at Empson's idea of the conceit. Second, Mr Smith's description, if we take account of formal features, is applicable to Eliot's use of the disconnected image-complex, and is thus what he got from Donne, and what links Donne to the poet as tribal outcast in this century.

First things being sanctioned first we shall look at Empson's remarks. 'Mr James Smith' he says,

> in an excellent essay . . . said that the metaphysical conceit was always built out of the immediate realisation of a philosophical problem such as that of the One and the Many. I should agree with this, but I think it was nearly always arrived at in the way I am trying to describe. The supreme example of the problem of the One and the Many was given by the Logos who was an individual man. In all those conceits where the general is given

a sort of sacred local habitation in a particular, so that this particular is made much more interesting than all similar particulars, . . . there is an implied comparison to the sacrificial cult-hero, to Christ as the Son of Man.[22]

In Donne's case, however, this 'sacred local habitation' occurs within the levels of a poem as the image-complex of the two lovers, of the beloved as the Separate Planet, or of Elizabeth Drury as the Logos. So that the external contexts and the level of meaning are already fed into the levels of Artifice. Donne was well aware of this when he made his famous retort to Jonson that he 'painted the idea of a woman, not as she is': that is, discursive imagery (the idea of woman) in control of empirical imagery and *a fortiori* in control of any external context. And this 'idea', of course, is the internal thematic synthesis built up from the way in which the image-complexes control the other levels of Artifice. In the two 'Anniversaries', for example, the movement of the refrain 'She is dead' is one formal device which takes us from an empirical situation to the conventional elegaic act. Since her death is admittedly fictionalised as a symbol it resembles Grishkin's maisonnette which is inserted between the image-complex and the thematic synthesis to stand for the mediating activity of the poet.

Before comparing the 'Anniversaries' with Eliot's major works let us first see what Eliot could have learnt from another of Donne's techniques: formal pattern as contributor to the image-complex. The example will be from 'A Valediction: Of Weeping':

> Let me p*owr*e f*or*th
> My t*ear*es bef*or*e thy f*ace*, whil'st I st*ay* h*ere*,
> *For* thy f*ace* c*oin*es them, and thy st*am*pe they b*eare*,
> And by this Mint*age* they are s*o*mething w*or*th,
> *For* thus they b*ee*
> Pregn*ant* of th*ee*;
> Fr*uit*s of much gr*ie*fe they *are*, emblemes of m*ore*,
> When a t*eare* f*a*lls, that th*ou* f*a*lst which it b*ore*,
> S*o* th*ou* and *I* are n*o*thing then, wh*en* on a divers sh*ore*.

> On a r*ound* b*a*ll
> A w*or*kman th*at* h*ath* c*opi*es by, c*an* l*ay*
> An *Euro*pe, *A*frique, and an *A*sia,
> And quickly m*a*ke th*at*, which was n*o*thing, *A*ll,
> S*o* d*o*th each t*eare*,
> which th*ee* d*o*th w*eare*,
> A globe, y*ea* w*or*ld by th*at* impression gr*ow*,
> Till thy t*eare*s mixt with mine d*oe* *overflow*
> This w*or*ld, by w*a*ters sent fr*om* th*ee*, my h*eaven* diss*o*lved s*o*.[23]

I have italicised the dominant key of *o* which is reinforced by long *ay* and slurred *r*, all are marked in the rhyme-words (conventional level)

·and extended into the body of the line in the comparison of the flood and weeping. In fact a battle takes place between this image-complex—incarnated on all levels as the verse moves through them and across the arrangement on the page—and the 'coining' image with its *i c*. And it is interesting to note that this contrast extends to the formal opposition between 'You' (oo) and 'I', for thus is indicated that the personae required for the fiction of parting are absorbed in the greater unreality of the formal pattern. This opposition is overborne, though, by the similarity between the tidal wave of the *o* pattern and the lengthened 'mee' and 'thee'. The reader is made aware that the tensions in the formal patterns are more important than the tensions in the meaning, and that the warring image-complexes will produce an internal thematic synthesis.

Empson, of course, produces a skilful external Naturalisation.[24] He extends the image-complexes in the two first stanzas quoted above so that the 'nothing' which the two lovers will become implies that she will be unfaithful to him (or vice versa, one might think) during his absence. Empson can do this because he will not admit non-semantic evidence that the 'coining' image-complex is overborne on the formal level, just as the 'I/You' opposition is overborne. Note, in passing, that we are agreed that 'nothing' is a key-word, but that I can use it to distinguish these internal patterns while Empson has to use it to provide an external expansion. Being conscious that the matter is not as simple as that—a man about to depart from his wife for some time and anxious to control grief on both their parts does not bother to write a very complicated poem—Empson finds ambiguities in the syntax. These are explained with reference to an ambivalence in the author's state of mind (remember Gascoyne and Sitwell): the author is trying to disguise the fact that he will really be relieved to be gone and free of their emotional bond.

The argument to stress here is that *prima facie* no arrangement of words so skilfully blended and presented *as a poem* in an age noted for its self-conscious attention to rhetoric could possibly be reducible to such an external limitation. (It is a sad fact about our own age that this should have seemed the critic's job.) Empson's bad Naturalisation is this: let me indulge my grief in your presence because it creates an emotional bond between us which I am not at all sure will last when I leave. And then, with a complete volte face, Do not weep so much because it upsets me terribly.

But even on the level of meaning this interpretation accounts for only one of the image-complexes. Her face reflected in his tears gives them value like a stamped coin; when they weep apart this will not happen and the tears be spent in vain—'So thou and I are nothing then when on a divers shore'. In the next stanza we see Donne's Artifice overtaken by another image-complex, dependent on imaginative possibilities seen in

the interaction between form and meaning. The idea of 'nothing juxtaposed with the idea of 'teare' leads to their common property of round-
ness; and this leads to the idea of another object, originally 'nothing' but
made 'All' by the mind: a globe of the world. Already Donne has stopped
following the logic of an argument that would be true to a 'state of mind'
and taken up the logic of poetry which tests discursive imagery through
the apparatus of non-semantic levels by placing it against empirical
imagery.

The astronomy, or geography, of the Separate Planet, takes charge.
The stress on geography plus cartography as symbol of the human condition reminds us slightly of 'Letter V'. Only slightly though, for Donne
uses non-semantic complexities as Empson does not. And Donne's attention to these prevents clogging obscurity on the level of meaning since
one cannot do everything at once.

Empson, however, must locate any complexity on the level of meaning, and works to develop an ambiguity. The second stanza tells us that
'On a round ball a workman . . . can lay an Europe (etc.) and quickly
make that which was nothing All,'

> So doth each teare
> which thee doth weare,
> A globe, yea world by that impression grow,
> Till my teares mixed with thine doe overflow
> This world . . .

The first 'doth', Empson argues, may be an independent verb: each tear
behaves like a workman, is active, makes whatever was nothing all, produces water which will drown the whole world. If, on the other hand,
'doth' is an auxiliary of 'grow' then the tear is not active but passive, not
like the workman but like the ball: it, when imprinted with your image,
grows into a globe or entire world, just as the ball imprinted with images
of continents becomes a globe.[25]

It seems very suspect to take 'doth' as an independent verb, but
Empson wants a potentially active tear so that he can make 'thee' (thou/
she) a passive object on which the tear works or which it at least controls.
He wants to make 'thee' into a full-fledged character so as to work out the
meaning of an empirical situation. But in fact 'thee' has nearly vanished
in the process of working out the image-complex. 'Thee' remains only as
a residue of external context which attempts but does not, it seems, succeed in keeping off an external expansion; she has never been a 'real' person in the poem and now she has become by her non-semantic properties
very much more. The Separate Planet has taken over and absorbed the
rationalist assumption of continuity into a technical device. We can see
this very clearly in the final stanza:

> O more than *Moone*,
> Draw not up *seas* to *drowne* me in thy *sph*eare,
> Weepe me not dead, in thine arms, but forebeare
> To *teach* the *sea*, what it may *doe too soone*;
> Let not the *winde*
> Example *finde*,
> To *doe* me more *harme*, then it *purposeth*;
> Since th*ou* and *I* sigh *one anothers breath*,
> *Who* e'r sighes *most*, is *cruel*lest, and ha*sts* the *others death*.

It is hardly necessary to italicise the *o* pattern and to note how, by feeding into the other levels it indeed overflows the pattern of *ay ee i* so as to make the voyage allegorical. The contrast between 'I' and 'thou' makes the formal pattern mirror the thematic situation of the voyage and the leave-taking between two lovers. And the conventional level helps by presenting the reader with a complicated stanza spaced across the page in alternating short and long lines.

Empson fastens on an external Naturalisation in terms of extended meaning: 'she is *more than Moone* because she is more valuable to him than anything in the real world to which he is being recalled; because she has just been called either the earth or the heavens and they are larger than the moon.' She controls the tides of emotion which are more important than the tides of the sea; she makes the world more 'hushed and glamorous than does moonlight'; she is more powerful because closer, she shines by her own light; she is more powerful than the moon because more constant or more inconstant (this harks back to the forgery extrapolation Empson has made from the coining image-complex).[26]

All these things are strands in the eventual thematic synthesis, but we can see that they are only strands because irrelevant levels have been used to distance the poem even while the level of meaning has maintained continuity with the reader's world. It is possible, therefore, both for Donne to talk about more universal themes than his love-life and for the reader to perceive this. He does meditate on the universal connection between love and knowledge and how separation can affect this ('And when I love thee not chaos is come again'). He can go further and relate this separation to the ultimate separation of death, not simply death that separates lover from beloved, but which separates any and all men from the known, and transports them into the unknown. As in 'Letter V', 'You are the map only of the divine states / You, made, nor known, nor knowing in, make known.' By accepting that love is transitory, as all things, Donne can say that the precariousness of love is an emblem of the whole of human life—'the shadow of death', as Swinburne says. And as poet he can make it less transitory by putting the argument into a poem where the interaction between image-complexes can develop internally. Empirical

images—the tears, the voyage, the compasses—can 'prove' the argument
that love is a symbol of knowledge and is precarious.

'Letter V' does the same thing; its empirical image-complexes—envelopes, letters, the beloved's face—can be conjoined
with discursive scientific imagery as in the line, 'Yet if I love you but as
Cause unknown, Cause has at least the form that has been shown', and in
the complicated puns of 'Principle/Principal' whose mathematical sense
has been explored. But because Empson is scornful about the non-
meaningful elements, he cannot use them so thoroughly as Donne uses
his sound patterns in *o* and his complicated stanza and rhyme-scheme to
make a thematic point. Donne has no need to say 'You are a metaphor
and they are lies' for the reader to see that this is the case. Because the
reader can see this, Donne may then go on to use the levels of Artifice to
produce his internal thematic synthesis about love, death, separation,
and knowledge while knowing that it will remain internal. For it is what a
poet does with these ideas that interests us as much as the fact that he (in
common with the rest of mankind) entertains them. This is why every
poem on the thematic level is about the same thing—or about one or
more of about five basic things—while being different internally: a different way of looking at the same thing. The microscope of technical
detail makes possible the telescope of thematic synthesis. In 'Letter V',
Empson's microscope is dimmed by congestion of meaning.

There is no need to go on with this, and I wish simply to mention a fas-
cinating and unjustly neglected study of Donne published in 1906 by Mr
Weightman Fletcher Melton. His book presents the thesis that the whole
poem 'Of Weeping' may be seen as a symphony in the key of varying *o*
sounds, with minor patterns—such as those in *ay i ee*—rather than as a
descriptive utterance referring to a real situation. Mr Melton finds a similar pattern in lines 251–260 of the second Anniversarie and adduces the
find as support for his claim that Donne's poems as a whole show an
'artistic monotone' which brings us to see a new category of meaning
'counterpart to the accepted use of figurative language in verse'.[27] This is
very near to my own position, though I should prefer 'new perception of
arrangement' to 'new category of meaning'. But Mr Melton probably felt
that he had been audacious enough.

This, then, is what Eliot learnt from Donne: the conventional and
formal features of poetry can be used simultaneously to assert and to
deny continuity with the past and with the assumptions of contemporary
society. That 'proof' in poetry is a matter of validating discursive imagery
with empirical imagery or, in more general terms, that at least two levels
must be shown to interact internally if the outside world is to be challenged. Eliot chose the conventional level and sound/look to assert his
continuity and this led him to his radical creation of the disconnected

image-complex which is totally different from Donne, as we shall shortly see. But it is small wonder that he chose to canonise the earlier poet who had shown him a way of juggling innovation and security in his verse style. And small wonder that this expertise has proved the resource of later poets who began in the early 'sixties to realise the extent of the problem and the extent to which intervening manoeuvres had concealed it.

I wish now to compare passages from Donne's Anniversaries with parts of 'The Waste Land' and *Four Quartets* as a way of showing more clearly the qualities of the disconnected image-complex and leading thereby into the restatement of the poet's position as tribal mediator.

III   *These fragments I have shored against my ruins*

Pound gloried in the 'épater les bourgeois' revolutionism of Imagism, Vorticism, the 'technique of the Ideogram', but to Eliot ruin was ruin. And if all that could be shored against it were fragments, so much the worse. Anxious always to integrate himself with his society and his literary past by assuming the public role of 'the poet', he was too much of a poet to be unaware that his survival as a poet depended on detachment from society's idea of 'poetry' and on re-creation of the literary past. He could never, as did Pound at what cost we know, ignore contemporary society to the extent of setting up as one man literary tradition. I intend this not as a biographical statement (though it is that also) but as a way of expressing the crucial differences between these two. Crucial differences, because while Pound is overtly the defiant innovator to whom young poets turn, he remains a traditionalist at heart, as an examination of the *Cantos* will show. And it is Eliot who from the very beginning re-created the forms and substance of English poetry; which is why he stands where he does in this book and in this century's literature.

We do not, however, begin at the beginning, for in the quatrain poems the technique of the dislocated image-complex is already far advanced. 'The Waste Land' takes it further in the obvious sense of breaking with rhymed stanza but also paradoxically takes it back. The poem is shot through with ghosts of Eliot's progenitors, but they do not attain that ideal condition, expressed theoretically in 'Tradition and the Individual Talent', where the new work of genius modifies the existing monuments. Eliot, as I said above, has got beyond irony by innovating on the contract of intelligibility between poet and the reader where irony cannot operate, but he maintains his position by the skin of his teeth. Compare the last passage of 'The Waste Land' with one of the most celebrated passages from the first Anniversary, and it will become obvious why Eliot turned to Donne, who could express chaos by a new order while he must express order by a new chaos:

                              I sat upon the shore
          Fishing, with the arid plain behind me
          Shall I at least set my lands in order?
          London Bridge is falling down falling down falling down
          Poi s'ascose nel foco che gli affina
          Quando fiam uti chelidon—O swallow swallow
          Le Prince d'Aquitaine à la tour abolie
          These fragments I have shored against my ruins
          Why then Ile fit you. Hieronymo's mad againe.
          Datta. Dayadhvam. Damyata.
                              Shantih shantih shantih[28]

     And new Philosophy calls all in doubt,
     The Element of fire is quite put out;
     The Sun is lost, and th'earth, and no man's wit
     Can well direct him where to looke for it.
     And freely men confesse that this world's spent,
     When in the Planets, and the Firmament
     They seeke so many new; they see that this
     Is crumbled out againe to his Atomies.
     'Tis all in peeces, all cohaerence gone;
     All just supply, and all Relation:
     Prince, Subject, Father, Sonne, are things forgot,
     For every man alone thinkes he has got
     To be a Phœnix, and that then can bee
     None of that kinde, of which he is, but hee.
     This is the worlds condition now, and now
     She that should all parts to reunion bow,
     She that had all Magnetique force alone,
     To draw, and fasten sundred parts in one;
     She whom wise nature had invented then
     When she observ'd that every sort of men
     Did in their voyage in this world's Sea stray,
     And needed a new compasse for their way;
     She that was best, and first originall
     Of all faire copies, and the generall
     Steward to Fate; she whose rich eyes, and brest
     Guilt the West Indies, and perfum'd the East;
     Whose having breath'd in this world, did bestow
     Spice on those Iles, and bad them still smell so,
     And the rich Indie which doth gold interre,
     Is but as single money, coyn'd from her:
     She to whom this world must it selfe refer,
     As Suburbs, or the Microcosme of her,
     Shee, shee is dead; shee's dead: when thou knowst this,
     Thou knowst how lame a cripple this world is.[29]

The Eliot passage hides an extreme discontinuity beneath the new convention of the five stress free verse line; it drags in its bewildering variety
of allusions and gives the reader very little help in forming any image-

complex or any internal thematic synthesis. For if we try to think of defeatism, chaos, desire, to shore fragments against ruins, we have only two lines—'Shall I at least set my lands in order' and 'These fragments I have shored against my ruins'—to hang on to or to help us; and these are overwhelmed by the other phrases.

The passage, then, barely controls the associations evoked by its lines. And the control is not assimilated to the verse form other than as part of the conventional level and as literary allusion in an external reference, which the reader may, if he is bent on a thematic synthesis at all costs, make into an image-complex.

Arnaut Daniel in the *Inferno*, *The Golden Bough* and all that, 'Per-vigilium Veneris', Nerval, Kyd, Baudelaire, Swinburne ('Swallow, my sister, O sister swallow' from 'Itylus'), and the *Upanishad* are not modified by Eliot's mention of them. On the contrary they tend to run away with the verses themselves (if Jessie Weston is modified it is only because we had never before heard of *From Ritual to Romance*). Dante is a special case and will be considered later when we find in Eliot a techni-que that by transcending irony is able to absorb allusion.

It is quite otherwise with Donne's passage. This, though having the same thematic synthesis as we could force on 'The Waste Land'—' 'Tis all in peeces, all cohaerence gone'—keeps the traditional resources of rhyme, metre, image-complex. In fact, we could say that it succeeds in presenting an order in chaos, in maintaining continuity with the reader while stressing the poet's role as seer. The refrain—'Shee, shee is dead'—as a traditional poetic device helps enormously here. Where Eliot could use only new techniques, thus exposing himself to the danger of unintelligibility, Donne with confidence relies on the traditional, thus holding with his society's idea of poetry. And note that this contrast is not confined to the thematic, or even to the image-complicated level, for it uses formal pattern, poetic convention, and sound/look as well. Donne has no need of the disconnected image-complex so amply illustrated in the Eliot lines, since he can use traditional image-complexes—'poor Elizabeth Drury as the Logos'—to set up his usual relation between dis-cursive and empirical imagery. One death is made a symbol for the theme of chaos in 'And new philosophy puts all in doubt'.

It was a long time before Eliot was able to use the disconnected image-complex to create a new thematic absorption in this way, because he had to start from the destruction of his society's notion of poetry, while Donne starts from acceptance of it. Reach it, however, Eliot did, in *Four Quartets*. And we can see this once again by comparison with the Anniversaries:

Words move, music moves
Only in time; but that which is only living
Can only die. Words, after speech, reach
Into the silence. Only by the form, the pattern,
Can words or music reach
The stillness, as a Chinese jar still
Moves perpetually in its stillness. . . .

And all is always now. Words strain,
Crack and sometimes break, under the burden,
Under the tension, slip, slide, perish,
Decay with imprecision, will not stay in place,
Will not stay still. Shrieking voices
Scolding, mocking, or merely chattering,
Always assail them. The Word in the desert
Is most attacked by voices of temptation,
The crying shadow in the funeral dance,
The loud lament of the disconsolate chimera. . . .
Love is itself unmoving,
Only the cause and end of movement,
Timeless, and undesiring
Except in the aspect of time
Caught in the form of limitation
Between un-being and being.
Sudden in a shaft of sunlight
Even while the dust moves
There rises the hidden laughter
Of children in the foliage
Quick now, here, now, always—
Ridiculous the waste sad time
Stretching before and after.[30]

Here, in the fifth section of 'Burnt Norton', is found what was sought in
'The Waste Land', and in intervening poems that I have no space to consider. The disconnected image-complex has been brought to such a pitch
that it is almost ready to be discarded ('The poetry does not matter') in
favour of a new union, a greater communion. Such a technique, in which
the conventional level varies easily with the thematic level and is signalled by feed-back from the image-complex, is full of perceptible relations, while the disconnected image-complex destroyed these. Observe,
for example, the use of punctuation, needed by the syntactic level, for
conserving a balanced rhythm in the first seven lines quoted. Note, also,
that the level of image-complex is developed in these lines along with the
syntactic and conventional, and that through this development we get
the thematic synthesis. The level of meaning is invoked, beckoned, and
then absorbed by the pattern so that the traditional relation between
levels has been re-established, with this difference: a new tradition takes
place among them. Note, further, that the traditional relation between

discursive and empirical image-complexes, by which the latter served to 'prove', imaginatively, the arguments set out in the former, is used on a new level of abstraction. This very relation is itself made to prove that 'Words, after speech, reach/Into the silence. Only by the form, the pattern,/Can words or music reach/The stillness'. The Chinese jar analogy, the theological imagery, themselves serve as symbols for the way in which poetry takes over the external world through its forms of language. And so it is with the whole of *Four Quartets*. The disconnected image-complex has served its purpose of maintaining contact with the social idea of poetry and with the poetry of the past, through innovation on the technical level, while all other levels served to disconnect twentieth-century poetry from these. So much did Eliot succeed that, despite our eagerness to rehearse its thought and theory, his technique is quite beyond irony and he can again speak straight in his capacity as poet, because he began by parodying it.

So much was not demanded of Donne; he did not live under conditions that seemed unpropitious. Nevertheless we can find an analogy, in that Donne's verse also keeps firm control over whatever external Naturalisation in terms of other discourses ('Shrieking, mocking, or merely chattering') he has to use. And he does so not by the dangerous pyrotechnics of the disconnected image-complex, but by the simple and perennial insistence that internal expansion will take place through the image-complexes, and thus that poetic Artifice will dominate even the discourse of religion on which he relies so much. His claim, 'blessed maid/Of whom is meant what ever hath been said/Or shall be spoken well by any tongue/Whose name refines coarse lines, and makes prose song', echoes Eliot's resolution of his fire/water/earth/air symbolism—'And the fire and the rose are one'—in *Four Quartets*, and its prefiguring in the symbolic children at the end of the passage quoted. Moreover both claims meet the eternal claim of Artifice: 'Not marble, nor the gilded monuments of princes, shall outlive this powerful rhyme'.

We can see this with one more quotation from the first Anniversary:

> Here therefore be the end: And, blessed maid,
> Of whom is meant whatever hath been said,
> Or shall be spoken well by any tongue,
> Whose name refines coarse lines, and makes prose song,
> Accept this tribute, and his first yeares rent,
> Who till his darke short tapers end be spent,
> As oft as thy feast sees this widowed earth,
> Will yearely celebrate thy second birth,
> That is, thy death; for though the soule of man
> Be got when man is made, 'tis borne but than
> When man doth die; our body's as the wombe,
> And, as a Mid-wife, death directs it home.

> And you her creatures, whom she workes upon,
> And have your last, and best concoction
> From her example, and her vertue, if you
> In reverence to her, do think it due,
> That no one should her praises thus rehearse,
> As matter fit for Chronicle, not verse;
> Vouchsafe to call to minde that God did make
> A last, and lasting'st peece, a song.[31]

Donne here combines the techniques noted in the previous passage with the canonical claim that death is life, and he transforms this into a symbol for the artificial claim that poems are the only true reality. His task was easier than Eliot's for the reasons already given. In fact it would be most accurate to say that, far from being the point from which Eliot started his development of the disconnected image-complex, the metaphysical conceit is the point at which he arrived ('In my beginning is my end').

We can see this briefly in the differing uses Eliot makes of Dante, when he is beginning and when he nears his goal.

In the cancelled parts of 'The Waste Land' there occurs a passage describing Ulysses' final, fatal voyage, which is written in a clumsy forerunner of the free verse line of *Four Quartets*; many echoes of iambic pentameter haunt it. But the passage is redeemed by its final two lines which, while containing a direct echo of Dante and insisting that the voyage is allegorical, are yet sufficiently part of 'The Waste Land' imagery to free both poet and reader from the constraint of meaning:

> And if Another knows, I know I know not,
> Who only know that there is no more noise now.[32]

We recognise our favourite key of *o* and the balancing of paradoxical phrases which recalls the more skilful balance of 'Burnt Norton' and which is enough to hold up our progress towards abstraction. Moreover, the passage is immediately followed by that section of 'The Waste Land' which most clearly presents the astronomy of the Separate Planet: 'Phlebas the Phoenician, a fortnight dead'. Phlebas, as Pound said, 'is needed ABSOlootly'.[33] In this section IV we are most clearly aware that individuals as separate beings are destroyed together with the external world according to the needs of formal and conventional pattern, and that these needs may be reconciled more easily to discursive imagery than to descriptive writing.

Indeed that is why Eliot needed Dante, for in the *Commedia* more strikingly than anywhere else is such a conjunction brought about. The extremes of exact physical description are reconciled to the extremes of abstract thought through the medium of a highly stylised and artificial verse form: *terza rima*. From the quatrain poems or earlier, Dante's conjunction of thematic abstraction and technical skill was necessary to the development of the disconnected image-complex. Only in the 'familiar compound ghost' passage of 'Little Gidding' do we get the other levels in play at all and this is in order to make another poem.

It is helpful to look at Dante's lines with the above observations in mind before reaching the 'Little Gidding' passage:

> Tre volte il fe' girar con tutte l'acque
>   alla quarta levar la poppa in suso,
>   e la prora ire in giu com'altrui piacque,
> infin che il mar fu sopra noi richiuso.

> Thrice it|[the storm] turned us together with the whole ocean
>   at the fourth the poop was lifted up
>   and the prow went down as pleased another [God]|
> until the sea closed over us.   (Canto XXVI, my translation)

With Dante we feel the presence of all levels of organisation so that the isolated formal pattern of Eliot's lines is present as part of a whole. We feel also that Dante can afford to allow place to the external world— Ulysses as a speaking individual, the reader's knowledge of his myth, of sailing even—because he is so firmly in control of the thematic synthesis. That control ensures that the reader will not remain with his external Naturalisation; there is consequently no need for anxiety about disconnecting one's poem from the reader's presuppositions. Anxiety of that kind leads, as we have seen, to the development of the disconnected image-complex, to Grishkin's maisonnette, to Phlebas the Phoenician, to the modulations in *o* in Eliot's cancelled passage.

Unlike formal patterns in Dante which are part of a whole which can include references to God as well as a mannered style, Eliot's modulations in *o* stand out on their own, rather than as part in a whole design, because they are not mediated by the other levels of Artifice, whose operations are blocked by the disconnected image-complex. And the isolation of the reference to God—'And if Another knows I know I know not'—is the counterpart on the thematic level of the isolation of formal patterns. By forcing the reader to note that formal pattern and conventional disposition of phrases are more important than 'ideas' or 'themes' or 'message', more important even than 'reality' to the poet, the poem prepares the way for the reader's re-initiation into the rites of mediation. By deliberately omitting the levels of Artifice which 'normally' make poetry interesting to persons who cannot recognise a sestina when they see one, the way is prepared for their readmission and recreation. Dante could take this part for granted, and so could Donne; Eliot could not, and, unlike the majority of poets and critics and readers in this century (Empson is a case in point), he knew that he could not. Hence the dis-

connected image-complex, the tendentious obscurity, the transcendence
of satire; hence:

> In the uncertain hour before the morning
>   Near the ending of interminable night
>   At the recurrent end of the unending
> After the dark dove with the flickering tongue
>   Had passed below the horizon of his homing
>   While the dead leaves still rattled on like tin
> Over the asphalt where no other sound was
>   Between three districts whence the smoke arose
>   I met one walking, loitering and hurried
> As if blown towards me like the metal leaves
>   Before the urban dawn wind unresisting.
>   And as I fixed upon the down-turned face
> That pointed scrutiny with which we challenge
>   The first-met stranger in the waning dusk
>   I caught the sudden look of some dead master
> Whom I had known, forgotten, half recalled
>   Both one and many; in the brown baked features
>   The eyes of a familiar compound ghost
> Both intimate and unidentifiable.
>   So I assumed a double part, and cried
>   And heard another's voice cry: 'What! are *you* here?'[34]

This is the transcendence of the disconnected image-complex, the recovery of the lost levels of Artifice, and in a profound as well as obvious
sense, a re-creation of Dante. Eliot's development as measured against
the examples from Donne, from Empson, and incarnated in the passages
quoted here, is the type-case of the poet as metaphysician/metaphysicist:
as he who has to remake his poems out of the dead language of his contemporary society and, as part of that society, to mediate the new
imaginative vision to his readers, assuming a double part in order to tread
between innovation and intelligibility.

That it is not easy may be seen if we recall that some critics think it
adequate to remark that this passage refers to Eliot's occupation as a
fire-watcher during London in the second war, while others (what brave
fellows, to be sure!) adversely criticised the passage since 'the dark dove'
would then refer to a German bomber. Needless to say, such a reading is
assumed and discarded, like other external contexts, by the poem itself.
And if I say that from the internal thematic synthesis of *Four Quartets*,
'the dark dove' takes on a much more important meaning—it is the dove
of the holy transformed into the mystic's dark night of the soul—I shall
be accused of pandering to the desire to naturalise. Rather than demonstrate exhaustively and exhaustingly once more how such a Naturalisation differs from reference to the external world—it goes through all
the levels of Artifice and expecially concentrates on how the image-

complexes are developed—I shall be the pattern of all patience; I shall say nothing.

But that I hope this chapter has illustrated the difficulties of mediation, the problems of questioning and upsetting order while remaining within an order of intelligibility. This, given the nature of language and of society, is no easy matter. Some more extreme strategies for coping with this double part will occupy the rest of the book, but none has yet proved as successful as Eliot's. Insofar as they are successful at all they follow, consciously or unconsciously, where he has been.

In a chapter devoted so much to the problem of linguistic mediation to puns of physics and metaphysics, to the myth of the poet as outcast and tribal hero and to its reality, it is fitting that the last word should go to one who has played a crucial part in my argument both as theorist and as poet. 'It is clear', says Empson, 'that the view of the poet as outcast and unacknowledged legislator . . . puts him exactly in the position of the mythical tragic hero . . . No doubt this ancient dramatic theme becomes a nuisance when the artist persists in acting it all the time. [. . .] But in a milder form it is almost the only myth still in active use for poetry.'[35]

CHAPTER FIVE

Pastoral
and parody

you come through but
are incomparable the lovely tent
mystery you don't want surrounded the real
you dance
in the spring there was clouds

John Ashbery

In speculation
I would not willingly acquire a name
For ill-digested thought;
But after pondering much
To this conclusion I have come:

A. E. Housman 'Fragment of a Greek Tragedy'

And now, ladies and gentlemen, I have asked you to come here tonight for one purpose: to tell the truth. The truth has, of course, been clear to me from the beginning, the employment of the little grey cells, as my friend Hastings amuses himself by scorning, has made everything plain to me. While the inevitable running round the countryside has been inimitably performed by my good Japp. Naturally, one of you has been in possession of some version of the truth from the beginning. But that one has reckoned without Hercule Poirot and his little grey cells: never a wise thing to attempt and, of course, impossible to achieve. For the rest, assembled here, I, Hercule Poirot, shall now clear up this most distressing mystery . . .

Agatha Christie

Each of my three epigraphs applies to one aspect of poetic Artifice. To take the last first, a parody of Hercule Poirot and the obligatory clearing-up at the end of a detective story: my system is not designed to tidy loose ends; it will be enough if some people learn from it which questions to ask and how to ask them in their dealings with poetry. It will be enough if someone gets the right idea of the relation of poetry to other language and, through language, to the world and back. The second epigraph parodies both the normal 'conclusion' to a book or argument and the way in which the conventions of verse allow one to say nothing at considerable length. Especially as the conclusion is 'Life is uncertain'. The first epigraph combines the functions of the two others; it uses the conventional level to establish continuity and the other levels to destroy it; it recognises that the most important level to destroy is the syntactic. For it is through syntax—the suggestion that a coherent proposition is being offered—that external meaning smothers words. Ashbery, therefore, produces a sequence of words which is meaningless if the reader tries to extend syntax into an external naturalisation but not meaningless if the reader realises that the level of meaning is being used as part of the formal organisation. Further, in order that the reader be in no doubt about what is going on in the process, this sequence includes an obviously ungrammatical sentence: 'in the spring there was clouds'.

Ashbery, like the Dadaists, Surrealists, and Eliot before (all of whom have influenced his work) has undertaken what Tristan Tzara attributed to Mallarmé: the attempt to dissolve 'the hard cement of an apparently impregnable fortress: syntax'[1] Moreover he, realises as do the others with whom this chapter will be concerned, that this destruction of syntax, this breaking of the links between words and the world, must be accompanied by assertions of continuity with the reader if the poem is to remain powerful and intelligible; and that these assertions can best be made on the level of theme at one end and of convention at the other. Thus stated the association of Parody with Pastoral seems inevitable. For Pastoral is the genre which asserts connection on the conventional level, which is granted, by convention, the right to put the complex into the simple, to unify the natural with the highly artificial, to bring together the tribe and the poet. Parody is its counterpart, as a technique stressing connection on the thematic level by taking another language as its theme.

Pastoral is to the thematic level what Parody is to the conventional; and we have seen with what deadly skill Eliot wielded this fact in the quatrain poems, with what bland destruction of the image-complex he went through his development of the disconnected image-complex. We have seen how this development transcended irony and eventually, in *Four Quartets*, created a new world and made the old explicit by reappropriating the other levels of Artifice. The enterprise might, of course, have been even more deadly: man does not challenge the gods with impunity, nor a poet invoke the myth of the poet as metaphysical tribal outcast. These myths have their actualities (the case of Ezra Pound is archetypal) and it is not very likely that Eliot, for all his continuous compounding with deities, escaped. However, we have to do not with the man who suffers but with the mind which creates. And with one exception—Sylvia Plath, of whom more later—contemporary poetry is doing well if it questions and transcends; it is not in much danger of producing society's effective scapegoats.

For this there are many reasons: conditions are even less propitious than in the earlier part of the century; Leavis, Richards, even Empson, have left their mark on millions of readers who may never have heard their names; the elevation of the novel, whether in its more 'realistic' or 'unrealistic' forms, to the dominant literary genre, has allowed us to get away with much slovenly reading of poems and has encouraged poets themselves to neglect artifice. Social and political, even educational problems are not, however, my concern here. Those 'poets' of the 'fifties, 'sixties, and 'seventies who ignore the demands of Artifice will appear only as counter-examples. In any case for us there is only the trying; the rest is not our business.

Geoffrey Hartman says that

> the formality of art becomes a central issue in any literary history. How do we ground art in history without denying its autonomy, its aristocratic resistance to the tooth of time? Is it not a monument, rather than a document; and monument, moreover, of the soul's magnificence, and so richly solipsistic or playful edifice?
> To understand the 'art' in art is always essential. But it is even more essential today, for we have clearly entered an 'era of suspicion' in which art seems arty to the artist himself. The artist, indeed, is often the severest critic of his own medium which turns against itself in his relentless drive for self-criticism.[2]

Quite so. But Professor Hartman does not apparently realise that this criticism and suspicion of his own medium is endemic to the condition of being an artist at any time. His phrase 'the era of suspicion' is a translation of Mme Nathalie Sarraute's 'L'ère du soupçon', which her admirers (associated with *Tel Quel*) make the focus of a traditional argument: this present time is characterised by such self-consciousness in content as well as form that the poet cannot by definition write about anything except writing poetry. Further, Professor Hartman goes on to claim that Eliot, Yeats, and Pound had an 'elitist view of culture' and that Pound's *Cantos* 'remain a nostalgic montage, without unity, a picaresque of styles'.[3] Though on the right lines theoretically, Professor Hartman's comments suggest that he cannot see how such montage of styles, such internal criticism of ordering languages, could ever be more than a simple distrust of art. And if he views the distrust of art in modern literature as something the historian of literature should investigate, he will not go beyond it. This is not a very comfortable position for a Professor of English and Comparative Literature, but it is even less comfortable—that is, useful—for the poet. My system may have looked as if I were saying that one may write only about writing, but I have tried to insist that in so doing one is writing about a great many other things as well; in fact one can only be interesting about writing by concerning oneself with something else. To be told that one may write only about writing and to be censored when doing anything else is enough to discourage anyone. If all that poets can tell readers is how agonising it is to write poems then readers also are likely to rebel. No. As we saw at the end of the last chapter poets have to undergo a development which is both stylistic and thematic; and they have to be quite sure that this development will allow them to present, however altered by technique, their most important thoughts on life, love, and cookery. The reader needs a corresponding assurance, for he too is interested in life, love, and cookery; and the reader lacks the poet's compensating creative fascination with technical problems.

Before turning to an investigation of contemporary techniques, we should consider the resources of Pastoral and Parody as they were developed and exploited by Pound's and Eliot's late nineteenth-century predecessors. Whatever manoeuvre Eliot and Pound performed, it took account of the contemporary resources of artifice, and whatever useful manoeuvre later poets have performed, they have done so through Eliot and Pound's manoeuvres.

I The garden of Proserpine

This is not the place for a survey of nineteenth-century poetry nor even of selected 'Pre-Raphaelites'; it is the place for a demonstration that all the operations of Artifice are available to poets in this century. Previous poets have coped—with very different results, of course, since they were very different men living in different societies—with the problem of great technical innovation and achieved considerable thematic complexity while keeping the attention of the reader by use of the conventional level. Eliot developed the disconnected image-complex and its eventual transcendence. But there is another who did the same. Who should this be but the poet most scorned by the middle-of-the-road people; who should it be but the poet they accuse of wishy-washiness, of verbalising (as if to be a poet were not, in a very actual sense, to verbalise), of being unable to cope with an abstract thought, a concrete 'image', a 'deep emotion' or a complicated rhyme-scheme; who, in fact, should it be but Algernon Charles Swinburne.

I shall quote two pieces of Swinburne, one from a 'straight' poem, one from a self-parody. Examining the differences will rid our minds of any notion that Swinburne can justly be accused of any of the faults mentioned in the above paragraph; it will also, which is more germane to the question, restate our system of Artifice.

> Thou has conquered, O pale Galilean; the world has grown grey from thy breath:
> We have drunken of things Lethean, and fed on the fullness of death.
> Laurel is green for a season, and love is sweet for a day;
> But love grows bitter with treason, and laurel out-lives not May.

Sleep, shall we sleep after all? for the world is not sweet in the end;
For the old faiths loosen and fall, the new years ruin and rend.
Fate is a sea without shore, and the soul is a rock that abides;
But her ears are vexed with the roar and her face with the foam of the tides.
O lips that the live blood faints in, the leavings of racks and rods!
O ghastly glories of saints, dead limbs of gibbeted Gods!
Though all men abase them before you in spirit, and all knees bend,
I kneel not neither adore you, but standing, look to the end.
All delicate days and pleasant, all spirits and sorrows are cast
Far out with the foam of the present that sweeps to the surf of the past:
Where beyond the extreme sea-wall, and between the remote sea-gates,
Waste water washes, and tall ships founder, and deep death waits;
Where, mighty with deepening sides, clad about with the sea as with wings,
And impelled of invisible tides, and fulfilled of un-speakable things,
White-eyed and poisonous-finned, shark-toothed and serpentine-curled,
Rolls, under the whitening wind of the future, the wave of the world.[4]

And again:

Surely no spirit or sense of a soul that was soft to the spirit and soul of our
   senses
   Sweetens the stress of suspiring suspicion that sobs in the semblance and
      sound of a sigh;
Only this oracle opens olympian, in mystical moods and triangular tenses—
   'Life is the lust of a lamp for the light that is dark till the dawn of the day that
   we die.'
Mild is the mirk and monotonous music of memory, melodiously mute as it
   may be,
   While the hope in the heart of a hero is bruised by the breach of men's
      rapiers, resigned to the rod;
Made meek as a mother whose bosom-beats bound with the bliss-bringing
   bulk or a balm-breathing baby,
   As they grope through the graveyard of creeds, under skies growing green as
   a groan for the grimness of God.[5]

Of course it is easy to see which is the parody. I have given the matter
away by including in the first quotation some of the most illustrious lines
from Swinburne's 'Hymn to Proserpine': 'Thou hast conquered, O pale
Galilean; the world has grown grey from thy breath'. But how anyone,
reading that poem or others in the same volume, could accuse their
author of looseness, empty and meaningless phrases, lack of concrete
imagery or abstract argument or technical skill is hard to believe. Mr
Dwight Macdonald, editor of the collection of parodies, actually says
that the self-parody 'seems to me rather self-sparing; Swinburne only
mocks his mechanical alliteration, but there was much else to be criticised.'[6] Not only does Swinburne parody much else besides his alliteration but his alliteration itself is far from being mechanical. This may
be seen by his very sparingness of alliteration in the first passage quoted

above; he uses it to support the level of meaning, of rhythm, of theme, of rhyme; he dispenses with it when it is needless—as in the first part of the first line, of the second line, of the third line, of the fourth line; he can include a parody of it, in lines nine and ten, to make a thematic point and to stress how awful is the Christian God. He can immediately follow this, in line eleven, with a total absence of alliteration and a concentration on the syntactical level: the line follows an exclamation mark, which is the strongest possible grammatical pause, and leads to a conditional clause in the next line which is the strongest grammatical contrast to apparently uncontrolled emotional utterance. This syntactic contrast, in con-junction with conventions of rhythm, metre, and symbol, helps to effect an internal thematic synthesis.

How Swinburne achieved a reputation for verbosity when his lines are composed almost entirely of monosyllables would remain mysterious if we were not sufficiently alert to note that the monosyllables 'the', 'of', 'and', are what create his characteristic anapaests. Similarly, his reputation as a dweller entirely among words would remain a puzzle, given his themes of love, life, death, faith, and fame, if we did not know that his monosyllabic simplicity—his use of these words themselves—gives an appearance of ingenuousness which he is very far from deserving. Observe the delicate balance between syntax, theme, form, and metre in 'Sleep, shall we sleep, after all? For the world is not sweet in the end', and how here the alliteration is used to help the mixture. Similarly, in 'I kneel not neither adore you, but standing look to the end', the syntactical level is blended with the formal level to sum-up the thematic synthesis on 'standing': and imagined scene is led back to an abstract argument and both meet in ver-bal form. The sea and shipwreck images remind us of Eliot, and, though they are not here so developed as in 'The Triumph of Time', they are vivid enough to do away with any notion that Swinburne was incapable of the relation of discursive to empirical imagery that we saw in Donne.

A major difference between Swinburne's 'straight' poem and the parody lies in the relation between content and form. In the latter content is produced, by a show of virtuosity, as if by the formal level itself, as a pretext for alliteration. Or rather, in an important sense in the parody there is no content, no resistance from the external world, and con-sequently no development of the formal level since this would arise only as a manoeuvre to deal with new content. There must, as in Pastoral and Parody, be two levels in relation to create the tight-rope between Artifice and reality. In the Swinburne self-parody we approached—however unlikely this may seem—the condition of bad Naturalisation in which both form and content are given in advance, as something outside the poem in terms of which it is to be understood. We naturalise the poem by reading it as parody, as an extreme version of certain techniques and associations. Consequently, irrational obscurity on the technical level and external Naturalisation in terms of the poet's mind are inevitable. In the first passage, contrariwise, there is constant movement both forward and backwards: a forward development of the image-complexes, of the anapaestic line, of the thematic synthesis, and a backward, retrospective, almost casual, handling of symbols like the shipwreck and the sea and of the conventions of metre and rhyme which re-create the future in the present through the past. Compare the artificial subtleties of the first passage with the mocking passage of the parody: 'Surely no spirit or sense of a soul that was soft to the spirit and soul of our senses/Sweetens the stress of suspiring suspicion that sobs in the semblance and sound of a sigh.' Or compare the passage in the parody celebrating (one cannot call it bemoaning) the passing of love, of hope, of life, with Swinburne's earnest engagement with such themes elsewhere. It will be clear that the real Swinburne is not the figure of caricature. Swinburne is often called a self-indulgent poet, but if we read him properly we shall see that he is, in fact, given the exuberance of which he was capable, a poet of consummate self-restraint.

However, my purpose is not simply to assert that Swinburne was a good poet but to consider his versions of pastoral, his success in creating, through formal techniques that fictionalise external contexts, an artificial world both continuous and discontinuous with the world of experience. It is a world which simplifies and exalts but also, and by the same token, parodies. We can grasp two moments of the pastoral/parodic mode in the nineteenth-century through a comparison between Edward Lear's 'Akond of Swat' and Swinburne's 'Faustine'.

These two creatures are clearly denizens of Pastoral and they are equally strands in Parody which has overcome its direct parasitic dependence on a particular model. It may seem odd to call the ferocious Faustine a rustic swain, but remember that her creator has assumed the responsibilities of poet as mediating metaphysician who must be also tribal outcast. She exists, then, not simply as a necessary fiction but as subject to that goddess who rules the realm of Artifice. She is Persephone, queen of the dead and bringer of life, both one and three. Faustine can thus be used by her poet—as her poet is used by his goddess—not simply to escape the external world nor even to criticise it through its language but to create new orders of imaginative freedom which have their own strict rules. She seems simple as a 'real' person and simple too as a necessary fiction. Only when considered as an organising principle in the verse is her true complexity perceived.

Lear's 'Akond' as pastoral swain is less puzzling. Wherever the 'real' realm of Swat and its Akond might be (it's probably an oilfield by now and the Akond a millionaire) in the poem it is accepted as part of the bric-à-brac of the world of Victorian children (and adults): an imagined realm through which this disintegrating world is criticised.

To claim that these poems illustrate Parody transcending itself is more elaborate. In 'Faustine' it amounts to saying that Swinburne's style, with its detached and passionate craftsmanship, is a parody of traditional 'lyric love poetry'. The parody of lyric deals with the formal levels while that of love poetry deals with the thematic. The very details that have seemed to people to sweep the verse along arrest the onrush and make us examine them as technique. We saw this in our previous Swinburne self-parody. Lear, of course, is less subtle; he parodies the anecdotal, easily-rhymed verse narrative, like Chaucer's 'Sir Topas', while his pastoral strategy permits him to retain this mode as means. Both poems, in fact, by conjoining pastoral with parody preserve continuity in discontinuity. They provide something for the reader's Naturalisation to work on while undermining it on another level.

Take, for example, 'Faustine':

> Did Satan make you to spite God?
>   Or did God mean
> To scourge with scorpions for a rod
>   Our sins, Faustine?
>
> I know what queen at first you were,
>   As though I had seen
> Red gold and black imperious hair
>   Twice crown Faustine.
>
>   . . .
>
> Was life worth living then? and now
>   Is life worth sin?
> Where are the imperial years? and how
>   Are you, Faustine?
>
> Your soul forgot her joys, forgot
>   Her times of teen;
> Yea, this life likewise will you not
>   Forget, Faustine?
>
>   . . .
>
> What sterile growths of sexless root
>   Or epicene?
> What flower of kisses without fruit
>   Of love, Faustine?
>
> What adders came to shed their coats?
>   What coiled obscene
> Small serpents with soft stretching throats
>   Caressed Faustine?

E*

> But the time came of famished hours,
>   Maimed loves and mean,
> This ghastly thin-faced time of ours,
>   To spoil Faustine.[7]

That thin-faced time had not come for Swinburne when he wrote these stanzas; there is nothing mean about his arrangement of rising and falling rhythm, rhyme, and imagery which extends to a thematic synthesis of which they are a part. Faustine is an image-complex; her career and even her name are altered for the sake of a rhyme or cadence—and she again alters them. Sometimes she is addressed directly; sometimes she is a person in an historical story. Sometimes a strong speech cadence—'Hullo, Faustine, how are you today?'—is overborne by the rhythm and metre (and how/Are you, Faustine?); sometimes—as in the last stanza which I do not quote—the name is merely tagged onto the line with the most tenuous semantic connection.

Always Faustine is part of Swinburne's larger theme of love, death, and life all lost, but always too she is part of his larger Artifice: a world which allowed him to parody the hated 'thin-faced time' while consoling him with the delights of transforming pastoral into parody. Artifice substitutes its own complexities for the threatening complexities of individual existence. This is a pastoral seclusion more secure than that offered Swinburne by Mr Watts Dunton at 'The Pines' because it can encompass evil in its own questioning mode and give it an ambiguous disembodied status.

But sometimes Faustine appears part of a vision of life which, as Eliot says of the choruses in 'Atalanta in Calydon', is 'effective because it appears to be a tremendous statement, like statements made in our dreams.'[8] Eliot, of course implies that the statement only *appears* powerful. But given the context, which we have examined, of the overt assertion of continuity and bad Naturalisation, and the covert re-creation of convention requiring secret discontinuity and eventual good Naturalisation, we can note the fact while rejecting the implication. Eliot also claims that 'only a man of genius could dwell so exclusively and consistently among words as Swinburne.'[9] We can see what degree of truth this comment has: Swinburne is a craftsman of genius but he never lets his form run away with his content. His content is great, spanning almost the whole spectrum of human preoccupations, but it would be nothing if his form were not able to support it. His subtleties of perception, his esoteric sensibility, would be no more use to him than to Ella Wheeler Wilcox if he could not translate them into subtleties of technique by presenting the disingenuous appearance of talking about simple things. This is the essential manoeuvre of pastoral and parody combined: put the complex into the simple and then the complexities will become stylistic and can be dealt with accordingly. The poet will keep, by this appearance of simplicity, some contact with his tribe of readers, while his real complexity will give him contact with the important he—the innovating poet—and with his literary past. This way of dealing with the world may be the difference between life and death to the individual. To Swinburne it was the difference between life and life in the protective seclusion of Watts Dunton. In the twentieth century the question has been given more immediacy by the suicide merchants who say, in effect, 'no one can become a great poet unless he has at least tried killing himself.' It is obvious that this springs from external expansion and complicity with bad Naturalisation, from an insistence that innovation in 'experience' is the only innovation possible. But people are still taking-off at such a rate . . . Why, only the other day John Berryman, who was at least enough of a poet to know quite a bit about formal innovation . . .

Swinburne, however, did not dwell exclusively among words; he would not have been a great poet had he done so. Is it necessary to insist on Eliot's 'statements made in dreams' as part of the Surrealist *rêve*—that area of reverse priorities where the looking-glass world transforms our ordinary hierarchies of extended meanings? Is it necessary to recall that Swinburne was for a time stranded in the everyday world of action by his interest in the Italian risorgimento, and produced a lot of bad verse in consequence? Is it necessary to insist that Swinburne knew how to absorb the forms of external discourse and to use these for poetic ends, thus fulfilling Jacob's statement that 'a work is not valuable by what it contains but by what surrounds it'?[10] And what surrounds it is primarily the discourse of the critic who goes between it and other languages in his interpretive reading. It should not, for example, have been necessary to remark, as I did above, that form must support content.

Too many literary theorists, however, have taken this to mean that form and content are fused in such a way as to make it impossible for us to distinguish levels in a poem or to find it good on one level though ill on another. If form must support content, it is no less necessary, as we have seen from the relation between the semantic, the image-complicated, and the thematic levels, that content should support form. There must be as much or as little power in the theme as transmitted through the image-complex—that is, through a mixture of meaning and the non-semantic levels—as is appropriate for the formal convention. In other words, themes appropriate for the villanelle will not suit the sonnet, still less the ode or the epic. This does not imply that form and content are identical, still less that they are fused; on the contrary, it implies that they must be different, distinguishable in order that their relations may be judged.

But let Swinburne himself speak on this topic:

a writer conscious of any natural command over the musical resources of his language can hardly fail to take such pleasure in the enjoyment of this gift or instinct as the greatest writer and greatest versifier of our age must have felt at its highest possible degree . . . But if he be a poet after the order of Hugo or Coleridge or Shelley, the result will be something very much more than a musical exercise; though indeed, except to such ears as should always be kept closed against poetry, there is no music in verse which has not in it sufficient fullness and ripeness of meaning, sufficient adequacy of emotion or thought, to abide the analysis of other than the purblind scrutiny of prepossession or the squint-eyed inspection of malignity.[11]

Precisely. Swinburne is aware that expansion of the level of meaning and imposition of Naturalisation are inevitable constituents of the process of reading poetry and must be allowed for in the process of writing it. He is further aware that in making such allowances one can find ways of making a poem transcend its initial Naturalisation and impose its own world of imaginative possibilities, simply because it has made technical allowance for the reader's initial realistic expansion/limitation.

In a cruder form this may be seen in Lear's 'Akond'. A violent juxtaposition of the convention of rhyme and of pseudo-descriptive narrative produces an artificial effect, an impression that the whole discourse is governed by the need to find a rhyme, to find the world of Artifice in the nurseries of Victorian England:

> At night if he suddenly screams and wakes,
> Do they bring him only a few small cakes or a LOT
>   The Akond of Swat?
>
> Does he live on turnips, tea, or tripe?
> Does he like his shawl to be marked with a stripe, or a DOT
>   The Akond of Swat?
>
> Does he like to lie on his back in a boat
> Like the lady who lived in that isle remote, SHALLOTT
>   The Akond of Swat?
>
>   . . .
>
> Some one, or nobody, knows I wot
> Who or which or why or what
>   Is the Akond of Swat![12]

Of course this is less skilful and complicated than 'Faustine', but perhaps, for that same reason, we can see more easily what is going on. The conventions of pastoral are used with the conventions that parody normal poetic discourse—where poets try to conceal the fact that a rhyme is more important than a philosophy—in order to assert the autonomy poetry grants to the imagination in language. Oddly enough only the difference in subtlety separates Lear's reference to Tennyson and 'The

Lady of Shalott' itself: that lady is also a creature of pastoral and inhabits the world of unrealism:

> She left the web, she left the loom,
> She made three paces thro' the room,
> She saw the water-lily bloom,
> She saw the helmet and the plume,
>   She look'd down to Camelot.
> Out flew the web and floated wide;
> The mirror crack'd from side to side;
> 'The curse is come upon me,' cried
>   The Lady of Shalott.[13]

Contact with reality destroys her fantasy world, but not the poem, for she is more than a creature of fiction; she is an organising formal principle, and her abode has been chosen by the need to find a rhyme for 'Camelot'. Like Faustine, she is secure in her internal relations even if her external relations are destroyed. In fact there is a good deal in common between these two ladies—though both their creators would be shocked to be told so. They have been selected for the flexibility in organising rhymes which will feed into the formal level and for their ability as personae to link the formal to the thematic level; while the Akond of Swat with his restriction to hard *k t* and sibilant *s* comes, like Lepidus, a poor third.

I hope I may be excused here for quoting two of my own poems which illustrate how these techniques may be put to use in twentieth-century poetry. The first, called 'The Lady of Shalott', is self-conscious to the degree implied by the choice of such a title and stresses its formal level by having one completely meaningless line, but these sacrifices to parody and disconnectedness enable it to combine pastoral with parody. I quote it here because of its aptness and its illustration of this point.

The Lady of Shalott

> The child in the snow has found her mouth
> And estate-agents must beware,
> For if what we seek cannot be truth,
> And we've only a lie to share,
> The modern conveniences won't last out;
> Bear tear flair dare
> And the old ones just don't care.
>
> Back and forth she moves her arms,
> Forth and back, her legs.
> No one would care to say:
> Her lips are red, her looks are free,
> Her locks are yellow as gold.
> Whether she's very young or old,
> The nightmare life-in-death is she
> Who thicks men's blood with cold.

What of the future is in the past
Channels towards us now.
Present and future perfect past
Makes no tracks in the snow
Turn the tap and the water will come
For five seconds.
And then the sand
Flows into our ever-open mouth.
What was it we understand?

She does not stand in the snow; she kneels:
A parody of prayer.
Lucretius said it long ago:
Why think the gods care?
When the telephone goes dead,
The fridge is broken, the light . . .

Why should we think of knowledge as light?
There is enough to see her.
And, having seen, the message is plain
To those who wish to know
(They are not many.):
Run quickly back to darkness again;
We have seen the child in the snow.[14]

Here the poet (having had the effrontery to use my own poems as examples I now hide behind my role) is able to use extremely traditional regular iambic rhymed verse with anapaestic variation (in lines, 1, 3, 7, 16,
20, 23, 25, 28, 37) plus extremely conventional symbolism ('the child in
the snow'). He combines this with a traditional use of literary allusion—
the title and the Coleridge lines of the second stanza—which is made into
the allusiveness characteristic of twentieth-century poetry by the support
of specifically twentieth-century conventions: a deliberately extra-
metrical line, 'for five seconds', and the ellipsis ('. . .') which stands for
'the light (fails)'.

Thus the conventional and formal levels contribute to a thematic
synthesis as old as the hills: 'Fate is against mankind'. Yet it takes on a
new aspect when set in relation to poetry as a cognitive instrument: 'It is
impossible for poetry to work when we have no standards of knowledge'.
The best is obtained from both worlds and the levels of Artifice are
restored to their old power by getting new power. The poet is not
restricted to the insistence on formal dominance stressed in line 6—'Bear
tear flair dare'—an insistence that seemed his only resource in other and
earlier works. These had the same theme of being unable to escape from
language into the 'real' world and they made this imprisonment tolerable
only by accepting the non-meaningful aspects of language. Here he can
combine strength of content with strength of form given by all the trad-

itional levels of Artifice, as Eliot and Swinburne do; that is, the man-oeuvre is similar. I have said it is typical of all twentieth-century poetry written in what is, according to the theoretical position set out in this book, the tradition of innovation.

In another poem, 'Pastoral', I was restricted very much to the stress on non-meaningful aspects of language as the only escape from the into-lerable theme:

Pastoral

They are our creatures clover, and they love us
through the long summer meadow's diesel fumes.
Smooth as their scent and contours clear however
less than enough to compensate for names.

Jagged are names and not our creatures
neither in sense or fullness like the flowers.
Raised voices in a car or by a river
remind us of the world that is not ours.

Silence in grass and solace in blank verdure
summon the frightful glare of nouns and nerves.
The gentle foal linguistically wounded,
squeals like a car's brakes, like our twisted words[15]

If one writes a line like the first line of this poem one is obviously alerting the reader to the fact that sound resemblance—'clover'/'love'—is more important than meaning. The second line furthers the process in making it clear that the extension of meaning is less important than the way external contexts—the meadow, the flowers, the cars, the voices, the river—feed back into the thematic synthesis which is given in the fourth line and developed through the other two stanzas. This is particularly noticeable in the last two lines where the 'gentle foal' is important for his *entle oal* sounds rather than for his physical being. For these sounds are taken up in 'linguistically wounded', which is a crucial phrase both for the theme and for the rhythm. That is, the foal's physical being is trans-ferred to the sound of the names we give him. A pretty paradox in view of the poem's theme; since the poet is saying (thematic synthesis) just that: pre-occupation with linguistic problems prevents contact with the phy-sical word.

The ninth line provides a linguistic equivalent for the idea of blankness in 'blank verdure'; b d n, especially the conjunction of k and v (which makes the latter almost hard), and the annulment by hard a of the e u softening vowel sounds all make the verdure particularly blank. The sound pattern of the line thus offers a direct challenge to the dominance of 'abstract' theme and 'concrete' senselessness, but the alliteration and assonance in 'Silence in grass and solace' help to combat any non-poetic extension at this point. The rest of the poem is strong enough on its own to resist such extension. Much of its strength comes from its use of regular metre, half-rhymes—'fumes/names'—and stanza form. Indeed it is half-way along the path which leads to 'The Lady of Shalott' in its willingness to call on some of the traditional resources of technique; the foal looks remarkably like a traditional symbol used to give the kind of empirical instance in a discursive argument that we saw in Donne and Eliot.

But if 'Pastoral' is half-way along the path to 'Lady of Shalott' it also resembles, in some of its apparent concrete meaninglessness, another form of artifice, whose examples can be grouped under the loose heading of Dada. This is only one incarnation of the perennial god of Artifice, who like other deities, has different names at different places. Whatever the relation of Dada to Swinburne, Lear, Tennyson, and Forrest-Thomson, however, I am not calling them Dadaists in the historical sense. Before expanding Dada to include the central moments in the renovation of Artifice we must turn to the historical Dadaists and their achievement.

II   Dada and its avatars

Dada's revolutionary fervour was always ambiguous. On the other hand it is obvious that a theory of poetry is a theory about poetry; Breton refrained from firing his celebrated revolver for that reason. On the other hand, the Dadaists and Surrealists were fully aware both of the danger of taking their movement as a purely literary, formalised game, and of the impossibility of its being anything else. Consider the scorn Aragon heaps on those who did think it purely a literary movement:

> I have no desire—and everyone should be quite clear about this—that surrealist texts, and even 'le rêve' should become part of a classification of fixed forms, as if they were the perfection of freedom taking out a patent on liberty, just like those classifiers who find that free verse is already to be deplored. One more step in the advance of free verse! That is how some people see and speak of surrealism![16]

Consider, on the other hand, Maurice Nadeau's statement that surrealist rigour 'is based fundamentally on language, that is, ultimately, on words, their meaning, which is not that of the dictionary, but the explosion of each letter, each syllable.'[17] And what, or course, is exploded in the process are the comfortable assumptions about the intelligibility of the world, as mediated by language, that constitute Realism as a literary mode.

But what can contain the explosion, give it powerful agents to reconstitute the destroyed world or to make a new one, to preserve continuity

as 'Pastoral' and 'The Lady of Shalott' preserve it, is solidarity with the
tools of past Artifice. Lack of this vitiates much historical and Dadaist
writing, just as it vitiates the productions of more recent French 'Structuralist' writers like Philippe Sollers and Marcelin Pleynet; presence of it
wins some poetic achievement from Denis Roche, another 'Structuralist'
destroyer of poetry. However I have argued this elsewhere[18] and wish
now to turn to a poem which introduces the traditional poetic device of
the refrain: Tristan Tzara's 'L'homme approximatif', whose first
movement at least is a positive achievement.

The first section revolves round three phrases which subtly alter the
traditional function of the refrain as they exploit it. These phrases are
part of a complicated rhythm established and maintained by an interaction between surprise and expectation; it characterises all poetry but has
come to be the held base of poetry in this century. As always with long
poems one can only quote the crucial lines and hope that the reader will
look up the rest:

> *l'eau de la rivière a tant lavé son lit*
> que même la lumière glisse sur l'onde lisse
> et tombe au fond avec le lourd éclat des pierres
> *les cloches sonnent sans raison et nous aussi* . . .
>
> sans amertume sans dette sans regret sans
> les cloches sonnent sans raison et nous aussi
>
> pourquoi chercher le bout de la chaîne
> que nous relie à la chaîne
> sonnez cloches sans raison et nous aussi
> nous ferons sonner en nous les verres cassés[19]

I have italicised the first two of these refrain phrases. We shall reach the
third shortly, but first I want to try a bad Naturalisation in terms of
external limitation/expansion:

> The poet is giving in gracefully to a rather gloomy view of human life as
> totally deterministic; we can never find a reason in our lives any more than
> bells have a reason for ringing. His logic is rather faulty since bells usually
> do have a reason for ringing; that's why they are rung. But poets are
> allowed to make illogical statements provided they don't try to make us
> take them seriously. He compares life to a river, which is a very well-worn
> simile originating in Heraclitus, who probably got it from the Sanskrit
> grammarians, who probably got it from . . . However he's a good little
> poet and gives the old simile a new polish with that comparison of a light
> being cast with the heaviness of a stone—just the right kind of concrete
> sensuous detail that we are told to expect from poetry though that simile
> too is pretty traditional. Why, even Ernest Dowson . . .

Now, even that bad Naturalisation has gone directly counter to the evidence of the lines themselves. For the fifth line quoted—'sans amertume

sans dette sans regret sans'—shows that the poet is deliberately playing
variation on the *sans/sonnent/sonnez* key and that this is more important
than ordinary logic. There is no need, however, to suppose that these
evocations need be absent from a good Naturalisation. As I keep saying,
twentieth-century poetry that is really innovatory builds on the assumps-
tions of bad Naturalisation and transcends them to the extent that they
become practically harmless—to poet and reader—if not insisted on by
critics. We can think of 'All things are a flowing sage Heracleitus says';
we can think of Baudelaire's 'Je suis une cloche fêlée'. What we must not
do is think that if Tzara, or any other good poet for that matter, were
asked for his views on life he could come up with nothing better than
'Well, I think everything changes, if you see what I mean'. Only the
Larkins behave like this; and they have their best apologue in the
smothering subtleties of Wallace Stevens.

It does no harm to have such associations, but we should not think that
the value of Tzara's lines depends on them. 'Bells ring for no reason and
so do we', 'The river water has so much washed its bed', are not among
anyone's 'great thoughts for the day'. What they do, in their original
French, is to organise and control the movement of sound—which means
the selection and ordering of words—throughout the poem. The context
of throwing a stone into a river is invoked, provoked by the other sounds
its linguistic expression suggests, and suddenly transformed into the
sound of bells because the form of the poem requires the transformation
as it required the provocation: 'même', lumière', 'glisse', 'l'onde lisse',
tombe au fond', lourd éclat', 'cloches'. The second context—of accepting life's flow and simultaneously asserting oneself against it (why write
poems if everything will drift away like the waters)—is equally removed
from reality by the changes rung on *sonner/sans*.

The poet, then, having set up a complicated apparatus of rhythm,
internal rhyme, and sound/look to absorb meaning cannot easily destroy
it in favour of a banal comment on life. And—shall I say it again? I shall
say it again—if the critic tries to make the poem do so he commits a grave
crime against poetry and against his own function as transmitter of the
poet's visions to the inarticulate reader. If the critic tries to do it with an
overtly Dada poem it will completely slip his grasp and elude him. This is
not to say that, like our earlier examples of irrational obscurity, such
poems cannot have a 'message' wrenched from them. As we saw with
Eliot's disconnected image-complex, it is part of their purpose to provide
a wrenchable message for those who like wrenching and messages. In the
present case our villain might want to say that the last two lines of this
first section of 'L'homme approximatif' summed up its message:

> je pense à la chaleur que tisse la parole
> *autour de son noyau le rêve qu'on appelle nous*

I have italicised the third of the refrain lines; and the fact that this is the third of the refrain lines should give even our message-merchant pause. For a line cannot be everywhere at once; if it is so important on the thematic scale, it is very unlikely to be the backbone of the formal organisation, and vice versa (this is where critics who think form and content ought to be coterminous are making a big mistake).

What Tzara's poem offers is much more than a few banal reflections or expected literary manoeuvres; it offers a voyage through the untravelled bourn where poetry is re-forged in the smithy of language. The ticket is cheap: the reader must merely accept the stance of 'content as form', of 'aesthetic distance', and join the poet in his escape from involvement with action and suffering (which does not mean denying them). We do not want more poems about everyday life; there are enough and more than enough poems that do that; but never today enough Dada poems.

Poetry maintains the sublime in the old sense by creating the sublime in the new, because to create new techniques is to insist on the dominance of non-meaningful aspects of language and to absorb even the conventions of fictional writing. As an Arab writer of the ninth century says of Moorish poetry,

> it is accounted an imperative rule that the poet, breaking off from the subject matter of the lyric, should pass on to the *kharga* without any transition, and that he should represent it as being uttered by characters who speak in their own names, or, if they remain silent, are connected with a theme other than that of the poem. The *kharga* is frequently couched in childish language or in a foreign tongue. In any case it is a customary convention that it should produce the effect of meaningless jargon.[20]

It may seem a long way from Ibn Sana al-Mulik to our present problems but the *kharga* in Moorish poetry is the nearest equivalent to the Western refrain; it was the model for the Troubadour coda; and it is nice to know that the disconnected image-complex, simultaneously distancing and absorbing society into the poem by quoting its discourse with the conspicuous irrelevance of disconnected imagery, is so universally recognised.

Moreover, the Dadaist point of view is simply an extension of that aesthetic distance which produces the 'meaningless' *kharga*. Its discovery is a fundamental aesthetic experience. Artifice involves two crucial notions: 'aesthetic distance' and 'content as form'. These two concepts find their analogy in pastoral as content (thematic level leading to artificial limitation/expansion) and parody as technique (the levels of Artifice which provide a kit for transforming the non-poetic into the poem). When we combine parody as technique and pastoral as content we are in a position to grasp the truth of the Dadaist claim that everything, from the point of view of Dada, *is* Dada. From the point of view of

Artifice every poem as such is an incarnation of Artifice.

Indeed this must be so. For once we have established the combination of detachment from content and minute attention to form that is essential to pastoral and parody, the whole system of language as communication about the socially-given real world dissolves and with it the dominance of extended meaning, realistic limitation/expansion, bad Naturalisation.

Some instances. One: In September 1972 an exhibition of 'The Surrealist Revolution' is held, under the auspices of the French Government, in the Musée de l'Art Decoratif in Paris. Two: the proprietor of 'L'Hotel de France' tells me that in order to enter my room I must insert the key upside down and turn it counter-clockwise. Three: the latest thing at the Louvre is a series of jig-saw puzzles of famous works of art, including the 'Mona Lisa'. Four: also at the Louvre are empty pedestals solemnly labelled 'Aphrodite' and 'Nymphe?' Five: at the Surrealist exhibition is a Miro canvas, empty except for the 'Photo' at the top left and a blue patch at the bottom right with the words, 'Ceci est le couleur de mes rêves', while beside the canvas an official notice instructs us 'Défense de photographier'. Six: a dog hurls itself across the pavement to leap into the Seine and must be forcibly embraced by its master who then allows the dog to stand on the parapet and gaze into the water.

These examples could be multiplied indefinitely; you will find them in your own everyday experience. Indeed you would have difficulty in avoiding them once you had adopted the Dada/Artifice/'form as content' perspective. The point is that, as with the extended meaning of words in a poem, we are quite well aware of their significance outside the realm of artifice. The locality and sponsoring of the exhibition, the official notices, the manufacture of puzzles, may, from a political or sociological viewpoint, be sinister. The dog's longing for the water and its master's care of it were certainly vivid experiences for them. I was certainly much annoyed by the recalcitrance of the lock on my door. Finally, Miro's witty self-reflexiveness in exploiting the audience's pictorial expectations—which was taken further by Desnos and Dali in the same exhibition—is the acme of parody and pastoral combined. Desnos has two canvases that show the artist in aesthetic detachment from his own external context, including that of the interpretive critic, transmuting these into technical devices. His 'Mort d'André Breton' represents Breton's pontifical persona by including the words 'Moi je sais', 'Vous vous trompez', and represents the surrealist magazine *Nord-Sud* by a circle with these two words at its poles. His 'Mort de Paul Éluard' absorbs critical Naturalisation by the words 'Je me trompe', 'Dieu aussi est mort' and, on the coffin, 'Ci gît Paul Éluard qui fut bleu et fluide'. For is not Éluard praised by critics for his scepticism, his humility, and the almost simplistic lyricism of his verse. Dali goes one step further; his canvas is entitled 'The Surrealist Revolution in New York' and includes these words on it as part of formal pattern.

This is the famous Surrealist 'L'humour' at its best, and is not to be confused with 'a sense of humour' or frivolity or tolerance. There is nothing funny about the lives of Rimbaud and Lautréamont or the deaths of Jacques Vaché and René Crevel. But there is a pattern in which these things form a part. How else could we bear them; how else could we risk the same? The point about the empirical examples is simply that from artificial detachment and aesthetic distance we can see this pattern in little in the events of our own lives. And, having done so, we are better fitted to appreciate Artifice as readers of poetry, without Naturalisation that insists on the Wallace Stevens type of 'deep thoughts' while ignoring formal creativity and innovation. To poetry then I shall now return.

The example of the jig-saw puzzle is perhaps instructive. Before me now as I write is the puzzle of 'La dame à la licorne' which I shall shortly re-assemble. Each of these fifty scraps of shape and colour (verbal sound and meaning) has its place in the design of the whole (thematic synthesis). However, the design in each must be known to match it with the finished reproduction on the lid, before the picture is re-created. So it is with words, phrases, impressions, experiences, ideas from which the poet will assemble his poem: he doesn't know until the poem is finished what its design and its thematic synthesis will be. (It is customary at this point to refer to Michelangelo's remark that the sculptor simply reveals the statue hidden in the block of marble. Nevertheless, like most truisms, this is true.) Eliot is right to say that we can only learn to get the better of words for the thing we no longer wish to say, though the statement should be qualified by noting that the way in which we no longer wish to say it is absorbed in the new way, and hence we say a new thing.

The critical analyst is slightly better placed than the poet. Like me with my jig-saw puzzle he has the finished article in front of him. Nevertheless, he must still participate in the activity of first dismantling, then fitting together the correct strands and levels into an internal thematic synthesis, and this is not easy. This has been done throughout with the system of Artifice and the concept of the disconnected image-complex. We must now explore the problem further in relation to the techniques of Dada. We know by now that the interpretive reader is committed simultaneously to a synthesis between meaning and form (resulting in an internal thematic synthesis) and to keeping the levels apart while doing so. The extension of meaning into the external world must find its own place and be absorbed by the disconnected image-complex, which is the only viable strategy to cope with poetry in the twentieth century.

It may have seemed so far that the slogan of this book was 'Words of the world, unite! You have nothing to lose but your meanings.' But, of course, even in Dada there can be no question of dispensing with meaning; it is necessary as a technique. We can see this clearly in a final example of bad Naturalisation that short-circuits the non-semantic. I take it from a book on Max Jacob by Mr Gerald Kamber.

Of Jacob's famous line, 'Dahlia! dahlia! que Dalila lia', Mr Kamber remarks, 'we are left with an incongruous picture of Dalila tying up drooping dahlias'.[21] Why does this reading seem so comical? Because it returns us to the outside world of everyday experience, while it is poetry's function to transcend this world? Because canonically poetry does this by using artificial organisations—'A more than usual order with a more than usual intensity' as Eliot puts it'? Perhaps. Although the vast majority of poetic theorists since Plato have held that Artifice serves the representation of 'reality', not many are quite so blunt about by-passing Artifice as Mr Kamber. The evidence is not lightly to be set aside. Perhaps Peter Stern is right when he claims, in his book *On Realism*, that the evidence of the centuries put the onus on the anti-realistic people to prove their case. At any rate we have seen, in the Introduction and first chapter, that anti-realism need not imply, as certain French theorists might claim, a rejection of meaning. All that Artifice requires is that unmeaningful levels be taken into account, and that meaning be used as a technical device which makes it impossible as well as wrong for critics to strand poems in the external world. And even Professor Stern admits that lyric poetry falls (or rises) outside his province.[22]

We have to remember conventions here; particularly the rhetorical devices used in suspending Naturalisation. It is more likely that we find Mr Kamber's reading absurd because we ourselves dwell on the poet's conscious skill. Our pleasure in the line comes from a realisation that what seems at first a complete surrender of the conscious mind to an impersonal network of meaningless verbal resemblances in fact reveals the latent intentionality of poetic language. The net of language catches, as it were, the acrobatic poet. Graham Hough, in his essay 'An eighth type of ambiguity', discusses the vexed question of the dichotomy between the poet's intentions as someone who writes 'poems' and the intentionality revealed in the structure of any actual poem's language. The 'meaning' of a poem may have more to do with the 'intention' to write a poem with reference to particular variants in convention than with the utterance itself. That is, as I said of Shakespeare, a poet wants to write a *poem* not a love letter or a description of his surroundings or a philosophical treatise. Professor Hough says: 'The life is in the detail; and the cumulative effect of the detail is something different, even contrary, to the primary intention'[23] (it is part of the latent intentionality of poetic language). The *significants* in poetry have a complexity that is equal to (though quite different from) the complexity and variety we find in actual speech situations. I am not suggesting that the poem characteristically tries to act as surrogate for its own empirical context—though some poems do seem to attempt this, and some critics seem to admire it. The poems that do attempt it are those which act in complicity with external limitation and expansion, as if Eliot had just said (as he does in the cancelled drafts) 'Life seemed so futile' instead of writing 'The Waste Land'. The critics admire it because it makes their job easier; they can say 'What Eliot really means is that life seemed so futile'.

I, on the contrary, so far from thinking that poems act as surrogates for their empirical situation, believe that they use their empirical situation (extension of meaning into the external world) in such a way as to change the meaning of 'empirical situation'. Indeed, the impatient reader might object that what I want to say is 'Eliot may have thought he was expressing life's futility, but all he really wanted was an excuse to arrange that marvellous pattern of *o*'s'.

We have got rather far from Jacob, however. Even Mr Kamber admits the importance of artificial conventions: 'this little poem is shot through with conventional poetic devices in spite of its surface unconventionality.'[24] Of course it is. Dada also developed the art of the disconnected image-complex. Here is 'this little poem':

> Comme un bateau naufragé est le poète âgé
> ainsi qu'un dahlia le poème étagé
> Dahlia! dahlia! que Dalila lia.[25]

The second line shows that the poem is self-reflexive; it is layered like the petals of a flower. This makes the reader think of the first line as self-reflexive also: it uses the traditional comparison to turn content into form. We cannot think of poets as boats without thinking of Rimbaud's 'Le bateau ivre': that is already to place the poem in a tradition. Jacob omitted 'naufragé' in subsequent versions so that the line read—'Comme un bateau est le poète âgé'. That omission suggests that Jacob was aware of the phrase's inevitable connotation and wished to play it down.

He does not succeed, however, for any mention of boats and poems is bound to bring in not only 'Le bateau ivre' but the reader's knowledge of Rimbaud's shipwrecked life. This is an example of external knowledge converted into technical skill by the disconnected image-complex which makes a poem's form part of its theme. The same thing happens in the second line—there is no flower so scentless, so deprived of the external properties of flowers, as a dahlia, which therefore is most useful for the process of being absorbed into the artificial garden of 'content as form' where toads question our idea of the poetical. Moreover, not only is the poem self-reflexive in using traditional comparisons to absorb external contexts, not only does it take this a step further in saying that a poem is layered like a flower, but it also uses the form of this particular flower to take a new leap in the third line. 'Dahlia' is linked to 'Dalila' because both contain 'lia' (linked). The interaction between a similarity in meaning and a similarity in form is made into a link to bind the poem together. Technique stresses the non-semantic aspects of language as creative in a way that is more than merely fictional: it brings our knowledge of language itself into a thematic synthesis.

Thus Jacob's 'little poem' shows the build-up of levels common to all poetry and goes beyond, into disconnected unrealism through which twentieth-century poetry must go in order to be able to use the traditional levels again — and eventually to speak out 'straight'. Stressing its difference from other languages and working on those differences, poetry enters a pastoral unrealism which enables it to resist or at least to postpone, external naturalisation by directing the reader to internal naturalisation.

Of course, it is difficult to maintain continuity in discontinuity but it is especially important to try . Especially since movements such as Dada, associated with the predominance of form over extended meaning, did not, with some rare exceptions, develop the techniques of unrealism strongly enough to combat their eventual evaporation into a bad Naturalisation. Dada, for example, succumbed to Surrealism's stress on the unconscious, which is by definition a pre-verbal area. And Structuralism has now evaporated its initial stress on verbal form in the heavy air of political revolutionism—again an external context.

The most prominent exponents of formal priority in English criticism have also ended by locating the domain of poetry beyond language or articulated thought. W. K. Wimsatt, for example, says that 'behind metaphor lies a resemblance between two classes, and hence a more general third class. This class is unnamed and most likely remains unnamed and is apprehended *through* metaphor. It is a new conception for which there is no other expression.'[26] And John Crowe Ransom concludes: 'I should say that we might call the poet's piety a "natural" piety, his gift for finding the natural world not merely mechanical but hospitable to moral Universals'.[27] So I must sit on my fence, feet on the bars of the scale of relevance, head in the air of Artifice, bottom perched—very hesitantly—on the disconnected image-complex. I must maintain that Wimsatt's 'third class' and Ransom's 'moral Universals' can be brought into new poetic techniques through 'content as form', that things external to language may be brought into the formal order of poetry, which thus becomes a mode of action. As Francis Ponge puts it, 'le seul moyen d'agir est le moyen que j'ai choisi: d'écrire'. And even the poetry of chaos evokes imagined alternatives. We should remember Tzara's statement that 'this necessary chaos that Rimbaud talks of already implies a nostalgia for a past order or the anticipation of an order to come.'[28] It behoves us to try to discover this order (we might ask King Arthur—*rex quondam rexque futurus*—who is fabled to awake when England has need of him). This can only be a matter of literary study, of poetic theory such as that here set forward, of writing and reading according to these principles.

Of course these principles can also be discovered or applied in non-literary experience, making it literary. I remember a graffito I found on the bell of Notre Dame de Chartres, which said 'Marcel Duchamp, Karl Marx, and Winston Churchill were here', and a metro ticket shoved into the glass case at the Surrealist exhibition. These show that the spirit of Dada, or parody and pastoral, of Artifice, still lives. The dissolving parody of artifice and the value it offers lead to the reflection that those who deny the validity of the old dichotomies—idealism/realism, idealism/nominalism, idealism/empiricism, capitalism/communism, form/content—are on the right track; that what is needed is another set of relations and concepts in which these old quarrels will be dissolved. Moreover it is poetry's duty to show use of these relations and to bring to our notice the third area which has always existed and is always in the future:

> To build the city of Dioce
> whose terraces are the colour of stars
> (Canto LXXIV).

This book is an attempt to state and argue the case of Artifice. Neither the psychopathological and political emphases of French literary theory associated with the journal *Tel Quel* nor our native breed of rank theoretical ignorance will explain why the idea that poetry gives us special contact with external reality has been so popular in the past. Nor will either explain why we feel constrained to re-examine, perhaps to reject, certainly to re-formulate, that idea now. Only an examination of the power of poetic organisation can do that.

The question is not one of causes but of reasons which we give for perceiving and relating one level of organisation in a poem to another. One of the main reasons that distinguishes real poetic innovation in the century from poetry of the past, even while on another level it asserts continuity, is the notion that language in poems not only works differently from the way it works in other discourse but also works against other language by absorbing it into its formal structure. Hence the stress on the disconnected image-complex. Eliot remarks, 'I don't think good poetry can be produced in a kind of political attempt to overthrow some existing form. I think it just supersedes. People find a way in which they can say something. "I can't say it that way, what way can I find that *will* do". One didn't really *bother* about the existing modes.'[29]

But this statement was made in 1959 long after Eliot had found his
way. Moreover he relates it directly to the claim that 'the form gave
impetus to the assertion', and if Eliot had 'bothered' a little more to
explain earlier what he was doing in his innovations we might have been
spared the whole profitless controversy about the style of 'The Waste
Land' and *Four Quartets.* One must bother sufficiently about the existing
modes to know *why* they will not do (which is why I shall shortly have to
bother about the productions of Mr Ted Hughes). If Eliot had bothered
to explain a little earlier why he could not say what he wanted in the existing modes, we might even have been spared Dr Leavis' apologetics (it
was not enough to say 'then fools' approval stings' twenty years later).
We might have been spared Leavis' claim that 'Mauberley' is Pound's
greatest poem, or the slogan of 'back to Hardy' attributed to Mr Larkin,
and (since we are indulging utopian prospects) we might even have
avoided the 'Movement', the 'Group', and the apologetics of Mr Alfred
Alvarez. We might even have avoided the 'fifties and 'sixties altogether
(though it would have been a pity to miss Mr Kingsley Amis' 'Shaving
this morning, I look out of the window').

Nostalgia, however, will get us nowhere. I write now in loving memory of all the minor poets, driven to suicide, religion, drugs, divorce and
giving up smoking because they felt they had to innovate and could not
do so on the technical side, incapable of 'the least emendation of the
better tradition'. It is high time to realise and not to be afraid of saying
that it is—sometimes literally—fatal to justify the banality of one's form
by the purity of one's experimental extremities. (I am not speaking of the
banality in content necessary to such stylised forms as villanelle and
sestina.)

The realisation of this fact by the poets I loosely call 'Dada', their
awareness that they must take account of this type of bad Naturalisation
as well as others, makes their work particularly interesting. (It is not for-
gotten that some did succumb to the suicide craze; one of the first ques-
tionnaires distributed by *Nord-Sud* is 'Le suicide est-il une solution?'.)
However, the way they cope with other kinds of bad Naturalisation, by
building on their conventions, is more interesting to examine because it
has provided help for those who want to live rather than die for their art. I
shall take an example from a writer not normally considered Dadaist in
the historical sense but who has formulated some of its most useful
devices even though he called himself a Cubist: Max Jacob. In 'Roman
Feuilleton' Jacob parodies the conventions of narrative technique:

> Donc, une auto s'arrêta devant l'hôtel à Chartres. Savoir qui était dans
> cette auto, devant cet hôtel, si c'était Toto, si c'était Totel, voilà ce que
> vous voudriez savoir, mais vous ne le saurez jamais . . . jamais . . .[30]

Jacob is helped in his parody by the formal level of language (Toto, Totel), just as in Dahlia, albeit in a primitive fashion. We may, however, let him speak for himself about this quality:

> artistic emotion is neither a sensory act nor a sentimental act; if it were nature would suffice to give it to us. Art exists, and therefore it must correspond to a need; strictly speaking art is an *amusement*. . . . The will cannot exercise itself except through the choice of means, for the work of art is nothing but a set of means, and thus we arrive at the definition of style in art which I wanted to give: art is the will to externalise oneself by chosen techniques . . . Style here is considered as a putting to work of materials and as the composition of the whole, not as the language of the writer. And I conclude that artistic emotion is the effect of an act of thinking [pensante] on an activity thought [pensé]. I use the word 'thinking' with reluctance, for I am convinced that artistic emotion ceases where analysis and thought intervene; it is one thing to make people think but quite another to give them the feeling of beauty.[31]

No one should make the mistake of believing that either Jacob or myself is advocating stupidity or that intellect is out of place in artistic matters. Indeed Jacob's insistence on the will in his definition of style would do away with any such misapprehension. His claim that art is the will to externalise oneself by technical details supports my claim that through details of technique both artist and reader find their most secure self. Further remarks from the same source can give us a clue to this elusive quality of Artifice: 'Let us distinguish the style of a work from its situation. Style or the will creates, that is, separates. Situation distances, that is, excites artistic emotion; one recognises that a work has a style when it gives the feeling of closure; one recognises that it is situated by the small shock received from it, or, even better, from the margin that surrounds it.' Clearly this 'style that separates' is the same old separate Planet of Artifice which makes us aware that language in poems is used differently from any other kind of language. Clearly also this 'situatedness' is the same old 'content as form', 'aesthetic distance', and detachment that I have been claiming is characteristic of twentieth-century poetry. Jacob's stress on the small shock and on the surrounding margin shows that he is talking about continuity in discontinuity, innovation in tradition.

The historical Dadaist, however, rarely took this step in practice; it remains rudimentary in Jacob, Tzara, Arp. The possibility of combining parody with pastoral to create a new technique was largely neglected. Until John Ashbery found it and took it up with results like this:

> On the secret map the assassins
> Cloistered, the Moon River was marked
> Near the eighteen peaks and the city
> Of humiliation and defeat—wan ending

> Of the trail among dry, papery leaves
> Grey-brown quills like thoughts
> In the melodious but vast mass of today's
> Writing through fields and swamps . . .
>
> Your plan was to separate the enemy into two groups
> With the razor-edged mountains between.
> It worked well on paper
> But their camp had grown
> To be the mountains and the map[32]

This is from a long poem entitled 'Rivers and Mountains'; if we juxtapose it with a stanza of Auden's 'Mountains' we shall be able to see where Ashbery has learnt his various skills and what he has made of them:

> I know a retired dentist who only paints mountains,
>   But the Masters rarely care
> That much, who sketch them in beyond a holy face
> Or a highly dangerous chair;
> While a normal eye perceives them as a wall
> Between worse and better, like a child, scolded in France,
> Who wishes he were crying on the Italian side of the Alps:
>   Caesar does not rejoice when high ground
>   Makes a darker map,
> Nor does Madam. Why should they? A serious being
>   Cries out for a gap.
>
> And it is curious how often in steep places
>   You meet someone short who frowns,
> A type you catch beheading daisies with a stick:[33]

This is a meditative verse, the very opposite of Dada's savage nonchalance. All the same we can see a considerable technical skill in wielding the verse line through the intonations of speech forced on Auden by his intention to express his thought directly. He does observe a minimal requirement that a poem possess 'situation' as well as 'style', so that his work is not entirely ruled out of court as others are by his stress on extended meaning. The relation between lines 2 and 4, for example, with their rhyme—'care/chair'—so subdued that it is hardly noticed in the poem's anxiety to communicate, contains a subtle modulation of vowel sounds and phrasal rhythms that is very typical of Auden: 'a highly dangerous chair.' It can be found, for instance, in pieces as disparate as 'On this Island' and 'In Memory of W.B. Yeats':

> Look, stranger, on this island now
> The leaping light for your delight discovers,
> Stand stable here
> And silent be,
> That through the channels of the ear
> May wander like a river
> The swaying sound of the sea.[34]

> For poetry makes nothing happen: it survives
> In the valley of its making where executives
> Would never want to tamper, flows on south
> From ranches of isolation and the busy griefs,
> Raw towns that we believe and die in; it survives,
> A way of happening, a mouth.[35]

It is quite probable that the casual reader scarcely notices the skill in both these extracts: the way in which the resources of alliteration, pause, assonance, syntax, and metre are used, the effect of the rhyme of 'silent be' with 'sea' in the first extract and of 'south' and 'mouth' in the second as these rhymes feed back on the arrangement and selection of words. The reader is too anxious to find a profound 'message' to notice with what skill it is presented. Because of the former, Auden has had his reward of public success but because of the latter he has the deeper reward of having earned a place in the tradition, of surviving as 'a mouth'.

We can see that Ashbery learns from Auden what the latter learnt from Eliot: the management of a variable 'free verse' line which both distances the reader and involves him in its swaying sound. From the Dadaists and from Eliot's quatrain poems and *Four Quartets*, on the other hand, Ashbery learns to innovate by detaching himself sufficiently from his writing to include a reference to it in his lines—'melodious but vast mass of today's/Writing'—while retaining enough control to manage the details of movement from word to word and line to line. Entirely from himself he learns to use the 'I' and 'you' in detachment from any supposed individual and to maintain a lyrical quality while apparently destroying lyricism. He has no need of the desperate measures of 'Pastoral' to assert the predominance of form; and he has no need of the aggressive traditionalism of 'The Lady of Shalott' to produce, as we shall see in 'They dream only of America', a poem with the classic quality of the traditional lyric.

III Fallen from an obscure disaster

I spoke earlier of Tzara's praise of Mallarmé for destroying syntax; now I should like to examine an example in a poem written in the 'seventies, 'Printed Circuit' by Andrew Crozier. By seeing how this fulfils one requirement of the disconnected image-complex, and how the tendentious obscurity of J. H. Prynne fulfils another, we should be able to proceed to the final comparison. I stress that these are long poems, and although I extract the most relevant pieces, the poem should be read as a whole.

My section-heading refers to Mallarmé's line, 'Calme bloc ici-bas chu d'un désastre obscur', from his 'Le tombeau d'Edgar Poe'. It is not a coincidence that this same poem contains the line 'Donner un sens plus pur aux mots de la tribu' which Eliot re-absorbed in the 'familiar compound ghost' passage of 'Little Gidding'. Just such a purification is undertaken in their different ways by Andrew Crozier and J. H. Prynne. First Crozier's syntactic revolution, 'Coup de Main':

> Five quarters duck lofty club bar rubbish
> With a short but sound composition—secure.
> It's from the oldest opera. As a wise precaution
> Ten cat-men break the laws of pain
> In an old man's stride. As first offenders
> A portly body of nurses is detailed fast
> In a gross Roman style of wrestling.[36]

No one could claim that these lines are meaningless, but the reader is uncertain on two points: both how to extend their meaning into an external/limitation expansion and how to perform an internal limitation/expansion which would result in a good Naturalisation.

He is helpless because it is generally through syntax that we can reach towards the external context that is applicable, and if syntax is disrupted without compensating formal organisation we cannot determine the external context, for the relations necessary for fictionalising are absent. The non-semantic levels of Artifice, which would be the agents of reintegration of sense in an internal synthesis, are not perceptible in Crozier's lines, for he lacks any development of the level of image-complex that would show them up. Phrases are disconnected with each other both as form and as meaning. We have, therefore, to question each phrase in isolation. Is 'duck', for example, a verb—which it would have to be if the sentence is to be grammatically coherent—or a noun? What is 'a short but sound composition' or 'the oldest opera' or 'five quarters'? Why should their 'ducking'—if duck is a verb—of 'lofty club-bar rubbish' (And what is that too?) lead to security? What, in fact, have all these phrases to do with each other, and who, in fact, is writing or reading these lines? Who can be writing or reading them when we all know that both activities depend on knowing how to provide external contexts and to perceive how they are fictionalised by the levels of Artifice? (even if this process itself, as in the disconnected image-complex, is made part of both theme and convention). The reader's interpretation depends on knowing what counts as a coherent sentence, character, persona, image-complex, thematic synthesis, rhyme feed-back, and finally, at the bottom (which, we remember, as Eliot said of Arnold, is a great way down), on knowing what counts as a conventional formal pattern. In the villanelle and sestina, for example, subtlety of form and banality of theme insist on the artificiality of poetry. We know nothing about this in these lines, and are quite unable to constitute them as part of a poem.

This is the obscure disaster from (or to) which contemporary techniques have fallen; and the clam block can be built up only through the use of conventional, formal, and artificial techniques that insist on obscurity of theme as part of their repertoire. We shall see this in Prynne's work and in the work of Sylvia Plath. Conventional level alone is not enough—even when as in the disconnected image-complex it absorbs all other levels—to restore the complexities of Artifice. It is not then free to do its own job of feeding back through sound/look to show what aspects of meaning are appropriate.

But I anticipate. Perhaps we can achieve some Naturalisation of Crozier's lines. We do, after all, know about wise precautions, first offenders, portly bodies of nurses, the gross Roman style of wrestling (as opposed to the refined Hellenic style). Perhaps we can say that an offence has been committed by a stroke of the pen—'Coup de Main'—which other strokes of the pen put right. Thus, the poem's title, as is traditional, sums up its theme. Alas for our Naturalisation, too much is left unaccounted for. From what external context came the 'cat-men'—what is a 'cat-man' anyway?—how can they co-exist with the portly body of nurses, the five quarters, the lofty club-bar rubbish, the laws of pain? We know what the laws of pain might be in the external world but not when juxtaposed with these others. Only as words on a page arranged as verse can these things have reality; and their reality consists only in their relation to each other as words on a page arranged as poetry ('Not here, O Adeimantos, but in another world'). As another poem in the same sequence puts it:

> Forced to become an astronaut-animal
> Which makes the insect run away
> When earth's last picture is painted. And the
> (Fill in this blank) are twisted and dried.
> Repeat for the educated who have lost their heads
> Wanting to alter the system. Try making changes.[37]

The title, 'Grow your own', suggests that we are meant to take 'Try making changes' and '(Fill in this blank)' as an insistence that the reader organise the poem. But we can't tell even whether this Naturalisation can be taken 'straight' ('Repeat for the educated who have lost their heads/ Wanting to alter the system'). 'Try making changes' is ambiguous; it may mean it is impossible to make changes in society through innovation in technique (*de te fabula* to contemporary critics of English poetry); or it may mean that it is impossible to make changes in the system of the poem itself. The second interpretation is more likely. The self-conscious obscurity hides a stringent structure, just as the apparent surrender to chance in 'Dahlia' hides an extreme control over verbal relations in the poem.

But what of our much vaunted way out of this dilemma: the minute attention to technical detail which, together with tendentious thematic obscurity, gives the poet a way of recapturing the levels of Artifice, of restoring language to its primary beauty as a craft by refusing to allow its social comprehension? I have already said that this is Prynne's strategy. And, by definition, difficult to analyse or discuss. All the same Prynne's work in this line is the most important in English poetry since Eliot (I am classing Pound and Ashbery as American, though they belong in the tradition because they received their techniques and influences from Europe via England.) It allows us a glimpse of the future possibilities of poetry in its use of formal pattern to assert lyric continuity and of important themes to assert intellectual power. It behoves us, therefore, to take stock, however inadequately, of such work.

I choose part of a very important poem, Prynne's 'Of Sanguine Fire', whose thematic synthesis is nothing less than the re-capture of idealism through the formal detail which is the absolution (in every sense) of this century's poetry:

> The alluvium does not rise or fall; the
>   song is equipolar and the faces are
> conjoined in likeness, made of that an-
>   gelic evidence. Disposition sports in
> the stairwell. Pie speaks, it is a last
>   precultural eulogy: I'm buggered he
>   says if I care I
>   don't give a four
>   penny damn or
>   a blind fuck where
>   soever and now all the
>
>   mountain peaks sail by in handy likeness
> and pride & passion & moral precept/gurgle
>   like the honey Outwash expected to
> run busily with the milk. Pancreas strikes hard
>   into the valley floor. The adrenal cortex
> cannot fail to grab for the willow wand,
>   life's like that all round. Pie is
> chastened, grows more organs of a strictly
>   theoretic cast; wine runs in his head like
> stellar juice (like evidence, off again):
>   the path runs out to
>   the lip of my fear, for
>   you; the planets bow
>   their heads at every door
>
>   At fortitude they sing in unison
>   At appetite they knead into a lump
>   At protraction they shine like the letter D

like you, like me
wearing the three
garments of the animal soul.

Let's face it says Outwash you're some
        what gone in the head, an organ
contrived as a fancy at least, in the
        stairwell, like the proleptic comfort
of taxis in Euston Station. Draw off
        a sample of that spinal fluid,
take more care. Be trusty. Our true fate
        is post-alpine, our true place bounded by
small mountain ringlets:

> *who have therefore no weight or load upon*
> *their Faculties, nothing to dead or slacken*
> *the Spring of their Nature, no Concupiscence*
> *to darken their Understandings, or to pervert*
> *their Wills, no Indisposition, Languor or*
> *Weariness occasioned through crazy and*
> *sickly Vehicles*

                                    wait for it, Pie
conceives a whiff of apple, even short crust, wait for
        it, like one bold face too many, pyloric mill
racing; yet Outwash runs on for the cloud—
        but are always Fresh,
        Vigorous and Bright, like the life and
        quickness of the Morning, and rejoyce like
        the Sun to run their Course—

                                                    and
makes it through zero gravity, he too on the
        verge of deep narcosis. He slides his face
down three stairs, skipping the treads; he merely
        thinks abruptly of a red sexy pudding.[38]

It is a hard task even to try to analyse these lines, remembering what I
have said in the first chapter of Prynne's tendentious obscurity. But the
effort must be made if the whole concept of Artifice is not to fail.

Traditional devices assert themselves in the symbolic 'Pie' and 'Outwash' and in the allusions to the land flowing with milk and honey.
Allegory asserts itself in the landscape of mountains and staircase and in
the contrast between 'angelic', 'disposition' and the 'animal soul'. The
traditional role of the poet is invoked by the reference to Virgil's descent
into hell, 'cannot fail to grab for the willow wand', which in turn brings in
'The Golden Bough and All That'. There is a striking combination of
traditional poetic devices and themes and their twentieth-century versions. This may be seen in the handling of the line lengths, the variation
from long to short lines and the use of italics to produce movement along
the scale.

F

But the movement is regulated, for the conventional level is always in unison with the thematic synthesis in order that formal pattern, syntax, and image-complex may play their parts in restoring the other levels of Artifice. However abrupt the transitions—between the quotation of the angelic description and the symbolic 'Pie', for example—there is always control from other levels. In this instance we have an isolated quotation in an archaic diction juxtaposed with a colloquial diction in a distinctively contemporary idiom. But the use of Pie and the symbolic landscape to develop through the conjunction of theme and image-complex can make us aware of a deeper coherence holding the poem together. And this is also true of the use of 'I'm buggered', 'don't give a blind fuck': these phrases are held together with the 'last precultural eulogy'; both appear in a controlled verse line. That is, the conventional level has been freed from asserting its discontinuity and can therefore be used as part of the thematic contrast to support or to deny development to the image-complexes. Thus a degree of internal thematic synthesis can be reached, focussed on the word 'like'. This appears and disappears in various incarnations. 'Like you like me' is the equation of love and knowledge; this is lifted to another level of abstraction in '(like evidence, off again)' which reflects the constant give and take between the body and the physical world, action and language, which is allegorised by the introduction of the passage descriptive of angels.

Once again, the conventional level used in this passage gives space to the poem by using italics; and it can do this because it is free from thematic oppression. On the other hand the conventional level may be used to create thematic unity, as in the section beginning 'the path runs out to' and ending 'garments of the animal soul', where the same preoccupations are maintained through a change in line-lengths, Sometimes, while the conventional level remains apparently the same, meaning and syntax fall apart: in the first section quoted, for example, where the introduction of 'Pie' marks a change in implied speech situation and hence in the external contexts that must be naturalised. Always the relation between discursive and empirical imagery is supported by movement on the formal and conventional levels. The mountains, the stairwell, and sexuality are related to the more general theme of abstract versus particular; and this in its turn is related to the differing aspects of the problem of knowledge through language which must distort what it gives the mind. Always too, the movement of level shifts this idea through the poem but not, as we have seen from the different ways in which the conventional level may support the thematic through the image-complex, outside.

The conventional level and the level of image-complex must involve a third level in order to preserve the necessary thickness of medium to prevent a critical reading slipping outside the poem. In this case it is the constant interweaving of differing voices as the lines vary in length and in tone. The abrupt colloquialism of Pie's 'I'm buggered' speech contrasts with the lines in italics about the angels and both contrast with the narrative of 'Pie is/chastened grows more organs of a strictly/theoretic cast'. This is a use of formal pattern—rhythm and varied speech—which not only presents the necessary third level but also connects this with the theme. The various voices each represent a different kind of relation between language and the external world. The colloquialisms make that relation that of the everyday world and so does the narrative; the elevated tone of the passages concerned with angels introduces the idea of an ideal world different from that of everyday; the narrative holds the two together.

Discursive imagery is characteristic of the more abstract passages while empirical imagery appears most frequently in the narrative. Not just the italicised description of angelic essences but also the preparation for this beginning 'the planets bow/ their heads at every door' is discursive and therefore apt to be taken as a thematic synopsis of the poem's subject. Balance is maintained between this type of imagery and empirical imagery in the constant alternation between the two. The italicised description of angelic essences is followed immediately by 'wait for it, Pie/ conceives a whiff of apple, even short crust'. Thus, whenever the reader wishes to say this poem is about an ideal world of imaginative freedom from physical interference with perception, the physical world is brought in again so that we know that however the ideal world exists it must be part of the real everyday world. Yet this world also is presented in abstract aspect through the allegorical figures of Pie and Outwash; they inhabit a familiar world of apple-pies, stairwells, taxis, but they are not themselves entirely part of this world. Each of them sums up a complex idea of how the physical world may appear in a poem. Pie stands for the disillusioned imagination facing its own inadequacies while Outwash stresses rather the robust physical world asserting its independence. These two figures are the main image-complexes of the lines. It is difficult to distinguish others since the constant movement from one implied external context to another does not allow consistent development of image-complexes over several lines; they appear momentarily only to disappear again. This disappearing quality in the image-complexes brings the conventional and the thematic levels closer together as the thematic contrast between the angels and the physical world is seen in the contrast between the rhythm of the italicised lines and the rhythm of the long descriptive lines. Yet the very obtrusiveness of the formal differences make these into image-complexes in themselves; each different rhythm has its different theme.

This interaction between levels and the varying degrees of intensity in texture and movement to which it gives rise places 'Of Sanguine Fire' with traditional poems in its use of all the varying levels of organisation and thus the most modern of techniques leads back to a revifying of the old.

'Of Sanguine Fire' is as much beyond the disconnected image-complex, beyond mere irrationality, as *Four Quartets* is beyond 'The Waste Land'. In fact when approached from the standards of Artifice it must be classed as a very rational poem; rational, of course, in its deployment of poetic logic and absorption even of good Naturalisation, as something to be reckoned with, but by no means the only external context that is used as a technique. This poem restores both the resources of lyric and the resources of thinking in poetry. It does so without stopping at parody or pastoral—parody of 'meditative verse', pastoral of 'idealised landscape'—(though it includes these), simply by using all the resources of past and present Artifice to make poetry again capable of powerful order and powerful thought. But it does not make even this the end of poetry, for its end is—as it always is—in its beginning. The image-complex both leads the other levels up to a thematic synthesis (Prynne's great thought on life) and forces the thematic synthesis to take account of the non-semantic levels so that it is an internal synthesis where all is movement, and where the sheer beauty of the formal pattern may make a powerful contribution—as it cannot, when, as in Crozier's piece, the revolution is mainly syntactic—to Artifice and to its future.

To this, then, we now turn.

IV   Ted Hughes and John Ashbery; or, The triumph of artifice

There are two reasons why this particular subtitle should seem odd. I shall deal with them in order and re-state my own position by so doing. First, a sudden descent to personalities may surprise you, but it is not as 'personalities' that Mr Hughes and Ashbery concern me; they concern me as symbols. Ashbery has come to stand for everything in Artifice which is productive, innovatory and demands a good and suspended Naturalisation from the critical reader. Mr Hughes, on the contrary, has come to stand for 'sincerity' or 'naturalness'. This is both the opponent of Artifice as the determinant of role and technique, and the accomplice of Naturalisation that wants a 'message', and ignores technique. Second, 'The Triumph of Artifice' may seem a trifle premature, but I wish to evoke the ghosts of Shelley's 'Triumph of Life' and Swinburne's 'Triumph of Time', because both these poems are instances of how the abstracting power on the thematic level can work in conjunction with extreme technical innovation and virtuosity.

Having, then, justified (I hope) my title, I shall turn to Mr Hughes'

Crow and his justification for thrusting it down our throat:

> Crow saw the herded mountains, steaming in the morning.
> And he saw the sea
> Dark-spined, with the whole earth in its coils.
> He saw the stars, fuming away into the black, mushrooms of the
>   nothing forest, clouding their spores, the virus of God.
>
> And he shivered with the horror of Creation . . .
>
> Crow blinked. He blinked. Nothing faded.
>
> He stared at the evidence.
>
> Nothing escaped him. (Nothing could escape.)[39]

Nothing escapes Mr Hughes; nothing could escape, for his technique works entirely in complicity with bad Naturalisation. A minimum of conventional level is preserved in spacing of lines across the page but there is not sufficient use of the non-semantic levels to allow the reader to perceive a formal pattern. On the contrary the use of symbol—Crow as the powers of the universe—is so entirely traditional that the level of image-complex is led upwards to an external limitation expansion in which the landscape described is both allegorical and real: in the former case because traditional relations between the expected poetic symbol with its accepted place in the allegorical allow the reader to extract the accepted message; in the latter because the level of meaning strands the landscape as a description of the 'real', physical, non-poetic, world.

In both cases, then, the image-complicated level emphasises the already known world of the reader (how to read allegorical poems and how to read descriptive language). So that the thematic synthesis must be external, must be 'great thoughts' about the non-verbal world. And so indeed it is, as Mr Hughes is so obliging as to tell us:

> poetry is nothing if not . . . the record of just how the forces of the Universe try to redress some balance disturbed by human error . . . . Formal patterning of the actual movement of verse *somehow* includes a mathematical, a musically deeper world than free verse can *easily* hope to enter, . . . but it only works of course if the language is totally alive and pure and if the writer has a perfect grasp of his *real feeling*, [The aim in *Crow* is to] produce *songs of no music whatsoever*, in a super-ugly language which would *in a way* shed everything except just what he wanted to say.[40]

Of course, the phrases I have italicised give the game away. Their vagueness could not be tolerated by any poet conscious of the resources of his craft in the artificial and non-semantic levels of language. This 'formal patterning' by which Mr Hughes characterises rhythm, rhyme and stanza form as opposed to 'free verse' may be seen in another of Mr Hughes' *Crow* poems:

There was a boy was Oedipus
　Stuck in his Mammy's belly
His Daddy'd walled the exit up
　He was a horrible fella
                                                        Mamma Mamma . . .
Oedipus raised his axe again
　The World is dark, he cried
The World is dark one inch ahead
　What's on the other side?
                                                        Mamma Mamma . . .
He split his Mammy like a melon
　He was drenched with gore
He found himself curled up inside
　As if he had never been bore
                                                        Mamma Mamma[41]

If this is a specimen of Mr Hughes' 'mathematical, musically deeper'
technique said to characterise 'formal patterning' I can only say that Mr
Hughes' aesthetic is a wise move on his part. Such invocations on the
thematic level of the great mythologies of Greek tragedy, Christianity
and simplistic Freudianism certainly clash violently with the uninventive
jingle and spineless recitative in which, on the level of convention and
formal pattern, they appear.

We can find the mythologies in a more subtle and accurate form elsewhere; here, they are hardly absorbed, altered, questioned, by the verse
technique as they are in 'The Waste Land', or *Four Quartets*, or 'Of Sanguine Fire'. Even 'High Dive' and 'Letter V' use more Artifice than this.
Since, therefore, the stanza form is left on its own it can do nothing to
save the conventional level, as Eliot's quatrain poems save it by including
the thematic level as an image-complex, from total incompetence. For we
should remember another aspect of that rule of Artifice, of 'content as
form': that form becomes content. If we are forced to look at form by
itself, either in irrationally discontinuous poems or quite un-inventive
poems like the stanzas above, both it and the meaning we have dis-
counted as beneath consideration will look paltry.

The fact that Crow is an allegorical figure plays down the part assigned
to image-complexes; for the allegory is not developed in depth: it
expands in narrative so that image-complexes have very little chance to
appear. When they do appear it is on the comparatively trivial level of
'herded mountains, steaming in the morning' or 'He split his Mammy
like a melon'. This is dangerous for, without strong image-complexes, a
poem, especially if written in an uninteresting formal pattern, is very
vulnerable to a Naturalisation in terms of the external world. The only
chance for the formal pattern to develop internally in the above lines
comes in the refrain 'Mamma Mamma' but nothing is made of this. It

signifies just a single emotion—the child's cry 'Mummy!'—and does not change throughout the poem.

The absence of image-complexes make the relation between theme and form appear totally arbitrary. The most we could say would be that the nursery rhyme jingle echoes the theme of infantile helplessness; and this is, of course, the reduction of the formal level to its most slavish dependence on the external expansion of a bad Naturalisation. Similarly with the first example we should have to say that the staccato short statements reflect the suddenness of Crow's vision of the universe and that the clichés—'he shivered with the horror of Creation' for instance—reflect its banality.

This type of reading—which is required by the style—gives Mr Hughes' work affinities with irrational obscurity where the reader can only say 'this poem is chaotic and therefore reflects the chaos of modern society'. It is difficult to say more since the work matches exactly with already created critical assumptions; there is no room for an internal expansion of critical reading and consequently no chance for the style to develop internally interesting relations between levels. The thematic preoccupations are not questioned by their use in a poem; poetic language does not have to stretch itself to accommodate new kinds of discourse. In the first example the discourse is that of everyday language. The descriptive lines—'he saw the sea/Dark spined, with the whole earth in its coils./He saw the stars, fuming away into the black, mushrooms of the nothing forest, clouding their spores, the virus of God'—work tiredly like worn out tunes. There is no clue as to where they come from; does Crow make these formulations or does the poet? Nor, as in the Crozier example, are these questions interesting clues as to the disruption of our everyday world through disruptions of syntax; the syntax is quite correct. The lines are an indication of complicity between poet and reader, an indication that they share the common clichés of the 'poetical'; and these clichés are not parodied or distanced by the conventional level as they would have to be in order to form the basis for a new technique.

The conventional level itself is kept down to a minimum of freedom to develop, for the poet's and reader's ability to make sense of the form must not be challenged any more than their ability to understand the content. Both form and content refer us back to the already known world. Needless to say, no formal pattern can be distinguished beyond the jingle of rhyme in the second example. For formal pattern needs an inventive use of convention and image-complex to point up the sounds that are to be important. In the second example the rhyme 'cried/side', for example, is of no interest thematically or as part of an image-complex, so that we don't know whether a pattern of *i* exists or not, whether there is some connection between these two words and the *is* in 'inch' and 'is'. The obvious choice of 'bore' for 'born' is dictated by the need to find a rhyme for 'gore' and it gives a kind of grim colloquialism to the statement. This is a rudimentary instance of an interaction between form and theme but it is the only one and cannot be taken any further in analysing the stanza.

Nor is the distinction between empirical and discursive imagery creatively used here. Empirical imagery only is involved in the narrative part while discursive imagery is implied in the various discourses of mythology. But they have no common ground in an image-complex and so can interact with each other only in the fixed way established before the poem begins where we can imagine the poet saying 'I want to write a poem using the Oedipus myth in nursery rhyme language.' This initial step taken, the relation between form and content is absolutely fixed; they cannot develop together as the poem progresses.

Since form and content do not have a dynamic relationship formal pattern also can have no development since it requires their constant interaction in order to signal to the reader which words are important. The lack of important image-complexes shows that Mr Hughes has failed to make the necessary adjustment between the level of convention and the level of theme which produces, first, the disconnected image-complex, and then the recovery of previous literary techniques which we glimpsed in the Prynne example. Mr Hughes has assumed that these techniques may still be used without the initial severance that indicates a poem's contemporary creativity. Consequently he presents both his themes—the mythologies—and his forms—the jingle of 'Oedipus', the flat lines of 'Crow say the mountains'—in a fixed manner. He does not enter into any real dialogue with the reader.

Mr Calvin Bedient, whose article on Mr Hughes I shall have occasion to consider again, remarks that Mr Hughes' relation to his themes is 'one of sniggering voyeurism, a voyeurism of various forms of extravagance, for extravagance is rather a romantic refusal of a subject.'[42] It may be romantic to refuse a subject, and voyeurism may be one of various forms of extravagance, but that is hardly what happens in *Crow*. Its subjects are not refused—let alone romantically—they are accepted in order to be subjected to something like 'sniggering voyeurism'. This, however, is not because Mr Hughes wishes it to happen; it is because he cannot help it happening. When the levels of Artifice are not used with true innovation and, more especially, when the conventional, image-complicated, and thematic levels fail to interact, no alternative to the non-poetic world can possibly be presented. To quote Mr Bedient once more, Mr Hughes 'tosses words on the page where they are in continual danger—despite the lines in which they hang—of sagging into prose, so his conceptions fall too readily into the slots of nihilism.' That is, lack of technical skill in blending the levels of Artifice is accompanied by lack of thematic creativity which would lead to such re-creating. Despite this, Mr Bedient still considers Mr Hughes a 'master of language' and thus justifies Mr Hughes' manoeuvres.

How any 'master of language' could 'toss words on the page into lines that sag' is wonderful to consider. If we are talking of nihilism, Ball, Picabia, Duchamp, Tzara, Rimbaud, Baudelaire, Aragon, Breton—to mention only a few and obvious examples—make Mr Hughes' 'nihilism' look somewhat adolescent (if we had any confidence that adolescence would ever be outgrown).

Naturally it would be better to *guarda e passa* but we see too much of this apocalyptic insensitivity in Anglo-American verse for us to brush past with a clear conscience. Mr Hughes does not, alas, stand alone. Messrs. Lowell, Berryman, Gunn, Davie, Larkin, Alvarez, Hobsbaum and Mrs Sexton—again, to mention only the obvious—are implicated in this dangerous ignorance of the true function of poetry: that it must create a middle area where Artifice can open up imaginative possibilities in both the forms and contents of other languages, and thus transcend the world these impose. Which is why Mr Hughes is taken here as a type-case.

First we had better take a sample of Mr Hughes at his best, 'Crow and the Birds':

> Whĕn thĕ *éaglĕ sóare*d cléar thrŏugh ă dáwn dĭštíllĭṅg ŏf *émĕră*ld
> Whĕn thĕ *cúrlĕ*w tráwlĕd iṅ *séadú*sk thrŏugh ă chíme ŏf *wíneglăssĕs*
> Whĕn thĕ *swállŏ*w *swóo*pĕd thrŏugh ă wómăn's sóng iṅ ă *cávĕ*rn
> Aṅd thĕ *swíft flí*cked thrŏugh thĕ bréath ŏf ă *víŏlĕt*[43]

These lines are not going to break the bank at Monte Carlo but they are not bad; they give us a glimpse of what Mr Hughes' talent might have led him to, if he also had not fallen victim to the stance of 'visionary'. The lines do use the conventional level to highlight formal pattern metre and theme; the first I have italicised and the second I have marked. It is noticeable that it is insisted on by the skilful use of metrical expectation and variation (which I have also marked), and that it is in the familiar key of *o*, reinforced as usual with slurred *r* and *l*. There is a subsidiary pattern in *i* reinforced by *s* and the repeated '*When*', but because it is subsidiary I have not italicised it.

Thematically the image-complexes give us the contrast and the similarity between animal creation and the human mind. And this is done the more skilfully in that the image-complexes are all empirical; they describe actions in the external world and it requires, therefore, the more power to make them absorb and change that world into a discursive thematic synthesis. It is to Mr Hughes' credit that, briefly, he has been able to do this, and to do it in the correct way: by using the non-semantic

F*

levels of formal pattern and metre, and by innovating in the matter of placing his thematically important words—'emerald' 'wineglasses' 'cavern' 'violet'—where they are brought to the reader's attention by the conventional and image-complicated levels.

Such success, however, is short-lived; it cannot survive Mr Hughes' predatory visionary role; and in the very same poem exactly those powers of patterning and handling the tension between theme, form, meaning, and metre are overdone in Mr Hughes' desire to put across his 'vision' and connect it with contemporary society. The poem continues:

> When the owl sailed clear of tomorrow's conscience
> And the sparrow preened himself of yesterday's promise
> And the heron laboured clear of the Bessemer upglare
> And the bluetit zipped clear of lace-panties
> And the woodpecker drummed clear of the rotovator and the rose-farm
> And the peewit tumbled clear of the laundromat
>
> While the bullfinch plumped in the apple bud
> And the goldfinch bulbed in the sun
> And the wryneck crooked in the moon
> And the dipper peered from the dewball
>
> Crow spraddled head-down in the beach-garbage, guzzling a dropped ice-cream.

What was a skilful touch on the strings of the artificial lyre has become as monotonous and ugly a jingle as Mr Hughes could desire. The first two lines quoted retain some metrical skill in the suspension between anapaests and dactyls—'When the owl' 'And the sparrow'—and the resolution into a surprising spondee in 'sailed clear'. But the mention of 'tomorrow's conscience' and 'yesterday's promise' is a threat of heavy symbolism, duly carried out in 'Bessemer upglare' and 'lace panties'. It is noticeable that the technique of the dropped word is no longer used as a purely formal device: 'rose-farm' is extended meaning without re-absorption of external context, and 'dropped ice-cream' is not only extended meaning but part of the heavy theme: 'you may think the natural world is pleasant, but it is really brutal, and so are human beings. Just look, for instance, at my insistent symbolism and brutally insensitive poems'.

How different from Ashbery's acceptance of innovation in:

> the water beetle head
> why of course reflecting all
> then you redid you were breathing
> I thought going down to mail this
> of the kettle you jabbered as easily in the yard
> you come through but
> are incomparable the lovely tent

> mystery you don't want surrounded the real
> you dance
> in the spring there was clouds[44]

This is from the title poem of *The Tennis Court Oath* published in 1962, eight years before *Crow*. I have already commented on the skill with which the verse line is handled and on the way in which the disconnected image-complex comes to a climax in the sheer ungrammaticalness of 'in the spring there was clouds'. Ashbery, as well as Mr Hughes, can include empirical imagery ('kettle' 'yard' etc.) and can vary his rhythm to include the cadences of 'everyday' speech ('why of course') without leaving any doubt that his external contexts are absorbed. Ashbery can even include a reference to the whole process of Artifice and suspended Naturalisation, 'mystery you don't want surrounded the real', without letting that govern his thematic synthesis or obviating the suspension of Naturalisation to which it refers.

But, of course, it is precisely this 'mystery' that Mr Hughes does want; he wants to be mysterious thematically without letting it affect his technique; he will even let the reader into the secret provided he is conceded his due as 'visionary'. We are at liberty (though Mr Hughes clearly thinks we are not)[45] to reject a 'vision' of human existence where the 'forces of the Universe' are represented only by sadism, copulation, death, and destruction, and nowhere by the creative exploration of form, by which alone we can get down from intolerable content. (We might even think there was something in the 'liberal humanism' Mr Hughes affects to despise). We are reminded of Eliot's 'Sweeney Agonistes':

> You'd be bored.
> Birth, and copulation, and death.
> That's all the facts when you come to brass tacks:
> Birth, and copulation, and death.[46]

We *are* bored, very bored indeed when all the work of intellect or hand, all the complexity of human dealings with language and the world, is reduced to presenting such statements literally. We should note that Eliot does not do so; Sweeney is an image-complex in a fictional situation which explores a new kind of verse form. His clichés are absorbed into a new technique and distanced from 'true' statements, as are Ashbery's. Moreover, as we have discovered from the quatrain poems, 'The Waste Land', and *Four Quartets*, the extension of meaning has led to a new use of the conventional level, itself providing part of its own theme—even this is transcended in the new freedom of *Four Quartets*.

Two further statements by Eliot are apropos here. First, that no verse is free for the man who wants to do a good job. It appears from the specimens we have examined that Mr Hughes—whatever his wishes—never does. Second, that a man will not join himself to the universe if he has anything else to join himself to. It would appear that Mr Hughes has nothing else, but that is no reason for trying to convince us that we are all in the same desperate straits. We have, for example, all the levels of Artifice to recapture, including the limitations internal to good free verse of which Mr Hughes does not seem conscious; he passes over the question of mediation and the techniques of formal pattern: 'every writer develops outwards into society and history, using wider and wider material of that sort, or he develops inwards into imagination then beyond that into spirit.'[47] We have seen earlier what Mr Hughes would consider fit tools for such development; I think that we have also seen that they are such as to defeat their own ends, if, as has been the burden of this book, creative innovation must take place by disrupting social ideas of 'poetry' and recapturing the old levels of Artifice.

The idea that a poet should develop outwards into imagination by using his external contexts ('society and history') as techniques seems not to have occurred. This, however, is exactly what Ashbery does, as we shall shortly see in more detail.

Mr Bedient described Mr Hughes as 'a mind on the outskirts of civilisation . . . as a thinker he is a hangman, not a priest.' The evidence so far—except for the first few lines quoted from 'Crow and the Birds', and that isn't much to show for the reputation Mr Hughes enjoys—would seem to me to indicate doubt as to whether Mr Hughes as a poet thinks at all, let alone like a hangman. (Does either Mr Bedient or Mr Hughes or myself know how a hangman thinks?) But the important point is that any poet in this century is a mind on the outskirts of civilisation; he must be so in order to perform his canonical function of mediator between his tribe and society. (This makes him priest after all.)

But thinking poets realise that this requires a new and shocking revaluation of all that poetic language has been. One such is John Ashbery. This is his masterpiece, 'They dream only of America':

> They dream only of America
> To be lost among the thirteen million pillars of grass:
> 'This honey is delicious
> *Though it burns the throat.*'

> And hiding from darkness in barns
> They can be grown-ups now
> And the murderer's ashtray is more easily—
> The lake a lilac cube.

> He holds a key in his right hand.
> 'Please', he asked willingly.
> He is thirty years old.
> That was before

We could drive hundreds of miles
At night through dandelions.
When his headache grew worse we
Stopped at a wire filling station.

Now he cared only about signs.
Was the cigar a sign?
And what about the key?
He went slowly into the bedroom.

'I would not have broken my leg if I had not fallen
Against the living-room table. What is it to be back
Beside the bed? There is nothing to do
For our liberation, except wait in the horror of it.

And I am lost without you.'[48]

This has the power of traditionally great poetry, but that power is hard won; it is interesting to see how. From the pastoral point of view it has the quality of dream landscape and of putting the complex into the simple. In this case the chain of cause and effect is disrupted and questioned in a single sentence: ' "Please", he asked willingly'. Ideas about American society and about how environment influences emotion are dismantled. Parody comes in with all levels of Artifice to be distanced and used and finally made into something greater—'the limits of parody in the snowy cloud'—as a piece of Prynne has it.[49]

First among these is the conventional level, and here Ashbery uses that of writing in stanzas so that he may be assured of the reader's applying the convention of lyric poetry. Having aroused these expectations, these conventions, he proceeds to disrupt them. An apparently innocent connection of title with first line—quite usual for latter to repeat former—shows us that we have no idea what the poet is talking about. Who are 'They' and what does this mean? So far this is simply anticipating the bad Naturalisation that is customary when first lines repeat titles and signal that the poet knows what the reader knows and will talk about it. The second line introduces more complexity by being apparently an explanation of the first: it is their dream of America, but what dream? 'To be lost among the thirteen million pillars of grass'. What does that suggest? Whitman's *Leaves of Grass*; but these aren't leaves; they're pillars; but could anyone, specifically an American writing about America (though we don't really know it's about America at all) mention anything of grass without thinking of Whitman? Does Ashbery intend a reference to Whitman? We cannot know. Does the intentionality of the poem's structure intend a reference to Whitman? The questions lead nowhere, for it is not a poem of likes and dislikes.

In fact we are too ignorant about the poem's structure to know whether there should be a reference to Whitman in the second line or not. Obviously it occurs to readers, and obviously too they don't find it easy to justify. We get very easily lost in something, whether or not it is pillars of grass, once our conventional expectation of coherence, and therefore of initial extended meaning, is disturbed like this. So far this is the familiar disconnected ·image-complex. The punctuation is no help, and so we look to the level of meaning in the third line, where a colon does occur, giving, we hope, an equivalent for 'dream'. But the lines following are in quotation marks; someone other than the 'They' is speaking.

Nevertheless, 'They' reappear in the following stanza, with an 'And' moreover, which suggests that these first two lines are equivalent to, 'This honey is delicious' and therefore to the 'dream'. But the person who speaks about the honey is not the same person who speaks about the dream etc., since he appears in quotation marks. Such a use of the conventional level with punctuation suggests that the poet is talking about someone ('They') other than himself, and that he introduces this person by giving him quotation marks, but we don't know enough about 'They' to suppose this with confidence, especially because both the quoted statement and the second stanza's descriptions are meaningless if we try to make them into an extended image-complex. What is there left of it? The glory and the dream? There is left only the skill in handling the implication and the lyrical transcendence of disconnected imagery in 'This honey is delicious/*Though it burns the throat*'. The fact that an image-complex is not extended, that these stanzas present the minimum of meaning and a bewildering variety of external contexts, would make the poem no different from Crozier's lines, were it not for the use of lyric stanza.

The poem works on the assumption that, at first, the reader will take 'America' for granted. Whatever other external references are suspended we know about America; it is the continent across the Atlantic which has properties in our minds, of affluence, materialism, success—Whitman's American dream and also Norman Mailer's. But after the eighth line we can't go on taking even 'America' for granted. Even if our attempt at extended meaning had withstood the previous lines' insistence that we were not to make a premature external thematic synthesis, even if we had, with determination, tried to make a discursive image-complex concerning ambivalence about attitudes to America lead us to a thematic synthesis, here in line eight the use of formal pattern would arrest us. The phonetic solidarity of 'The *lake a lilac c*ube' asserts the dominance of a formal order, its block-like resistance to empirical contexts.

It is impossible to find an external connection between that line and those preceding except through the fact that these lines are held together as a poem; and this is an internal connection. Pastoral and parody work in conjunction; the conventions of the detective story are parodied ('And the murderer's ash-tray is more easily—') just as cause and effect are parodied in ' "Please," he asked willingly'. And Ashbery can do this because he also parodies the reader's presuppositions about the development of image-complexes through meaning and the other levels in stanza form. The seemingly logical connection between the third and fourth stanzas—'before/We could drive'— is destroyed by the ungrammatical combination of 'He is thirty/years old./That was before.' Just as with 'America', our assumption that 'He' who is thirty years old is the same as 'he' who 'asked willingly' is destroyed by the level of syntax which isolates phrase from phrase and line from line. But the conventional level holds each together in a stanza, so that syntax, formal pattern, and convention, working together, suspend the level of meaning and even prevent it from producing an image-complex, other than the fact of writing in this way. The effective image-complex is the activity of writing words which have meaning but no extended or thematic sense except that derived from the fact that they are arranged as a poem.

This is a type-case of the artificial destruction of external contexts. Ashbery needs meaning and the formal and conventional levels, but he can do without either the extension of meaning into non-verbal contexts or the development of a single pattern of sound/look. Thus he does not need either the image-complex or the thematic level of synthesis in order to reach his poetic language. Or rather, he needs them as part of his technique so that the scale of Artifice itself is parodied. Technique is made part of a technique to transcend technique; and the final stanza shows how the parodied world of poetry is restored to us through this process:

'I would not have broken my leg if I had not fallen
Against the living room table. What is it to be back
Beside the bed? There is nothing to do
For our liberation, except wait in the horror of it.

And I am lost without you.'

Ashbery is so detached that he can make two discursive image-complexes ('I would not . . . table' and 'There is nothing . . . horror of it'), an implied external context ('What . . . bed'), and an ordinary lyrical statement ('I am lost without you') into a new world of imagination. For these phrases are intermingled and cut in on each other through the verse line and the conventional level. This is possible because the first stanza has made the reader expect an internal thematic synthesis through image-complexes. That is, the reader is already with a good Naturalisation; then he finds that the good Naturalisation itself is part of the poem's structure. Ashbery tells us nothing about who is writing the poem, or why, or in what world; he makes certain that we won't assume we know by using the disconnected image-complex in the first stanza, and he builds his structure on this. So that finally he is not restricted to denying bad Naturalisation because, while preventing us from lapsing into unawareness that he is writing unrealistic artificial fiction, he does not restrict himself to that function; he uses both it and our awareness of it to give us both a new imaginative freedom and internal limitation/expansion.

'He', 'They', 'I', etc. are deprived of context outside the poem, but their meaning and existence as part of a poem gives them a context within it. Similarly with 'The lake like a lilac cube': it is necessary that the lake should have no external meaning—its lack of connection with the other phrases sees to that. But it must have a meaning in order to bring its vowel and consonant sounds into play. The same thing happens with the parody of discursive meditation in 'There is nothing to do for our liberation' and the parody lyricism of ' "And I am lost without you" '. These phrases are prevented from being descriptive poetic empirical imagery, unlike Mr Hughes' 'dark-spined sea', or from being a comment on a state of society, unlike Mr Hughes' 'forces of Nature', or from being personal lyricism, unlike Mr Hughes' Oedipal jingles.

At one level, of course, they are all these things, but the fact that they are has been made into a technique that can fight and prevent them from remaining such. It is a technique that can also, once the battle is over, reconstruct the mediative power of poetic language as deployed on the fields of Artifice against Realism.

We can see this again in 'How much longer will I be able to inhabit the divine sepulcher . . . ':

> How much longer will I be able to inhabit the divine sepulcher
> Of life, my great love? Do dolphins plunge bottomward
> To find the light? Or is it rock
> That is searched? Unrelentingly? Huh. And if some day
>
> Men with orange shovels come to break open the rock
> Which encases me, what about the light that comes in then?
> What about the smell of the light?
> What about the moss?
>
> In pilgrim times he wounded me
> Since then I only lie
> My bed of light is a furnace choking me
> With hell (and sometimes I hear salt water dripping).
>
> I mean it—because I'm one of the few
> To have held my breath under the house. I'll trade
> One red sucker for two blue ones. I'm
> Named Tom . . .

Who are you, anyway?
And it is the color of sand,
The darkness, as it sifts through your hand
Because what does anything mean,

The ivy and the sand? That boat
Pulled up on the shore? Am I wonder,
Strategically, and in the light
Of the long sepulcher that hid death and hides me?[50]

This is an extract from a long poem, but there is enough for us to see that Ashbery uses traditional poetic symbolism—light/dark— and traditional reference to previous poets—Eliot's 'If there were the sound of water only' and Yeats' 'Isle of Innisfree'—to make his new technique. And we see that this new technique can use all types of image-complex and thematic synthesis plus the complete detachment of the 'I' from supposed external reference. It is able to do this because it has passed through the technique of aesthetic/Dada detachment: 'I'm/Named Tom'.

This is due to the combination of conventional and semantic levels; its image-complexes are anticipations of good Naturalisation. The poet has performed his function as mediator for his tribe of readers by absorbing even good Naturalisation into a technique, so that Artifice may proceed by creative development through its traditional levels of language secure (some of the time) in the knowledge that the reader will follow. I do not want to repeat this, but I do want to turn to the one poet in the sterile England of the 'sixties and 'seventies who, surrounded by bad Naturalisation, took the same step and exhibits the same qualities as Ashbery and the more illustrious names we have earlier examined.

Here too Mr Hughes is the villain, for he has had the misfortune to be associated with her. I refer, of course, to Sylvia Plath. In justice to Mr Hughes it must be admitted that even he is capable of appreciating some of this quality; he says of 'Last Words' in her book *Crossing the Water*, 'it is a poem which would have been safer said by a persona in some kind of play.'[51] Perhaps so, if we are concerned with Sylvia Plath the individual, although the comment shows an inappropriate idea of a poet's relation to his poems even as 'lyrical utterance': it demonstrates the notion that the woman who suffers cannot relieve her suffering by becoming the mind which creates, and also the idea that deliberate distancing techniques, such as 'a persona in some kind of a play', can help to bring that fact home.

Since, however, our concern is with Sylvia Plath's poems as exponents of Artifice, we are pleased not to be deprived of a piece that so clearly indicates its own unreality:

> I do not want a plain box, I want a sarcophagus
> With tigery stripes, and a face on it
> Round as the moon, to stare up.
> I want to be looking at them when they come
> Picking among the dumb minerals, the roots.
> I see them already—the pale star-distance faces.[52]

I quote only one stanza, and the resemblances to Ashbery should be obvious. The reader's knowledge of death, of different forms of burial, of Egyptian tombs, of the traditional place held by the moon in poetic imagery and by death in poetic themes—all are absorbed by the new experimentation which yet knows that it must use these forms of continuity with the past in order to create in the present. These continuities are most easily seen in the handling of rhythm, line-length, initial capitalisation and their connection with syntax. It should be now unnecessary to stress the formal skill which does so much of the linking between levels and between the imagined context and the actual words on the page. Such skill may be seen, for example, in our favourite key of *o* ('Round', 'moon', 'Come'), in *m* and in *i* ('them' 'Picking among the dumb minerals'), both of which are brought together in the climactic 'roots/I'.

We can observe this detached 'I', which is part of an image-complex, a formal pattern, and a thematic synthesis all at once, in a poem famous for the wrong reasons: 'Daddy'. People praise this and other poems, 'Lady Lazarus' for instance, because they present extreme states of mind; unfortunately Sylvia Plath was not able to recognise this as a bad Naturalisation with extended meaning, external limitation/expansion, and devaluation of the non-semantic levels. She was unable to recognise in theory what she knew in poetic practice. We need not to be so blinded, however, and our recognition of the artificial skills in these poems is a tribute (although, like most laurels, it comes too late) to what she has done for this century's poetry.

> Daddy
> . . . I made a model of you,
> A man in black with a Meinkampf look
>
> And a love of the rack and the screw.
> And I said I do, I do.
> So daddy, I'm finally through.
> The black telephone's off at the root,
> The voices just can't worm through.
>
> If I've killed one man, I've killed two—
> The vampire who said he was you
> And drank my blood for a year,
> Seven years, if you want to know.
> Daddy, you can lie back now.

> There's a stake in your fat black heart
> And the villagers never liked you.
> They are dancing and stamping on you.
> They always *knew* it was you.
> Daddy, daddy, you bastard, I'm through.[53]

The extreme skill with which the situation of a hysterical woman, enough for the bad naturalisers, is stated and then made symbolic through the traditional level of the vampire image-complex shows 'content as form'. Similarly the implied empirical context of marriage, of the telephone off the hook, of torture, shows how these things are fictionalised by the insistence of rhythm and division into stanzas (formal and conventional level). Just so the 'direct utterance'—'Daddy, daddy, you bastard, I'm through'—is made part of the rhythm.

I do not mean (and may I say this for the last time) that the 'content' is not important, that Miss Plath's suffering, the invocation of concentration camps elsewhere in the poem, the lack of telephonic connection, even the vampire myth, are of no importance. Certainly they are. A thematic synthesis requires extended meaning, as a stage before it returns to the safe and separate planet of Artifice. I have been at pains to stress that total and irrational discontinuity has no chance of performing the necessary rites of mediation, since no Naturalisation can get near it except the bad kind. Whereas good poetry requires good Naturalisation (good critical reading) as one of its most important external contexts. Without this the telephone will be off the hook. But the reader should not know in advance what message will come through or even in what language it will appear; *a fortiori* the critical reader should not dictate to the poet either the message or the world which it is to concern. The 'message' in the old sense is not what is important; message in the new sense is a product of the re-creation of the old orders, primarily through non-semantic levels. The poet as tribal mediator does not himself know what world he is in until the mediation has taken place (the poem is written). The worst disservice criticism can do poetry is to try to understand it too soon, for this devalues the importance of real innovation which must take place on the non-semantic levels. Criticism's function is eventually to try to understand, at a late stage, even Artifice.

That is not easy, as the whole effort of this book has been to show. I shall take one final example from Sylvia Plath, from those later poems in *Winter Trees* where startling empirical imagery and extremely abstract inference are linked by the technique of the verse form. We should remember Max Jacob's 'style', which is the will to create, to separate, and his 'situation', which is the margin that surrounds, that 'gives the sense of beauty'. We should remember that the main current of poetry in this century is to associate style and situation, technique and the beauties of form, which can come only from true innovation on the scale of Artifice. 'Purdah':

> Jade—
> Stone of the side,
> The agonized
>
> Side of green Adam, I
> Smile, cross-legged,
> Enigmatical,
>
> Shifting my clarities . . .
>
> A concatenation of rainbows.
> I am his.
> Even in his
>
> Absence, I
> Revolve in my
> Sheath of impossibles,
>
> Priceless and quiet
> Among these parakeets, macaws!
> O chatterers
>
> Attendants of the eyelash!
> I shall unloose . . .
>
> I shall unloose—
> From the small jewelled
> Doll he guards like a heart—
>
> The lioness,
> The shriek in the bath,
> The cloak of holes.[54]

The bad Naturalisation of this world go as follows: 'The poet identifies herself with a woman in purdah, therefore she feels stifled. That is the external context of emotion and situation. She is a poet so she presents symbols of her state of mind—a jade buddha, green Adam, parakeets, a doll. The resentment gets too much for her; she identifies herself with Clytemnestra. A nice balance is maintained between the symbols of her smothered feeling and the symbols of her resentment and eventual revenge; this is a constant theme in Sylvia Plath's late work. In 'Lady Lazarus', for example, she makes fun of the suicide impulse and then, turning on the world she found so intolerable, she says 'I rise with my red hair/And I eat men like air.'[55]

Why she should have bothered to write poems if this was what she wanted to say is of course not explained; it is taken to be enough that she was a poet.

I cannot see, however, how such a critical reading (and it is not too much of a parody)[56] can take account of the striking use of the verse line to emphasise sound patterns as they feed into image-complexes and are then discarded for others. In the first three lines, for example, we have an external context of a jade buddha which never so much as mentions the word 'buddha', together with a pattern of *o* and *n*. This is then suddenly shifted to 'green Adam'—who can 'green Adam' be, on an external reading like that parodied above? On our reading he is the symbol of the natural world made static. Then just as suddenly this image gives way to 'I', which is isolated at the end of the line and continues so, either at the end or the beginning, throughout the poem. The 'I' is juxtaposed with the abstract 'Shifting my clarities', and that phrase is taken up by 'Sheath of impossibles'. Both phrases are very odd uses of abstract terms, and show how syntax is made to contribute to image-complex and convention. A bad Naturalisation might see this as the abstract versus the concrete, so that the explanation in terms of a 'state of mind' is preserved by saying that her imaginative freedom is reduced to stasis by her position.

But I cannot see that such a reading could possibly cope with the last three lines: a transition from a rampant beast (empirical imagery) to a mythological murder (discursive imagery) to 'The cloak of holes'. What can that last phrase mean except just what it says? I think we should all be agreed that a cloak of holes does sound rather terrifying, but why? Because it is a contradiction in terms; a cloak cannot be made of holes. The discursive imagery negates the empirical but simultaneously asks to remain partly empirical: a cloak. This is the level of meaning used to present a striking image-complex and a technical device which will bring the poem to its climax. And it is this that a limited external Naturalisation, with its stress on external interpretation as 'state of mind', is most likely to overlook. In its anxiety to get at the 'meaning' *behind* the words it would overlook the meaning *of* the words.

I think there is enough now said to show that this level of bad Naturalisation is simply one strand—a necessary strand if continuity is to be maintained—in a very much more complex process of internal limitation/expansion on all the scales of Artifice. This process begins with 'Jade', passes through, but never discards, the level of formal pattern, uses the conventional level to appropriate the level of meaning and make it into an image-complex in 'Shifting my clarities', 'Sheath of impossibles'; finally it brings all these things together with the traditional symbolic 'the' which suggests a symbol in the final line. This sends us back inside the poem again—to its fictionalised 'I' for an explanation of the 'cloak of holes'; the 'I' is clothed in its negation. But like all true artificers 'I' remains enigmatical, presenting only the words on the page.

REFERENCES

Introduction

1 *Tractatus Logico-Philosophicus* (Routledge, London, 1961), p. 150.
2 See, for example, Samuel R. Levin, *Linguistic Structures in Poetry* (Mouton, The Hague, 1965); Roman Jakobson, *Questions de poétique* (Seuil, Paris, 1973) and *Selected Writings* III (Mouton, The Hague, forthcoming); *Literary Style: A Symposium*, ed. Seymour Chatman (Oxford University Press, New York, 1971).
3 *Some Versions of Pastoral* (Peregrine, Harmondsworth, 1966), pp. 77 &79.
4 *An Essay on Shakespeare's Sonnets* (Yale University Press, New Haven, 1969), p. ix.
5 *Ibid.*, p. 154.
6 *Some Versions of Pastoral*, p. 77.
7 *Ibid.*, pp. 79–80.

Chapter one

1 'A Retrospect', *Literary Essays* (Faber, London, 1960), p. 11.
2 *Tractatus*, p. 115.
3 *Philosophical Investigations* (Blackwell, Oxford, 1953), p. 8.
4 *Ibid.*, p. 59.
5 *Ibid.*, p. 208.
6 *Metre, Rhyme, and Free Verse* (Methuen, London, 1970), pp. 17–18.
7 *Collected Shorter Poems*, second edition (Faber, London, 1968), p. 225.
8 *An Essay on Shakespeare's Sonnets*, p. 170.
9 See Whorf, *Language, Thought and Reality*, ed. J. Carroll (Wiley, New York, 1956).
10 *Ezra Pound and Sextus Propertius* (Faber, London, 1965), p. 80.
11 *Blindness and Insight* (Oxford University Press, New York, 1971), p. 17.
12 *Ezra Pound and Sextus Propertius*, pp. 17–23. Sullivan places the 'Homage' with Johnson's 'Vanity of Human Wishes' and Fitzgerald's *Rubaiyat* in the genre of 'imitation' ('creative translation' is what Eliot called it). One might add Pope's *Iliad* and Rossetti's 'Early Italian Poets'.
13 *Ibid.*, p. 3.
14 See Roman Jakobson, 'Shifters, Verbal Categories, and the Russian Verb', in *Selected Writings* II (Mouton, The Hague, 1971), pp. 130–47.
15 *Structuralist Poetics* (Routledge, London, 1974), chapter viii.
16 See my article 'Necessary Artifice: Form and Theory in the Poetry of *Tel Quel*', *Language and Style*, VI, 1 (1973).
17 *Seven Types of Ambiguity* (Peregrine, Harmondsworth, 1965), pp. 5 & 7.
18 *Ibid.*, p. 239.
19 *Ibid.*, pp. 239–40.

Chapter two

1 *Collected Poems*, ed. Robin Skelton (Oxford University Press, London, 1965), p. 24.
2 *Ibid.*, p. xi.
3 T. S. Eliot, *Collected Poems* (Faber, London, 1963), p. 65.

4 The relevant lines from Dante and Baudelaire will be found in Eliot's note, ibid., p. 81.

5 *Selected Poems*, ed. John Lehmann (Macmillan, London, 1965), p. 45.

6 *Ibid.*, pp. 17–19.

7 *Seven Types of Ambiguity*, p. 13.

8 *Concrete Poetry: An International Anthology*, ed. Stephen Bann (London Magazine Editions, 1967), p. 192.

9 *Ibid.*, p. 25.

10 *The Poet's Tongues: Multilingualism in Literature* (Cambridge University Press, London, 1970), p. 93.

11 *Ibid.*, p. 93.

12 *Brass* (Ferry Press, London, 1971), p. 37.

13 M. Long, Review of *Brass*, *Cambridge Review* 93 (19 November 1971).

14 *Collected Poems* (Faber, London, 1965), p. 76.

15 *Ibid.*, p. 75.

16 *Collected Poems* (Faber, London, 1965), p. 76.

15 *Ibid.*, p. 75.

16 *Collected Poems* (Chatto, London, 1955), p. 65.

17 *The Whitsun Weddings* (Faber, London, 1964), p. 10.

18 For one example among many, see Anthony Thwaite, 'The Poetry of Philip Larkin', in *The Survival of Poetry*, ed. Martin Dodsworth (Faber, London, 1970).

19 *Collected Poems*, p. 13.

20 *Ibid.*, pp. 97–8.

Chapter three

1 'Rhythm and Imagery in English Poetry', *British Journal of Aesthetics* 2:1 (January 1962), p. 36.

2 *Ibid.*, p. 37.

3 'A Retrospect', in *Literary Essays*, p. 3. Cf. note 1.

4 *Gaudier-Brzeska: A Memoir* (First published 1911, Marvell Press, Hesle, Yorkshire, 1960, p. 88.

5 *Collected Shorter Poems*, p. 119.

6 *Seven Types of Ambiguity*, p. 25.

7 *Gaudier-Brzeska*, p. 86.

8 *Canzoni* (Elkin Matthews, London, 1911), p. 6.

9 'Ideogram and Persona', in *New Approaches to Ezra Pound*, ed. Eva Hesse (Faber, London, 1969), pp. 359 and 362.

10 *Collected Shorter Poems*, p. 124.

11 *New Approaches to Ezra Pound*, p. 330.

12 F. H. Bradley, *Appearance and Reality* (Oxford University Press, Oxford, 1920), p. 485.

13 *Knowledge and Experience in the Philosophy of F. H. Bradley* (Faber, London, 1964), pp. 162 & 164.

14 See F. R. Leavis, *New Bearings in English Poetry* (Chatto, London, 1932), for the most influential account.

15 *Selected Essays* (Faber, London, 1951), pp. 18–21.

16 *Collected Poems*, p. 46.

17 'Pound and Eliot: A Distinction', in *Eliot in Perspective*, ed. Graham Martin (Faber, London, 1970). This is foreshadowed by F. O Matheisson, *The Achievement of T. S. Eliot* (Oxford University Press, New York, 1935), p. 130. But Matheisson still naturalises in terms of the poet's mind.
18 *Collected Poems*, pp. 46–7.
19 *Selected Essays*, p. 15.
20 *Collected Poems*, pp. 44–5.
21 *Ibid.*, p. 59.

Chapter four

1 Published in 1921. Reprinted in *Selected Essays*, pp. 281–91.
2 'Donne the Spaceman', *Kenyon Review* 19 (Summer 1957), pp. 336–99.
3 *Ibid.*
4 *Collected Poems*, pp. 55–6.
5 *Seven Types of Ambiguity*, p. 79.
6 'Donne the Spaceman'.
7 *Some Version of Pastoral*, p. 69.
8 *Ibid.*, p. 68.
9 *Collected Poems*, p. 6.
10 *Ibid.*, p. 94.
11 *Poetical Works*, ed. Grierson (Oxford University Press, London, 1971), pp. 302–4.
12 *Ibid.*, p. 45.
13 'Donne the Spaceman'.
14 *Ibid.*
15 *Collected Poems*, p. 41.
16 Ibid., p. 104.
17 *Ibid.*
18 *Ibid.*, p. 6.
19 *A Selection from Scrutiny*, ed. F. R. Leavis (Cambridge University Press, 1968), vol. II, pp. 163 and 167–8.
20 *Ibid.*, p. 169.
21 *Ibid.*, pp. 162–3.
22 *Some Versions of Pastoral*, p. 70.
23 *Poetical Works*, pp. 34–5.
24 *Seven Types of Ambiguity*, pp. 139–45.
25 *Ibid.*, pp. 141–2.
26 *Ibid.*, p. 143.
27 *The Rhetoric of John Donne's Verse* (J. R. First Co., 1906). This copy: University Microfilms, Ann Arbor, Michigan, 1971. This brilliant piece of work was almost entirely ignored between these two dates, presumably because it violated the orthodoxy of external naturalisation that prevailed in literary studies. Grierson mentions it in his introduction to his *Metaphysical Lyrics of the Seventeenth Century*, as does Saintsbury in his *History of English Prosody*. But then they knew everything.
28 *Collected Poems*, p. 79.
29 *Poetical Works*, pp. 213–14.

30 *Collected Poems*, pp. 194–5.
31 *Poetical Works*, pp. 220–21.
32 *The Waste Land: A Facsimile* . . . , ed. Valerie Eliot (Faber, London, 1971), p. 61.
33 *Ibid*., p. 129.
34 *Collected Poems*, pp. 216–17.
35 *Some Versions of Pastoral*, pp. 167–9.

Chapter five

1 'Essai sur la situation de la poésie', in *Le Surréalisme au service de la révolution* 4 (December 1931).
2 *Beyond Formalism* (Yale University Press, New Haven, 1970), p. 358.
3 *Ibid*.
4 *Poems and Ballads: First Series*, in *Poems* (Chatto, London, 1911), vol. I, pp. 69–70.
5 'Nephilidia' (First published in *The Heptalogia, or the Seven Against Sense*, 1880, where Swinburne parodies seven of his contemporaries, including himself). Reprinted in *Parodies*, ed. Dwight MacDonald (Faber, London, 1964), pp. 458–60.
6 *Ibid*., p. 460n.
7 *Poems*, p. 108–11.
8 'Swinburne as Poet', *Selected Essays*, p. 326.
9 *Ibid*., p. 327.
10 Preface to *Le Cornet à dés* (Gallimard, Paris, 1945), p. 11. First published 1916.
11 'Dedicatory Epistle', in *Poems*, pp. xxvii–xxviii.
12 *Complete Nonsense of Edward Lear*, ed. H. Jackson (Faber, London, 1947), pp. 258–9.
13 *Tennyson: Poems and Plays* (Oxford University Press, London, 1965), p. 27.
14 *Omens*, 1974.
15 *Fuse* 2 (November 1972), p. 38.
16 Quoted in Maurice Nadeau, *Histoire du Surréalisme* (Seuil, Paris, 1964), p. 117n.
17 *Ibid*., p. 117.
18 'Necessary Artifice: Form and Theory in the Poetry of *Tel Quel*', *Language and Style* 6:1 (Winter 1973), pp. 3–26.
19 *L'homme approximatif* (Gallimard, Paris, 1968), pp. 11–23. First published in 1931.
20 Quoted by M. Hartmann, *Das arabische Stropengedicht* (Frankfurt, 1905), pp. 100–101.
21 *Max Jacob and the Poetics of Cubism* (John Hopkins, Baltimore, 1971), p. 25.
22 *On Realism* (Routledge, London, 1973), p. 156.
23 In *William Empson: The Man and his Work*, ed. Roma Gill (Routledge, London, 1974).
24 *Max Jacob and the Poetics of Cubism*, p. 39.

25 *Le Cornet à dés*, p. 65.
26 *The Verbal Icon* (Kentucky University Press, Lexington, 1954), p. 79. My italics.
27 'Observations on the Understanding of Poetry', in *Poems and Essays* (Vintage, New York, 1955), p. 183.
28 *Le Surréalisme et l'après guerre* (Nagel, Paris, 1948), pp. 21–2.
29 'The Art of Poetry', interview, *The Paris Review* 21 (Spring-Summer 1959), pp. 55–6. His italics.
30 *Le Cornet à dés*, p. 93.
31 *Ibid.*, pp. 21–2.
32 *Rivers and Mountains* (Holt, Rinehart and Winston, New York, 1967), pp. 10–11.
33 *Collected Shorter Poems* (Faber, London, 1966), pp. 258–9.
34 *Ibid.*, p. 82.
35 *Ibid.*, p. 142.
36 'Printed Circuit', *Skylight* 2 (Winter-Spring 1972), p. 9.
37 *Ibid.*, p. 11. *Printed Circuit* was republished separately by Street Editions, Cambridge, in 1974.
38 *Brass*, pp. 38–9.
39 'Crow Alights', *Crow* (Faber, London, 1970), p. 17.
40 Interview with Egbert Faas, *London Magazine* (January 1971), pp. 103–21.
41 *Crow.*, pp. 63–5.
42 'On Ted Hughes', *The Critical Quarterly* 14:2 (Summer 1972), pp. 103–21.
43 *Crow.*, p. 31.
44 *The Tennis Court Oath* (Wesleyan University Press, Middletown, Connecticut, 1962), p. 11.
45 Interview, *London Magazine*.
46 *Collected Poems*, p. 131.
47 Interview, *London Magazine*.
48 *The Tennis Court Oath*, p. 13.
49 *Into The Day* (privately printed, Cambridge, 1972).
50 *The Tennis Court Oath*, pp. 25–7.
51 'Sylvia Plath's *Crossing the Water*: some reflections', *The Critical Quaterly* 13:2 (Summer 1971), pp. 165–72.
52 *Crossing the Water* (Faber, London, 1971), p. 63.
53 *Ariel* (Faber, London, 1968), p. 56.
54 *Winter Trees* (Faber, London, 1971), pp. 17–19.
55 *Ariel*, p. 19.
56 See, for example, Barbara Hardy, 'The Poetry of Sylvia Plath: Enlargement or Derangement?', in *The Survival of Poetry*, ed. M. Dodsworth, pp. 164–87.